RED ALC-CHINA
Red Académica de América Latina y el Caribe sobre China

CENTRO DE ESTUDIOS CHINA-MÉXICO
UNIVERSIDAD NACIONAL AUTÓNOMA DE MÉXICO

CHINA'S FOREIGN DIRECT INVESTMENT IN LATIN AMERICA AND THE CARIBBEAN

CONDITIONS AND CHALLENGES

Edited by
Enrique Dussel Peters

CHINA'S FOREIGN DIRECT INVESTMENT IN LATIN AMERICA AND THE CARIBBEAN. CONDITIONS AND CHALLENGES
Enrique Dussel Peters — *Coordinador*
Megan McLean — *Edición*
Socorro García — *Diseño y formación de interiores*

Primera edición: agosto 2019
ISBN: 978-607-8066-45-2

CHINA'S FOREIGN DIRECT INVESTMENT IN LATIN AMERICA AND THE CARIBBEAN

CONDITIONS AND CHALLENGES

Edited by
Enrique Dussel Peters

CONTENTS

INTRODUCTION

Enrique Dussel Peters

China's increasing international presence in the 21st century has resulted in substantial outflows of foreign direct investments (OFDI), parallel to foreign direct investment inflows. The scale and dynamism of China's OFDI have been explosive: in 2018 Chinese OFDI accounted for almost US$ 130 billion –a more than six-fold increase since 2005, and only second to the United States– and foreign direct investment inflows and outflows have been practically equivalent in the last years.

This book will examine the characteristics of China's OFDI in Latin America and the Caribbean (LAC) against the background of this global context. In addition to the size of China's OFDI in LAC –during 2011-2018 it accounted for $US 79.12 billion or almost $US 10 billion annually in average or 7% of LAC´s foreign direct investments during the period– both the dynamism and its characteristics are significant. China's OFDI accounted for less than $US 500 million until 2003 and increased to levels above $US 15.88 billion in 2016, i.e. rapid growth of China's OFDI globally and in LAC is one of its most important features in the 21st century. There are relatively few in-depth regional and country-level analyses of Chinese OFDI, and even less systematic analyses at the firm level. As several chapters point out, there are even very substantial different methodologies used to register statistics on China's OFDI globally and in LAC.In order to respond to some of these topics the book is divided in two sections, totaling 15 chapters. The first section discusses general trends of Chinese OFDI in LAC from a Chinese perspective and includes the most recent strategies and regulations of China's OFDI (Xiaoyu Song), while the other three chapters focus on destination countries for Chinese OFDI that provide relevant points of comparison with LAC: the European Union (Mikko Huotari and Thilo Hanemann), Africa (Linda Calabrese) and Australia, (Adrian H. Hearn). All three cases are significant in the sense that not only do they provide accounts of the different strategies driving of China's OFDI –the search for raw materials, exports, the domestic market, or the acquisition of technology– but they also reflect the respective extension and depth of China's OFDI and its economic, social, environmental and political repercussions.

Section II concentrates on country-level case studies of China's OFDI in LAC. In addition to the regional LAC experience (Enrique Dussel Peters), 10 analysts reflect upon country-specific experiences: Argentina (Leonardo E. Stanley), Uruguay (Gustavo Bittencourt), Brazil (Celio Hiratuka), Colombia (Benjamin Creutzfeldt), Venezuela (Carlos Eduardo Piña), Panama (Nehemías José Jaén Celada), Costa Rica (Rafael Arias R. and Luis Vargas M.), Dominican Republic (Eduardo Klinger Pevida), Jamaica (Jevon Minto), and Mexico (Enrique Dussel Peters). These chapters start with overviews of each country's diplomatic relations with China and also explore other factors that play into the bilateral relationship. These chapters ultimately seek to explain the regional and national strategies of China's OFDI in each country while also explaining the respective impacts. In some cases, Chinese OFDI has grown substantially and plays an important macroeconomic and political role, while in other countries Chinese OFDI has not accounted for a single transaction, although expectations are very high. Even in the cases in which China's OFDI has not been significant, the prevailing belief is that Chinese OFDI will become an important variable in the future. China's OFDI in the last decade has been characterized by its increasing diversity in terms of sectors, countries and property but it is also important to consider its overall decline in 2017 and 2018. Both LAC and China need to substantially invest and improve the quality of their respective institutions regarding OFDI. Public, private and academic institutions in LAC and China specializing in the study of Chinese OFDI are scarce and insufficient and in many cases, LAC institutions are not sufficiently prepared to enhance Chinese OFDI and host Chinese firms. Chinese firms are equally ill-prepared to understand the characteristics of the respective LAC country in terms of labor, environment, suppliers, clients and other significant socioeconomic factors. Unless both LAC and China make substantial efforts to improve these shortcomings, learning processes will be costly and have substantial political and diplomatic impacts. The book is also a continuation of the Academic Network of Latin America and the Caribbean on China's (Red ALC-China) more recent and systematic research highlighting the substantial differences between trade, financing, infrastructure projects, and OFDI. Red ALC-China has recently examined the former three topics and this book will focus on Chinese OFDI. The book also follows the research of Red ALC-China on a group of firm-level case studies (Dussel Peters 2014) and the annual publications on the *Monitor of Chinese* OFDI *in* LAC (Dussel Peters 2019). Institutional and individual contributions to these debates are most welcome.

References

Dussel Peters, Enrique (coord.). 2014. *La inversión extranjera directa de China en América Latina: 10 estudios de caso.* Mexico: Red ALC-China and UNAM/Cechimex.

Dussel Peters, Enrique. 2019. *Monitor of China's* OFDI *in Latin America and the Caribbean 2019.* Mexico: Red ALC-China.

SECTION I.

CHINA'S OFDI IN THE WORLD

REGULATIONS OF CHINESE OFDI

GENERAL TRENDS IN LATIN AMERICA AND THE CARIBBEAN (2000-2018)

Xiaoyu Song

In 2018, China celebrated the 40th anniversary of its economic reforms and opening up to the larger world economy. The economic successes achieved under these policies are closely linked to the world market. In 2015, China became a net exporter of foreign direct investment (FDI) for the first time in history. In 2016, Chinese outward foreign direct investment (OFDI) exceeded the amount of FDI received within China and this gap has widened further in the last few years. China's OFDI flows reached US$ 196 billion in 2016, an increase of 34.7% over the same period of the previous year, positioning China as the second largest source of FDI globally. That same year, the stock of the Chinese OFDI amounted to US$ 1357.39 billion, accounting for 5.2% of global OFDI stock raising China's position in the world from eighth to the sixth place (MOFCOM, NBSC, and SAFE 2017).

In China, official OFDI statistics have only been kept since 2003 given that before this date there was practically no significant outflow of capital. Up until that date, the priority was to attract investment from abroad as a major source of financing. China became an important FDI source in the world within a relatively short period of time and is the only developing country with a middle income level among the main world sources of FDI. We will discuss two features of China's OFDI to understand this particular phenomenon. In the first section, we will discuss the methodological aspects of gathering OFDI statistics and the high percentage of round-tripping investment and its implications. In the second section, we will survey the mesoeconomic factors that determine Chinese OFDI, such as the roles played by the main institutions of the Chinese public sector and their regulatory policies. And finally, the article will end with a group of conclusions.

The Methodologies of China's OFDI Statistics

Currently, most of the statistical frameworks adopted to measure OFDI are from the International Monetary Fund and the OECD and are taken from a balance of payments perspective (Galindo et al. 2007:15). The existing statistical information is mainly limited to describing the volume and direction of the FDI inflow and outflow. It does not allow deeper analyses, such as the sectoral distribution, motivations for the investments, or their repercussions. Generally, FDI is considered an investment that can bring benefits in terms of financing, knowledge and technology transfer, access via the foreign investor's distribution network, etc. But when foreign investment is really about funds channelled abroad by domestic investors and returned to the national economy (round-tripping), it does not generate many benefits for the economy that initially receives the FDI. A more accurate rendering of FDI impacts identifies the ultimate destination for FDI (UIC, ultimate investing country), as established by the OECD (Benchmark Definition of Foreign Direct Investment, BMD4). The size or percentage of FDI identified in this way avoids distorted interpretations.

According to the OECD's BMD4, FDI flows and stocks are best recorded according assets and liabilities and the directional approach. An assets and liabilities approach does not show the direction of influence of FDI and OFDI. Under the directional approach, flows and direct investments are measured according to the direction of investment in the reporting economy (both inflows and outflows). The asset/liability approach does not take into account the nature of the companies or the direction of influence or control between companies. In addition, assets and liabilities include capital flows that are channelled into Special Purpose Entities (SPE), for example, tax havens, as well as those operated between subsidiaries of transnational corporations on behalf of the parent companies. These statistics demonstrate an artificial increase or distortion in the amounts of FDI in the individual economies or in the total data at the regional or global level. Under the asset/liability approach, assets include both assets of the resident parent as well as assets of resident subsidiaries; liabilities include both liabilities of resident parent and liabilities of resident subsidiaries. In contrast, the directional approach only considers the positions of investments abroad of the resident parent, while FDI inflows only consider the position of resident subsidiaries (Ortiz Velásquez 2016:5, 6 and 8).

For OFDI in Latin American and Caribbean (LAC) region, the Academic Network of Latin America and the Caribbean on China (abbreviated to Red ALC-China in Spanish) has been making efforts to improve the understanding of OFDI through its Monitor of Chinese OFDI in Latin America and the Caribbean, published annually since 2016. Statistics are presented from various sources and at various aggregation levels, and include discussions of the various methodologies for collecting data on OFDI, which leads to a greater understanding of the statistical discrepancies in measurements of Chinese OFDI (Dussel Peters and Ortiz Velásquez 2016). According to the Monitor, there are three types of statistical sources of Chinese OFDI currently: international, national, and private agency sources. This chapter relies mainly on official Chinese sources of OFDI data.

The difficulty of measuring OFDI is particularly relevant in the case of China. Before 2003, there were no official statistics of Chinese OFDI in the country. In 2002, the Ministry of Commerce (MOFCOM) and the National Bureau of Statistics of China (NBSC) established China's first "Statistical Regime for Foreign Direct Investment," based on international statistical standards for FDI. Their first project measured China's OFDI in the non-financial sector. Until 2008, the State Administration of Foreign Exchange (SAFE) officially became the regulatory institution for the management of financial sector Chinese OFDI. Since then, the three institutions began joint development of a statistical framework for Chinese OFDI statistical data is released on a monthly basis. MOFCOM collects data on non-financial OFDI and SAFE on the activities of financial OFDI. NBSC reviews the research to ensure that the work complies with the established methodologies and standards. Currently, the "Chinese OFDI Statistical Bulletin" is published annually with complete data from the previous year in both Chinese and English (MOFCOM 2018[a]).

This statistical source still raises some concerns. The institutions (MOFCOM, NBSC and SAFE) that prepare the statistical registry still have limited experience. However, there has been a constant improvement: from 2002 to 2016, the Statistical Registration Regime of Chinese OFDI has been modified six times. The version published in 2015 announced that Chinese OFDI would be accounted for by its final destination instead of the first territory it touches (MOFCOM 2015). But at the September 2016 press conference announcing the publication of the last Statistical Bulletin of OFDI China, officials confirmed that the new criteria had not yet been applied. The monitoring institutions had tracked Chinese OFDI in SPEs since 2006 but this version was not public and would only be used internally. These institutions justified continuing to use the first destination of Chinese OFDI is: 1) it is more feasible to compare this data with other countries, as only the US and a few others work on OFDI statistics with final destination criterion and they do not publish these statistics; and 2) more work and time will be required to collect data by final destination criterion and the figures cannot be published annually. Even as late as 2018, MOFCOM made clear that if the first investment location is the British Virgin Islands, the Cayman Islands, or the Bermuda Islands, for example, those countries would still be counted as the first country to invest (MOFCOM 2018[b]: 2).[1] General OFDI statistics also do not reveal a great deal about the nature of the investments.

1 On May 8th, 2018, the Ministry of Commerce of China released the "Notice on the Accomplishment of the 2017 Statistical Bulletin of China's Outward Foreign Direct Investment" (《商务部办公厅关于做好2017年度对外直接投资统计年报等相关工作的通知》).

Many of the statistical reports do not differentiate between investments that have been effectively realized or only partially realized. The catalogue of Chinese companies authorized by MOFCOM to carry out OFDI (境外投资企业机构名录) (Lin 2013:205) could provide another tool for counting OFDI by number of projects. However, an update to the portal in 2016 made it more difficult to consult by projects using simple searches by country, authorization date and company name, etc.

Analyses of the qualitative nature of Chinese OFDI require distinguishing approaches and identifying the shortcomings of different sets of statistics. It is also important to highlight the Special Purpose Entities where they tend to be the destination of capital flows, because of their global strategy, low taxes and/or the preferential policies and instruments offered by the FDI recipient countries. In most cases, SPEs are empty companies that do not carry out productive activities. The inclusion of these flows can inflate the real figures. A relevant exception is in the case of mutual or cross investments that occur when a subsidiary invests in its parent company. In the directional approach, mutual investments must be subtracted to obtain the total amount of the reporting country. That is, loans or transactions between parent companies and their subsidiaries abroad are cross-company accounts and are often counted as FDI.

In 2016, China's OFDI accelerated to the Americas and Europe, with China's direct investment in Latin America rising rapidly to US$ 27.2 billion, an increase of 115.9% over the same period last year. Meanwhile, China's OFDI stock in the region is US $ 207.2 billion, accounting for 15.3% of the total. But at the same time, the geographic distribution of China's OFDI in the region is not balanced (see Table 1). At present, China has more than 2,000 overseas enterprises in Latin America, accounting for 5.5% of the total number of enterprises outside China, mainly concentrated in the British Virgin Islands, the Cayman Islands, Brazil, Mexico, Chile and Peru (MOFCOM, NBSC and SAFE 2017).

In terms of investment volume, the Chinese OFDI that flows to the two offshore financial centers –the Cayman Islands and the British Virgin Islands– still accounts for the majority of Chinese

Table 1. Main destinations of the Chinese OFDI in LAC (2009-2016) (stock, billion US dollars)

2009		2010		2011		2012	
Country/ Region	OFDI	Country/ Region	OFDI	Country/ Region	OFDI	Country/ Region	OFDI
LAC	30.6	LAC	43.88	LAC	55.17	LAC	68.21
The British Virgin Islands	15.06	The British Virgin Islands	23.24	The British Virgin Islands	29.26	The British Virgin Islands	30.85
The Cayman Islands	13.6	The Cayman Islands	17.26	The Cayman Islands	21.69	The Cayman Islands	30.07
Brazil	0.36	Argentina	1.95	Brazil	1.07	Venezuela	2.04
Peru	0.28	Brazil	0.92	Peru	0.8	Brazil	1.44
Venezuela	0.27	Peru	0.65	Venezuela	0.5	Argentina	0.89
2013		**2014**		**2015**		**2016**	
Country/ Region	OFDI	Country/ Region	OFDI	Country/ Region	OFDI	Country/ Region	OFDI
LAC	86.09	LAC	106.11	LAC	126.32	LAC	207.15
The Cayman Islands	42.32	The British Virgin Islands	49.32	The Cayman Islands	62.4	The Cayman Islands	104.21
The British Virgin Islands	33.9	The Cayman Islands	44.24	The British Virgin Islands	51.67	The British Virgin Islands	88.77
Venezuela	2.36	Brazil	2.83	Venezuela	2.8	Brazil	2.96
Brazil	1.73	Venezuela	2.49	Brazil	2.26	Venezuela	2.74
Argentina	1.66	Argentina	1.79	Argentina	1.95	Argentina	1.94

Source: author´s elaboration based on MOFCOM, NBSC and SAFE (2010-2017).

investment in Latin America (see Figure 1). An average of 90.9% of Chinese OFDI in LAC flowed to the Cayman Islands and the British Islands between 2009 and 2016. These two countries are SPEs, which implies that capital flows do not stop there. The home and host countries are the often the same one and "foreign" investments are not foreign but rather flow through SPEs like the Cayman Islands and the British Virgin Islands to enjoy certain local tax incentives and take advantage of preferential FDI policies

Figure 1. Participation of the Chinese OFDI in SPEs in Latin America and the Caribbean, 2009-2016 (%)

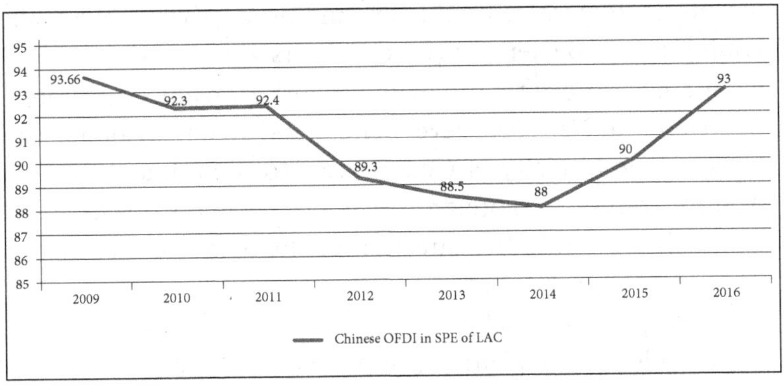

Source: author's own calculation and elaboration based on MOFCOM, NBSC and SAFE (2010-2017).

Note: The calculation is made by dividing the sum of Chinese OFDI directed to the Cayman Islands and the British Virgin Islands by the total of the Chinese OFDI in Latin America and the Caribbean.

These investment flows do not generate the respective benefits linked to FDI (financing, technology, upgrading and employment, etc.) in these Caribbean islands. It is relevant to identify this part of the round-tripping investment since its participation in the total of the Chinese OFDI in the region is absolutely high. And then, we can conclude that understanding the different methodologies on the registration of the OFDI is crucial, not only to understand the discrepancies between different statistical sources, but also to understand the qualitatively important discussions such as this case of the Chinese OFDI in LAC.

Regulating Chinese Public Sector OFDI, 2000-2018

A large part of Chinese OFDI is channelled through public companies with financing from public banks. China has a closed capital account and a controlled exchange rate regime and many multinational companies remain public. The public sector is omnipresent in China and in relations with other countries, directly (by ownership) or indirectly (by incentives, financing, procurement, etc.). The public sector has been able to generate massive incentives to increase production and productivity while maintaining public ownership (Dussel Peters and Armony 2015:52, 62 and 66). Currently the main authorities regulating Chinese OFDI are the National Development and Reform Commission (NDRC), the Ministry of Commerce (MOFCOM), and the State Administration of Foreign Exchanges of China (SAFE), all of which are under the direction of the State Council (NDRC 2018; MOFCOM 2018[a]). Chinese investors must register and obtain the approval of all three government authorities. NDRC is responsible for the planning, supervision, and coordination of projects, MOFCOM examines the investment proposal and SAFE reviews the sources and remittances of the currencies involved. Chinese acquirers must first register and obtain approval from SAFE, then request the corresponding NDRC ratification at the national or provincial level, and finally request certification from MOFCOM before remitting funds abroad. Investors must also obtain ratification from SASAC (State-owned Assets Supervision and Administration Commission) if the proposed acquisition involves property owned by the state (including state companies and those that are not owned by the state but where the government has a certain percentage of shares). Besides that, the Ministry of Finance, the SASAC, the Ministry of Industry and Information Technology, the People's Bank of China, the China Banking Regulatory Commission, and the China Insurance Regulatory Commission are also involved in the regulation of OFDI. Among them, the Ministry of Finance, the State-Owned Assets Supervision and Administration Commission and the Ministry of Industry and Information Technology mainly manage the state-owned assets that they are responsible for, while the People's Bank of China, the China Banking Regulatory Commission and the China Insurance Regulatory Commission mainly manage the financial institutions. In this document, we will focus on the approval and regulatory system of the National Development and Reform Commission and the Ministry of Commerce.

The first approval and regulatory system –laid out in Decrees No. 19 y No. 21 of NDRC[2]– for OFDI is based on the State Council's "Decision on Investment System Reform," adopted on July 16, 2004 (GRPCh 2004). This system established the transition from the examination and approval system to the approval system for overseas investment regulation and clearly stipulates that the NDRC is the responsible institution for the approval of overseas investment projects while the Ministry of Commerce is responsible for the approval of overseas investment enterprises.

The "Decision of the State Council on Investment System Reform" has three regulations for overseas investment. First, investment projects with a total of US$30 million and above and non-resource projects with investment of US$10 million and above should be approved by the National Development and Reform Commission. Second, for overseas investment projects other than the above projects, the projects invested by the central enterprises shall be reported to the National Development and Reform Commission and the Ministry of Commerce and the projects invested by other enterprises need be approved by local governments in accordance with relevant regulations. Third, the domestic enterprises that invest in foreign companies (excluding financial enterprises) shall be approved by the Ministry of Commerce.

Based on the above decision, the National Development and Reform Commission issued the "Interim Administrative Measures for the Approval of Overseas Investment Projects" on October 9, 2004. In addition to detailed regulations on approval procedures and conditions, the approval authority was further subdivided. Natural resource projects of US$ 30-200 million and large non-resource projects with remittances of US$ 10-50 million need to be approved by NDRC. For resource projects below US$ 30 million and non-resource projects below US$ 10 million, the central enterprises do not need to be approved. They only need to go to

2 On September 15th, 2004, the National Development and Reform Commission of China promulgated the No.19th Decree "Interim Measures for the Approval of Enterprise Investment Projects" (《企业投资项目核准暂行办法》) and on October 9th of the same year, the No. 21st Decree "Interim Measures for the Approval of Overseas Investment Projects" (《境外投资项目核准暂行管理办法》) was issued.

the NDRC for filing and local enterprises are approved by the provincial development and reform departments. Prior to this, all foreign investment projects with a Chinese investment of more than US$1 million had to be approved by the State Council.

This document also provides relatively clear rules for the approval process. The approval period is generally 20 working days and a maximum of 30 working days. However, the approval period does not include the time that the consulting agency may need to be commissioned for evaluation and the evaluation time of the consulting agency is not clearly defined. For overseas acquisitions and bidding projects, the National Development and Reform Commission also issued the "Notice on Improving Issues Concerning the Management of Overseas Investment Projects" on June 8, 2009, stipulating that before signing a binding agreement and filing a binding quotation and an application with the government department of the other country, the project shall submit a project information report to the NDRC and copy to the industry management department of the State Council.

According to the "Decision of the State Council on Investment System Reform" of 2004, the Ministry of Commerce also issued the "Regulations on the Approval of Mainland Enterprises to Hong Kong and Macao Special Administrative Regions" on August 31 and October 1, 2004. These regulations stipulate that central enterprises shall be approved by the Ministry of Commerce and local enterprises by the provincial competent commercial administrations. On March 16, 2009, the Ministry of Commerce further defined the approval authority when the "Measures for the Administration of Overseas Investment" was revised. Chinese OFDI of more than US$100 million should be approved by the Ministry of Commerce and local enterprises with a total investment of US$ 10-100 million shall be approved by the local commerce authorities. Others can be approved only by filling in the application form in the "Overseas Investment Management System" of the Ministry of Commerce.

This new regulatory framework significantly reduced the approval time for OFDI projects and eliminated some of the criteria amount of investment. The exchange rate regime was further relaxed during this period. The regulatory approach went from restricting OFDI amounts to evaluating the performance of OFDI. To improve the support of the OFDI projects, a national data bank was set up to disseminate general information of the Chinese OFDI although the quality of the data is still limited even today.

Prior to 2016, the regulatory policies for overseas investment in China focused on the promotion . In 2000, the state proposed a "Going global" strategy, which encouraged Chinese companies to invest directly overseas. The corresponding implementation rules were introduced in 2004. Subsequently, in 2009 and 2011, the authorities further relaxed restrictions on overseas direct investment, gradually decentralizing audit authority, simplified audit procedures, and improved the efficiency in term of time. In 2014, China's OFDI entered an era of renewed regulation. Since then, the procedures for approval and filing of foreign direct investment have been further standardized, processes have been streamlined, and efficiency has been continuously improved. In 2015, China further simplified the foreign exchange management policy for foreign direct investment, and banks can directly review foreign exchange registration under overseas direct investment.

However, 2016 became a turning point. That year, global OFDI fell by 2% while China's OFDI increased by 34.7% year-on-year and its non-financial OFDI increased by 49.3%. Debt instrument investment was 4.6 times that of the previous year. From the industry point of view, OFDI in some industries is extremely overheated. For example, foreign direct investment in the accommodation and catering industry increased by 124.8% year-on-year, 121.4% in the culture, sports and entertainment industry, and 95.8% in the real estate industry (Wang and Zhang 2018).

Such large-scale and unbalanced foreign investment activities, especially in the context of the weak Renminbi exchange rate and the rapid shrinkage of foreign exchange reserves, resulted in greater vigilance on the part of the Chinese government. By the end of 2016, the regulatory authorities began to strengthen the authenticity review of overseas investment, clearly indicating that they should pay close attention to irrational overseas investment behaviors in real estate, hotels, cinemas, entertainment, sports clubs and other fields. Under a series of temporary measures, from January to November 2017, China's new non-financial foreign direct investment fell by 33.5% year-on-year. In November, there was no new investment in real estate, sports and entertainment industry. Rational foreign investment was largely contained (Wang and Zhang 2018).

In the second half of 2017, the overseas investment policy entered a period of intense review. On August 4th, the National Development and Reform Commission, the Ministry of Commerce, and the People's Bank jointly issued the "Opinions on Further Guiding and Regulating the Direction of Overseas Investment," clarifying the categories of overseas investment in encouraged, restricted, and prohibited categories. On December 18th, the National Development and Reform Commission, the Ministry of Commerce, and the People's Bank of China jointly issued the "Code of Conduct for Overseas Investment and Management of Private Enterprises," which covered five aspects: management, compliance, social responsibility, environmental protection, and risk prevention and control. On December 26, the National Development and Reform Commission issued the "Measures for the Administration of Overseas Investment by Enterprises." The new measures came into effect on March 1, 2018 (Wang 2018).

The new regulations stipulate that within the scope of duties prescribed by the State Council, the National Development and Reform Commission shall perform the duties of the foreign investment authorities and provide macro guidance, comprehensive services, and full-scale supervision of overseas investment in accordance with the needs of safeguarding China's national interests and national security. The Chinese OFDI approving authority is the National Development and Reform Commission, which will carry out the approval process to all sensitive projects, including ones related to sensitive countries and regions and industries. Sensitive countries and regions are defined as: 1) countries and regions that have not established diplomatic relations with China; 2) countries and regions where war or civil strife occur; and 3) countries and regions that need to restrict enterprises' investment according to international treaties and agreements concluded by or participated in by China. The sensitive industries referred to in these measures include: 1) development, production, and maintenance of weapons and equipment; 2) development and utilization of cross-border water resources; 3) news media; and 4) other industries which are prohibited according to China's laws and regulations and relevant regulatory policies: real estate, hotels, the entertainment industry, sports clubs, and the establishment of equity investment funds or investment platforms without specific industrial projects overseas. This sensitive industry catalogue was issued by the National Development and Reform Commission in 2018 (NDRC 2018).

In 2017, China's non-financial OFDI fell by 29% year-on-year. This was the first time since China's foreign direct investment statistics system was established in 2002 that China's OFDI experienced negative growth. The Minister of Commerce pointed out that this decline was mainly due to the effective containment of irrational foreign investment. Future investments should focus on the fundamental improvement of its quality.

Conclusions

In this document, we analyse –the registration of statistics and the regulations of Chinese OFDI from a Chinese perspective. The statistical registry of OFDI is of the utmost importance, since it allows observations and analyses. FDI is considered an investment that can bring benefits in terms of financing, knowledge and technology transfer, and access of the foreign investor's distribution network. But when foreign investment is really no more than funds channelled abroad by domestic investors and returned to the national economy, it will not generate additional effects linked to FDI. The importance of the FDI registration method is the ultimate destination for FDI established by the OECD in the fourth edition of its Manual of Definitions of FDI. It is relevant to know the size or percentage of this type of investment because it can reflect the problems and avoid distorted interpretations of the policy towards FDI of a country. The capital flows channelled into SPEs, for example, tax havens, as well as those operated between subsidiaries of transnational corporations on behalf of the parent companies will cause an artificial increase or a distortion of the amounts of FDI in the individual economies or in the total data at the regional or global level.

In 2016, China's OFDI in LAC rose rapidly to US$ 27.2 billion, an increase of 115.9% over the same period last year. Meanwhile, China's OFDI stock in the region is US$ 207.2 billion, accounting for 15.3% of the total. At the same time, the geographic distribution of China's OFDI in the region is not balanced. At present, China has more than 2,000 overseas enterprises in LAC, mainly concentrated in the British Virgin Islands, the Cayman Islands, Brazil, Mexico, Chile and Peru. In terms of investment volume, the Chinese OFDI that flows to the two offshore financial centers –the Cayman Islands and the British Virgin Islands– still account for the majority of Chinese investment in LAC. An average of 90.9% of the Chinese OFDI in region has flowed to the Cayman Islands and the British Islands during 2009-2016. These are the round-tripping investment which only go to these places to enjoy certain local tax incentives and then they return to home country as a foreign investment in order to acceded the preferential policies for FDI of the "host" country. Therefore, these investment flows cannot generate the respective benefits linked to an FDI (financing, technology, upgrading and employment, etc.) in these Caribbean islands. It is relevant to identify this part of the round-tripping investment since its participation in the total of the Chinese OFDI in the region is absolutely high. And then, we can conclude that understanding the different methodologies on the registration of the OFDI is crucial, not only to understand the discrepancies between different statistical sources, but also to understand the qualitatively important discussions such as this case of the Chinese OFDI in LAC.

However, in 2018, MOFCOM still clearly emphasized to continue with the statistical principles about the countries and regions to invest based on the 2016 annual Bulletin: if the first investment location is the British Virgin Islands, the Cayman Islands or the Bermuda Islands, it will still be counted as the first country to invest, although from 2002 to 2016, the Statistical Registration

Regime of Chinese OFDI has been modified six times. And the latest version was published in 2015 where it announces that the Chinese OFDI will be accounted for by its final destination instead of the first territory it touches.

And in the second section, we talk about the regulations of the Chinese OFDI. It is essential to understand the Chinese public sector for a rigorous analysis such as this case of the Chinese OFDI. Currently the competent authorities of the Chinese OFDI are the National Development and Reform Commission, the Ministry of Commerce and the State Administration of Foreign Exchanges of China, which are three public institutions under the direction of the State Council. In a case of OFDI, the Chinese investor must register and obtain the approval of three government authorities: NDRC, which is responsible for the planning, supervision and harmonization of the projects; MOFCOM examines the investment proposal; and SAFE is responsible for reviewing the sources and remittances of the currencies involved.

Prior to 2016, we can conclude that the regulatory policies for overseas investment in China were still dominated by deregulation. In 2000, the state proposed a "Going global" strategy, which encouraged Chinese companies to invest directly overseas. The corresponding implementation rules were introduced in 2004. In 2009 and 2011, the competent authorities further relaxed restrictions on overseas direct investment, gradually decentralized audit authority, simplified audit procedures and improved the efficiency. In 2014, China's OFDI entered an era of reporting and approval. In the second half of 2017, the overseas investment new policy entered a period of intensive release. However, 2016 became a turning point. From the end of 2016, the regulatory authorities began to strengthen the authenticity review of overseas investment, clearly indicating that they should pay close attention to irrational overseas investment behaviours in real estate, hotels, cinemas, entertainment, sports clubs and other fields. On August 4th, the National Development and Reform Commission, the Ministry of Commerce, and the People's Bank jointly issued the "Opinions on Further Guiding and Regulating the Direction of Overseas Investment", clarifying the categories of overseas investment in encouraged, restricted and prohibited categories. And in the latest version of the regulation of NDRC and MOFCOM, a catalogue of sensitive projects is issued and it includes all the countries, regions and industries where the Chinese OFDI should be applied the approval process or be limited or prohibited. These recent regulations on China's OFDI in China will be revealing for Latin American countries, especially those that are about to initiate cooperation agendas in this area. The very specific catalogues will help the countries of the region to know the sectors where Chinese OFDI may or may not attract.

References

中华人民共和国中央人民政府。2004年.《国务院关于投资体制改革的决定. GRPCh (Government of the People's Republic of China). 2004. *Decisions on investment system reform of the State Council.* GRPCh: Beijing.

中国商务部，中国人民银行，国务院国有资产监督管理委员会，中国银行业监督管理委员会，中国证券监督管理委员会，中国保险监督管理委员会和国家外汇管理局. 2018年.《对外投资备案（核准）报告暂行办法. China's Ministry of Commerce, People's Bank of China, State-owned Assets Supervision and Administration Commission of the State Council, China Banking Regulatory Commission, China Securities Regulatory Commission, China Insurance Regulatory Commission and State Administration of Foreign Exchange. 2018. *Interim Measures for the of Outward Foreign Investment Filing (Approval).* MOFCOM: Beijing.

中国国家发展改革委员会. 2018年.《企业境外投资管理办法。China's National Development and Reform Commission. 2018. Measures for the Administration of Overseas Investment by Enterprises. CDRF: Beijing.

中国国家发展改革委员会。2018.《境外投资敏感行业目录. China's National Development and Reform Commission. 2018. *Catalogue of Sensitive Industries in Overseas Investment.* CDRC: Beijing.

Dussel Peters, Enrique. 2015. "The Omnipresent Role of China's Public Sector in Its Relationship with Latin America and the Caribbean Beyond Raw Materials". In: ¿Who are *the actors in the Latin America and Caribbean-China relationalship?* Red ALC-China, Friedrich Ebert Stiftung, University of Pittsburgh y Fundación Foro Nueva Sociedad: Mexico, pp. 50-72.

Dussel Peters, Enrique and Ortiz Velásquez, Samuel. 2016. *Monitor de la OFDI de China en América Latina y el Caribe.* Red ALC-China: Mexico.

Dussel Peters, Enrique (coord.), Luis Miguel Galindo Paliza, Edurado Loría, and Michael Mortimore. 2007. *Inversión extranjera directa en México: desempeño y potencial. Una perspectiva macro, meso, micro y territorial.* Centro de Estudios China-México/ Facultad de Economía/Universidad Nacional Autónoma de México, Secretaría de Economía, Siglo XXI Editores: Mexico.

MOFCOM (Ministry of Commerce of the People's Republic of China), NBSC (National Bureau of Statistics of the People's Republic of China) and SAFE (State Administration of Foreign Exchange). 2011-2017. *Statistical Bulletin of China's Outward Foreign Direct Investment (2010-2016).* MOFCOM and SAFE: Beijing.

商务部2015年版对外直接投资统计制度. MOFCOM. 2015. *The 2015 version of the Foreign Direct Investment Statistics Regime of the Ministry of Commerce.* MOFCOM: Beijing.

商务部合作司负责人负责解读《对外投资备案（核准）报告暂行办法. 2018年1月25日. MOFCOM[a]. January 25th, 2018. *The responsible in charge of the cooperation department of the Ministry of Commerce interpreting the "Interim Measures for the of Outward Foreign Investment Filing (Approval).* MOFCOM: Beijing.

《商务部办公厅关于做好2017年度对外直接投资统计年报等相关工作的通知》。2018年5月8日。MOFCOM[b]. May 8th, 2018. "Notice on the Accomplishment of the 2017 Statistical Bulletin of China's Outward Foreign Direct Investment".

商务部境外投资企业（机构）备案结果公开名录．2018年．MOFCOM. 2018. *Public Directory of Filing Results of Overseas Investment Enterprises (Institutions).* MOFCOM: Beijing. At: http://femhzs.mofcom.gov.cn/fecpmvc/pages/fem/CorpJWList.html

商务部关于印发《对外投资备案（核准）》报告暂行办法的通知. 2018年1月18日. MOFCOM. January 18th, 2018. *Notice of the Ministry of Commerce on Printing and Distributing the "Interim Measures for the of Outward Foreign Investment Filing (Approval).* MOFCOM: Beijing.

NBSC (National Bureau of Statistics of the People's Republic of China). 2016. *Press Conference of the 2015 Statistical Bulletin of China's Outward Foreign Direct Investment.* NBSC: Beijing.

OECD (Organization for Economic Cooperation and Development). 2008. *Definition of Foreign Direct Investment Framework.* OECD *Benchmark Definition of Foreign Direct Investment.* Fourth Edition.

Ortiz Velásquez, Samuel. 2016. *Monitor de la* OFDI *de China en América Latina y el Caribe. Aspectos Metodológicos (2000-2016).* Red ALC-China: Mexico.

姚枝仲，李众敏。中国对外直接投资的发展趋势与政策展望。国际经济评论. 2011年第二期. Yao, Zhizhong & Li, Zhongmin. "China's Outbound FDI: Trends and Policy Outlook". *International Economic Review* No. 2, pp. 127-147.

王碧珺，张明。2018。为何近期境外投资新政密集发布？FT中文网 。Wang, Bijun and Zhang, Ming. 2018. Why is the recent intensive overseas investment new policy? http://www.ftchinese.com/story/001075784?fu ll=y&archive

王碧珺. 2018. 对外投资要坚持高质量发展。中国金融新闻网. Wang, Bijun. 2018. Outward foreign direct investment must adhere to high quality development. http://www.financialnews.com.cn/hq/yw/201803/t20180322_135191.html

EU-CHINA FDI

WORKING TOWARDS RECIPROCITY IN INVESTMENT RELATIONS WITH CHINA

Thilo Hanemann and Mikko Huotari

Introduction

The European Union (EU) has become one of the favorite destinations for Chinese outbound foreign direct investment (OFDI). Annual Chinese OFDI in the 28 EU economies has grown from EUR 700 million in 2008 to EUR 35 billion in 2016. In 2017, Chinese investment in the EU dropped to EUR 30 billion, the first decline in four years, in the wake of China's regulatory crackdown on outbound capital flows.

Despite the drop, 2017 was still the year with the second largest inflow of Chinese FDI into the EU, and it was the year with the largest Chinese investment in Europe when counting the EUR 38 billion Syngenta takeover in Switzerland. Moreover, deal-making picked up later in the year, and the 2018 pipeline is filled with more than EUR 10 billion of pending acquisitions.

The growth and resilience of Chinese investment flows is eliciting both enthusiasm and anxiety in Europe. Some politicians are excited about the prospect of new investments to revitalize their local economies and better connect them with the booming Chinese consumer market. Others are concerned about potential security risks and negative economic impacts.

The discussions about potential risks from Chinese FDI have continued throughout 2017 and into 2018, despite the apparent slowdown of Chinese investment activity. One increasingly important concern is the lack of reciprocity in EU-China investment relations. While Chinese investors enjoy the same rights in the EU market as any European business, China still heavily restricts foreign investment in its markets, and it has not delivered on many promises to remove formal and informal hurdles for European companies operating in China.

This gap in investment openness raises concerns about detrimental economic impacts such as unfair competition and resulting market distortions but it also creates a sense among EU citizens and businesses that the playing field between Europe and China is not level. This strengthens protectionist sentiment and fuels political backlash against economic engagement with China. Thus, the resolution of reciprocity concerns will be critical for the future trajectory of EU-China economic relations.

The European debate about reciprocity is often guided by emotions and preconceived notions of an unfair China. There has not been much systematic effort to collect empirical evidence of reciprocity gaps. This lack of reliable information allows the debate to be politicized by special interests, which in turn undermines the argument *vis-à-vis* China.

In this report, we first explain what reciprocity means and what role it has played in creating today's institutional environment for global trade and investment. Then we describe why the emergence of China as a global investor is challenging those principles. Finally, we discuss the negative impacts for Europe from this reciprocity gap and illustrate the urgent need to address the existing gap. We conclude by offering recommendations to European policymakers.

The Diagnosis: EU-China Investment Relations Lack Reciprocity

"Reciprocity," or the lack thereof, has become the new buzzword in EU-China investment relations. The term is commonly used to describe an unfair gap between market access of Chinese investors in Europe and European companies in China. However, it is poorly defined and used in different contexts. In this section, we first clarify the basic concept of reciprocity, then review different metrics to help quantify the EU-China reciprocity gap, and lastly discuss why European leaders urgently need to address the gap.

Reciprocity is an important concept in social and political relations and has become the guiding principle in economic globalization. In the broader context, reciprocity refers to rough equivalence in "actions that are contingent on rewarding actions from others and that can cease when these expected reactions are not forthcoming."

Between sovereign states it is considered a standard of behavior which can produce cooperation and constitutes the foundation of international legal obligations. In the context of international economics, the concept of reciprocity has mostly been associated with liberal trade policies. Major international commercial treaties since the 18th century have referred to reciprocity in trade concessions. Most importantly, the reciprocity principle is the central norm of the General Agreement on Tariffs and Trade (GATT) and the World Trade Organization (WTO). In addition to serving as guiding principle for coordinated liberalization (upward convergence in openness), reciprocity can also refer to in-kind responses to both beneficial or harmful acts, such as countries or politicians lowering or increasing market access barriers in reaction to declining or increasing levels of protection in another country.

Historically, most bilateral and multilateral economic agreements were not based on absolute reciprocity requirements (i.e. full equivalence of market opportunities), but on the notion of relative equivalence of benefits that consider a country's specific characteristics and developmental situation. For example, the integration of developing and emerging economies into global arrangements such as GATT/WTO was based on relative reciprocity concepts that allowed phase out periods, grandfathering preexisting provisions and other exceptions.

While reciprocity principles have been the foundation for many trade agreements, their application on investment relations has remained rare. Rules related to reciprocity in investment relations inside the WTO framework remain limited and attempts to promote investment reciprocity in multilateral agreements in the late 1990s (the OECD Multilateral Agreement on Investment) have failed.[1] Today, international agreements on investment openness are limited to bilateral investment treaties and several regional arrangements with investment provisions.[2] In the absence of global agreements, global investment openness was mostly promoted by a coalition of advanced economies as well as unilateral measures to liberalize foreign capital inflows irrespective of the same treatment overseas. For instance, the EU treaties include the principle of free movement of capital toward not only EU members but also third countries on an explicitly non-reciprocal basis (Judgement of the Court 2007). Existing EU and OECD commitments explicitly rule out most forms of reciprocity conditionality regarding investment openness (OECD 2018).

For most of the past three decades, this status quo worked well since global cross-border investment flows were dominated by OECD economies that by and large followed those basic principles of mutual investment openness. Asymmetries in investment openness between OECD nations and China were a second order priority for policymakers. For one, China had few legal obligations under WTO/GATT to liberalize investment access. Two, the Asian Financial Crisis of 1997 and the Global Financial Crisis of 2008/2009 reinforced the notion that it was prudent for an emerging economy like China to only gradually liberalize its capital account. Third, multinationals were making handsome profits in China despite investment restrictions, and the Chinese government promised to continue liberalization of closed sectors. Fourth, as Chinese outbound investment remained negligible for the first three decades of reform, there were no Chinese companies that benefited from the tilted playing field outside of the Chinese market.

1 TRIPS, The Agreement on Trade-Related Aspects of Intellectual Property Rights; and GATS, the General Agreement on Trade in Services.

2 For example the North American Free Trade Agreement or the Vietnam-EU Free Trade Agreement signed in 2018.

Several of these variables have changed in recent years. Growth rates in the Chinese economy have slowed, increasing competition and thus the need for a level playing field. At the same time, Beijing has been slow delivering on FDI liberalization and other market-oriented reforms. Finally, Chinese outbound investment has soared, allowing Chinese corporations to enjoy European openness while being protected from foreign competition at home.

The reciprocity problem with China extends to restrictions at market entry (i.e. foreign companies are not allowed to invest in certain sectors) as well as formal and informal discrimination post market entry (i.e. companies can invest but face disadvantages operating in China compared to Chinese-owned companies). Recently announced policies to level the playing field are ambitious but they have not yet led to a measurable improvement of either dimension, and the recent track record casts significant doubts on the Chinese government's determination to fully implement them.

One dimension of openness is "de jure" openness to FDI, i.e. to what extent laws and regulations prohibit foreigners to invest in a country's economy. Using this yardstick, EU member states are considered among the most open economies in the world, in comparison to the global average as well as other advanced economies (Figure 1). China, on the contrary, despite its history of reform and opening up, remains heavily restrictive. On aggregate, China ranks as one of the most restrictive economies in the world, well below the OECD average and even below most emerging markets.[3]

A more detailed breakdown of FDI restrictions by industry reveals discrepancies across sectors (Figure 2). In virtually all industries, China is vastly more restrictive compared to EU economies. The discrepancies are especially large in the service sector, which remains heavily protected in China and restricted for foreign companies. Real estate is the only sector, in which EU economies, on aggregate, have restrictions similar to those in China.

3 The focus on formal restrictions distorts this perspective. If we were to take into account informal FDI discrimination, China would likely score better in a comparison with its emerging market peers.

Figure 1. Formal FDI Restrictions

FDI Restrictiveness (Index: 1=Closed / 0=Open),

Selected Economies and Country Groups, 2016

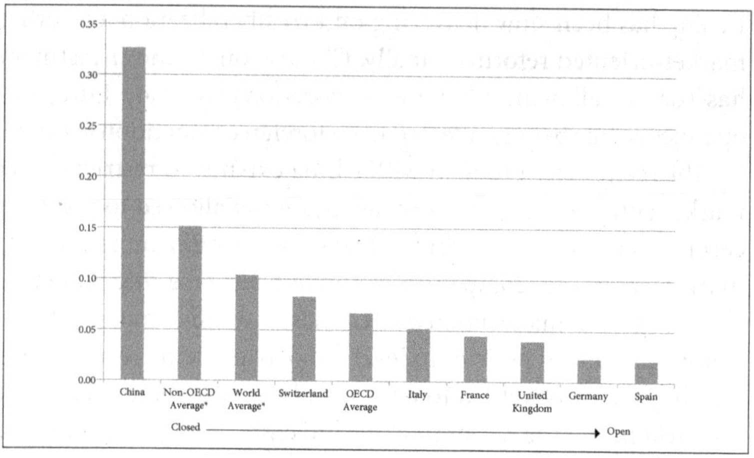

Source: author´s elaboration based on OECD. The index is compiled by measuring restrictions on foreign equity, screening and prior approval requirements, rules for key personnel, and other restrictions on operating foreign enterprises.

Figure 2. Chinese and EU Restrictions

FDI Restrictiveness Index (1=Closed / 0=Open),

EU vs. China, Sector by Sector, 2016

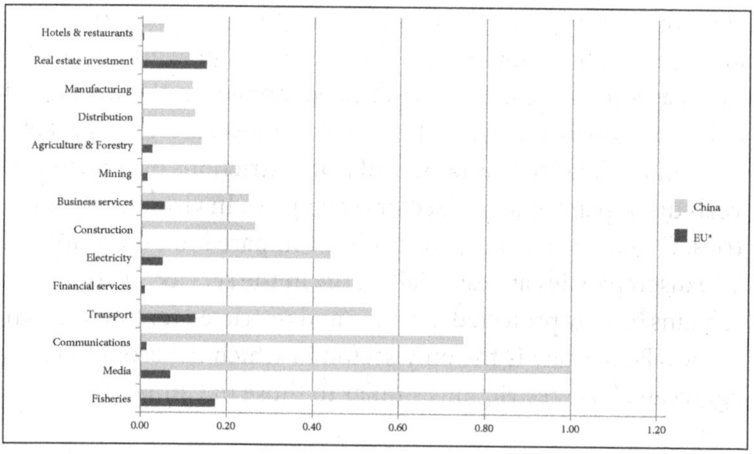

Source: author´s elaboration based on OECD:*Includes all available country in the OECD FDI Restrictiveness Index (Austria, Belgium, Czech Republic, Denmark, Estonia, Finland, France, Germany, Greece, Hungary, Ireland, Italy, Latvia, Lithuania, Luxembourg, Netherlands, Poland, Portugal, Romania, Slovakia, Slovenia, Spain, Sweden, and the UK).

Figure 3. FDI Liberalization

Formal FDI Restrictiveness Index (1=Closed / 0=Open) for China by sector, 2003-2016

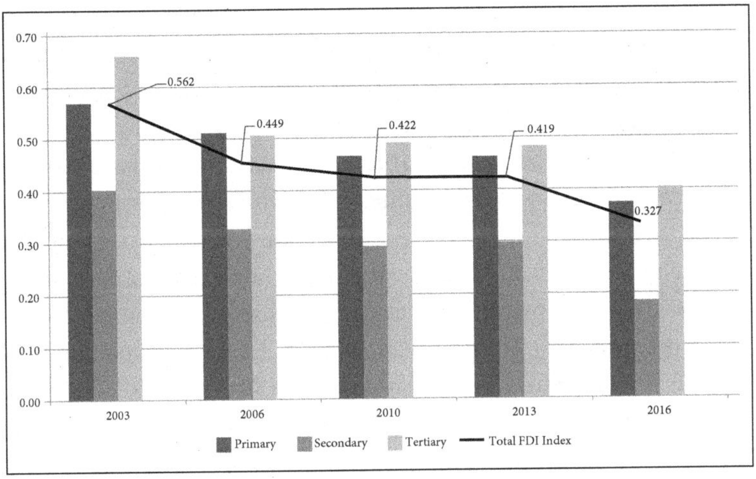

Source: author´s elaboration based on OECD.

Another useful perspective is the evolution of FDI restrictiveness over time. Figure 3 illustrates that China's FDI reform momentum was strong in the early 2000s but slowed since 2006. That progress virtually stalled until 2013. Since 2014, the pace of reform has picked up again. This reflects China's efforts to transition from an approval system (based on three lists of prohibited, restricted and encouraged sectors) to a new regulatory framework for FDI that will give foreign investors access to all sectors except ones defined through a negative list. If properly implemented, the new regime would legally abandon the distinction between foreign enterprises and local private firms in those sectors that are not on the negative list. In addition to this general administrative overhaul Beijing has recently made some progress in removing several sectors from the list of restricted or prohibited sectors.[4]

4 Relaxations included lifting of ownership percentage in steel, ethylene, oil refining, paper manufacturing; opening-up of non-ferrous metal smelting, small construction machinery manufacturing, and ordinary bearings manufacturing; and opening-up of import and export commodity inspection and certification, railway freight transport, insurance brokerage, accounting companies and trust companies.

A second important dimension of reciprocity is the treatment of foreign companies post market entry. While foreign companies enjoy equal rights and regulatory treatment in the European Union, China still discriminates against European and other foreign businesses. For decades, foreign-invested enterprises have been defined a separate group in the Chinese economy, which was subject to special treatment and different rules than domestic (i.e. Chinese-owned) companies. Informal discrimination against foreign-owned businesses continues to be widespread, especially on local government levels. There is abundant research documenting a wide range of administrative practices restraining foreign investors post-establishment.[5] Surveys among foreign businesses broadly confirm these findings. Over the past decade, companies have regularly complained about unequal enforcement of laws and other discriminatory practices (The European Union Chamber of Commerce in China 2018).

Notably, while formal FDI restrictiveness shows improvement since 2014, survey data suggests that informal discrimination has worsened in recent years. For the past four years, more than half of European companies have consistently reported that they are treated unfairly compared to domestic Chinese companies. Moreover, foreign businesses do not report high confidence that China will be able to implement substantial reforms that can address these problems in the coming years. There are significant concerns that new policies (such as Made in China 2025, ICT localization, cyber security or the implementation of the Anti-Monopoly law) will continue to tilt the playing field in favor of Chinese-owned businesses, even if China moves to legally abolish special treatment of foreign companies.

5 This includes measures such as a targeted enforcement of laws, financial support and other favorable treatment for local companies, and limited access to government procurement on all levels of the Chinese administrative system.

FDI Reform Announcements Warrant Skepticism

Since 2014, Beijing has made a push to re-ignite reforms that would address both market entry restrictions as well as post-market entry discrimination. China has made some progress on both goals in the course of 2017.

First, China has officially decided to abolish its traditional FDI regime and replace it with a framework that is based on pre-establishment rights restricted by a negative list only. This decision paves the way for China to abandon its planned economy approach to FDI and move closer to a modern approach for regulating FDI. While the negative list started out as an amalgamation of its lists of restricted and prohibited sectors, China cut it down throughout 2017 and demonstrated greater seriousness in reducing red tape for foreign investors. In July 2017, MOFCOM updated its regulation on the recording process for FIE establishment and change, formally eliminating approvals for foreign acquisitions in China (MOFCOM 2018). In August 2017, the State Council promised to open an additional 12 sectors, including electric vehicles and financial services, to foreign investment.[6] During U.S. President Trump's visit in November 2017, China announced to further open up foreign ownership in the financial services sector (The State Council of the People's Republic of China 2017). At the end of 2017, China announced to temporarily exempt foreign firms from taxes on profits reinvested in certain industries specified by Beijing (MOFCOM 2017/a). Other incremental changes in the past few months include further opening up of services sectors in the city of Beijing and regulatory changes to support opening up in the Free Trade Zones (XYZ 2017/a, 2018).

Second, China's leadership has vowed to address the discriminatory treatment of foreign-owned companies. At a central financial and economics Leading Small Group meeting in summer

6 The 12 sectors are: special-use vehicles and new energy automobile manufacturing, ship design, regional and general aircraft repair and maintenance, international maritime transport, rail passenger transport, gas stations, internet access service businesses (i.e. internet cafes), call centers, performance brokers, banking, securities, and insurance.

2017, President Xi himself stated the goal that "after entry, [foreign and domestic companies] should be equal in law and consistent in policy, and have national treatment" (Xinhua 2017). A State Council document on FDI reforms from August 2017 included the promise to "guarantee post-entry national treatment" for foreign companies. That same document also promised a range of policies aimed at tackling informal discrimination facing FIEs, including in taxation, personnel and visa, foreign exchange, intellectual property, and participation in initiatives such as "Made in China 2025" (MOFCOM 2017/b; XYZ 2017/b).

These steps are positive, and China's top leaders have promised to "exceed expectations of the international community" with further pushing forward reforms in 2018 (He 2018). However, serious concerns remain about China's ability to fully and timely implement the announced FDI reforms. In general, Beijing has made very slow progress on the market-oriented reform agenda it promised in late 2013 (Asia Society and Rhodium Group 2018). To the contrary, China under Xi Jinping has in fact moved backwards in some regards by replacing doubling down on industrial policies and greater party-state guidance in key sectors of the economy. Examples are the re-introduction of capital controls for foreign investors, the pursuit of industrial policies that discriminate against foreign companies, and the selective and sometimes mercantilist implementation of tools such as the Anti-Monopoly Law or the Chinese Intellectual Property regime. Ultimately, only with substantial progress towards more rule of law in China would foreign companies enjoy the necessary "contestability" for equal market participation. The past track record suggests that foreign skepticism about implementation of FDI reforms and their robustness is warranted.

The Impacts of the Lack of Investment Reciprocity

The described asymmetries in investment openness are not just a theoretical problem. They already cause major imbalances and distortions in capital flows between China and Europe, and they

Table 1. Chinese Acquisitions in Europe over $1 billion vs. the Permissibility of Similar Transactions in China

Date	EU Target	Chinese investor	USD billion	Sector	Notes
Dec-17	Logicor	CIC	14	Warehouses and logistics	Legally not restricted
Feb-17	NXP Semiconductors Standard Products Business	Jianguang AM, Wise Road Cap	2,8	Semiconductors	Legally possible but unlikely
Dec-16	Supercell	Tencent	8,6	Software / Online Gaming	Foreing ownership prohibited
Oct-16	Pirelli	ChemChina	7,7	Automotive Equipment/Tyres	Legally not restricted
Aug-16	KUKA	Midea	4,7	Industrial Machinery / Robotics	Legally possible but unlikely
Oct-15	Tank&Rast	CIC	3,8	Infrastructure / Gas Stations	Legally possible but unlikely
Dec-16	Global Switch	Chinese consortium	2,9	IT Services / Data Centers	Foreing ownership restricted
Jan-16	Avolon	HNA	2,5	Aircraft Leasing	Legally possible but unlikely
Dec-15	NXP Semiconductors RF Power Business	Jianguang Asset Management	1,8	Semiconductors	Legally possible but unlikely
Dec-16	Skyscanner	Ctrip	1,7	E-commerce	Legally not restricted
Feb-16	EEW Energy	Beijing Enterprises	1,6	Waste Incineration and Conversion	Legally not restricted
Dec-16	Urbaser	Firion Investment	1,6	Waste Management and Treatment	Legally not restricted
Oct-16	Groupe SMCP	Shandong Ruyi	1,4	Consumer Products / Textiles	Legally not restricted
Nov-16	Odeon & UCI Cinemas	Wanda	1,2	Movie Theatres	Foreing majority ownership restricted
Oct-16	BGP	CIC	1,1	Real Estate	Legally not restricted
Apr-16	KraussMaffei	ChemChina	1	Industrial Machinery / Automation	Legally possible but unlikely
Mar-17	11% Stake in UK National Grid Gas Distribution Business	CIC	1 (est.)	Utilities /Gas Pipelines	Legally possible but unlikely

Source: author´s elaboration based on Rhodium Group. *Analysis based on policy documents and authors' judgment.

cause real harm to European businesses and consumers. Finally, the perception of China as a free rider of the international trading system amplifies protectionist sentiment in the European public and undermines efforts for deepening economic cooperation with China. At the most granular level, the lack of reciprocity in market access leads to unfair competition between individual companies. Table 1 shows all Chinese takeovers with a value of US$ 1 billion or more in the period from 2000 to 2017. One quarter of those deals could not have legally been possible in the other direction at the same time as foreign investment in those sectors was prohibited or restricted. In half of the instances, the transactions would have been legally permissible but highly unlikely to be approved because of state control, industrial policies and other factors.[7] In other words, roughly three out of four of the largest Chinese acquisitions in Europe since 2000 could not have happened the other way around.

On an aggregate level, these existing barriers have already led to visible imbalances in EU-China FDI flows. Traditionally, EU FDI flows into China were significantly higher than Chinese outbound flows, which is in line with what economic theory would predict. Since 2010 the tide has turned rapidly, with Chinese FDI in the EU overtaking flows in the other direction since 2014. For the past three years, Chinese FDI in the EU surpassed EU FDI in China by a factor of three (Figure 4). These flows were almost exclusively driven by M&A activity, which remains heavily restricted in the other direction. Within a span of just five years, China's FDI stock in Europe has caught up to Europe's FDI stock in China (Figure 5).

Bilateral FDI flows are rarely perfectly balanced and reflect a host of macroeconomic, commercial, and firm-level factors including different development levels, comparative advantage, financial expectations, and other variables. However, there is clear evidence that political factors are causing imbalances that would not exist under free market conditions. In 2016, Chinese investment in the EU was higher than EU investment in China in 10 out of 15 industries. Chinese restrictions are a major factor for this

7 This classification is based on the authors' personal judgment, considering legal documents, empirical data (precedents of foreign M&A in those sectors) and conversations with M&A professionals in China.

Figure 4. Chinese FDI Flows to the EU Annual value of 3 -China Bilateral FDI Transactions (EUR million), 2000-2017

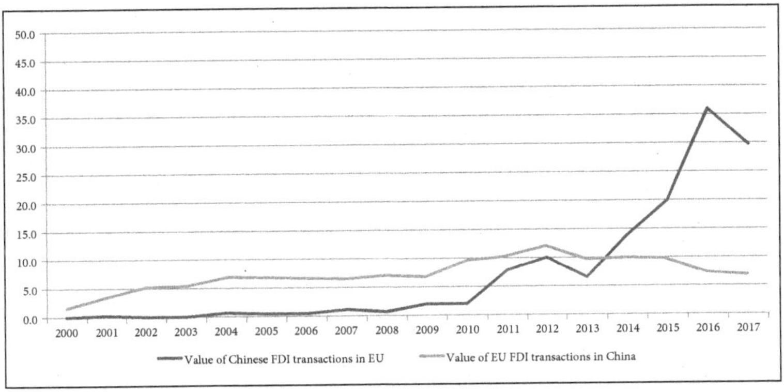

Source: author´s elaboration based on Rhodium Group.

Figure 5. Cumulative Chinese FDI in the EU has now caught up with EU FDI in China EUR million, 2000-2017

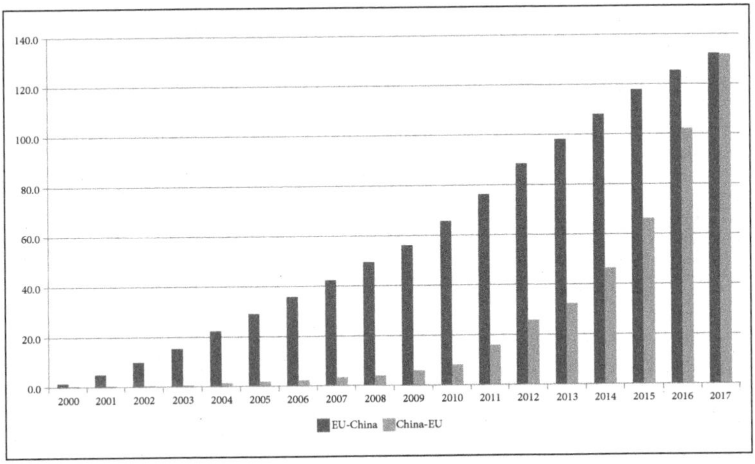

Source: author´s elaboration based on Rhodium Group.

imbalance, plainly visible for example in transport and infrastructure, entertainment, and energy and power generation (see Figure 6).

Moreover, the investment flows that are happening are clearly distorted by Chinese ownership restrictions that force foreign companies into minority joint ventures. Figure 7 illustrates that

Figure 6. Two-way EU-China FDI Dynamics by Sector

Annual investment 2000-2017, value in EUR million; EU-CN= ▒, CN-EU= ■

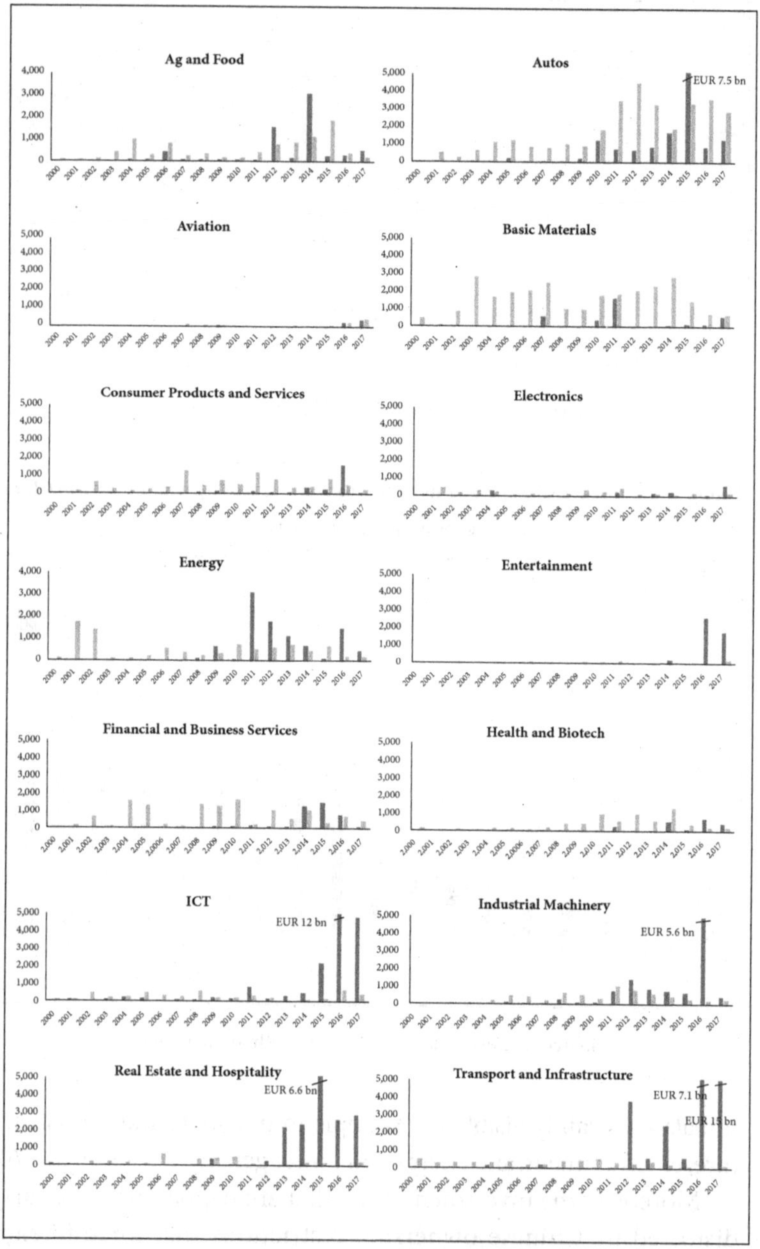

Source: author´s elaboration based on Rhodium Group.

at the example of two-way FDI in the automotive sector between Germany and China. Chinese investors mostly take majority stakes in in the German auto sector while German investors are forced to have more than half of their capital in China in minority stakes. Of the $27 billion of German FDI in the Chinese automotive sector, 55% was invested in joint ventures in which German companies were by law only permitted to have a minority stake of 49% or lower. Flows in the other direction were lower ($4 billion), but almost exclusively went into operations in which the Chinese investor held controlling ownership stakes.

Figure 7. Cumulative Value of FDI Transactions, 2000-2017

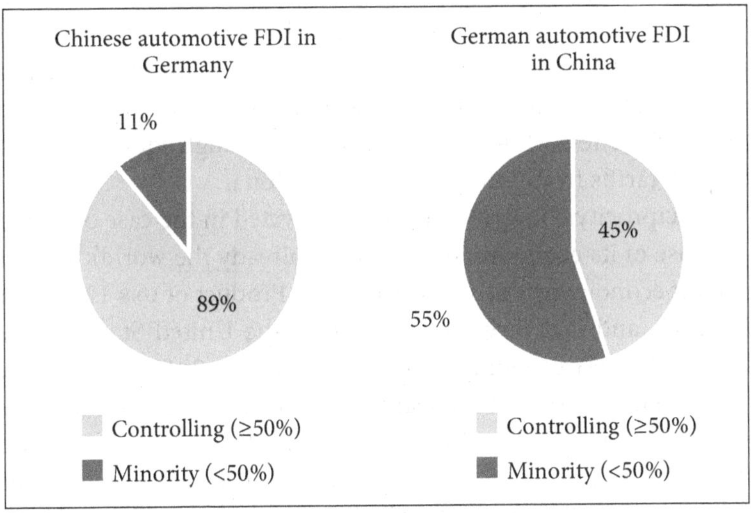

Source: author´s elaboration based on Rhodium Group.

If it persists, the lack of investment reciprocity can generate serious economic harm to European producers and consumers.

Uneven market access is a distortion of free competition, which poses a serious threat to the functioning of efficient markets. It protects less competitive Chinese firms from being defeated or swallowed by more productive overseas companies. It could even allow these less productive firms to acquire or defeat more productive overseas firms in their own home market, especially if additional subsidies and other distortions exacerbate the situation. If persistent, such patterns could lead to consolidation of an industry in the hands of inefficient but protected players. This in turn has serious negative implications for consumer welfare and innovation.

Take, for example, the automotive industry. European auto manufacturers face high tariffs of 25% and higher as well as taxes on car imports into China. For manufacturing and selling cars in China, they are required to engage in a joint venture with a Chinese company, which they cannot control (they can own a maximum of 49%) and are expected to share technology. Moreover, there are special requirements for localization of supply chains. Chinese companies on the other hand are free to enter the European market through 100% ownership of greenfield facilities, and they are free to acquire 100% ownership of existing European automakers as well as auto suppliers. In short, Chinese companies can utilize EU acquisitions and R&D operations to improve their competitiveness while they are protected through equity caps and import tariffs from European firms in China.

Reciprocity concerns get further elevated in the case of China because of its economic size. China is already the world's second largest economy with a Gross Domestic Product of US$ 12 trillion in 2017, and it is projected to surpass the United States as the world's biggest economy around 2032 (CEBR 2018). This is not a problem per se, but it means that China will have enormous weight and impact on global market structures and asset prices. If a country the size of China pursues policies that cause major market distortions, it could inflict serious harm on global markets.

In addition to these economic concerns, the EU-China reciprocity gap contributes to the erosion of support for a liberal economic order and plays in favor of those opposing greater economic cooperation between China and the EU.

Reciprocity has been a core principle of globalization in the past decades. While it was legitimate for China to open its capital account in gradual steps, many of China's provinces have now reached a development level that render arguments for protectionist policies, such as enabling the growth of infant industry, invalid. The rapid rise in outbound investment by Chinese firms must be interpreted as evidence that Chinese companies can now compete at levelly with foreign players. This erodes the argument that they need protection at home.

The perception that China, a major beneficiary of a liberal global trade and investment environment, is not playing fair undermines popular support for further integration and fuels the rise of protectionist sentiment worldwide (Chilton, Milner, and Tingley 2017). Foreign dissatisfaction with the lack of reciprocity coincides with serious concerns about Chinese trade practices. China has delayed or ignored several key WTO commitments (USTR 2018) and its aggressive industrial policies, like "Made in China 2025" which aims to replace foreign imports with domestic goods, violate the spirit of the WTO (Wübbeke et. al 2016). This behavior has escalated frictions between China and its trading partners in recent years. Many governments are re-configuring their external economic policies in response (Stevenson 2017).There is a problematic gap in FDI market access between the EU and China. Re-establishing a sense of relative reciprocity in investment relations is important from a moral perspective (fairness) but also for the sake of economic efficiency and, perhaps most importantly, to avoid further alienation between China and major OECD economies.

While Chinas has been moving in the right direction lately, there are many reasons to remain wary. China's track record of delaying economic reforms, of anti-foreign sentiment and top-down economic governance warrants caution. EU policymakers need to be more specific and realistic in defining what the EU can and should ask for to operationalize the principle of reciprocity. This needs to include sober considerations about the necessary political leverage and instruments of pressure. The following section describes several core principles for a "European Way" to approaching investment reciprocity with China and ntroduces a policy package that would move the EU forward.

The European Way

Europe is not alone in seeking the right response to the lack of reciprocity in investment and other aspects of economic relations with China. Many advanced economies (and increasingly also developing countries) are re-assessing economic relations with China in response to a perceived lack of fairness.

Perhaps the most radical re-assessment seems to be occurring in the United States, where the Trump administration has taken a more confrontational approach to certain Chinese practices, including trade defense cases and a far-reaching investigation into forced technology transfer based on a little known legal provision that can only be evoked under exceptional circumstances (USTR 2017).

European policymakers should pursue a more assertive economic agenda *vis-à-vis* China. They need to find policies that are effective but in line with European principles, values and political realities:

(1) Set realistic expectations. There are clear limits to what Europe and other advanced economies can expect from Beijing. For one, China will not converge with Western liberalism, and Beijing will not compromise on sectors it perceives as critical to the power of the Chinese Communist Party, for example media and communications. Two, China is facing tremendous economic challenges and it will maintain control over sectors that it perceives as critical for managing the transition to a new growth model, such as banking and other types of financial intermediation. These realities need to be considered when setting priorities for market access negotiations with China. Priority number one should be to push for Chinese convergence in sectors that have no national security dimensions and for equal treatment of foreign investors post market entry.

(2) Downward convergence should be the last resort. Europe has been a champion of investment openness and it needs to defend these values. It should still aim for upward convergence

in FDI openness and build up the necessary leverage to effectively pursue this goal. The feasibility of a "net benefit test" in the European context, a method employed by Canada that allows for incorporating economic considerations in the screening of investment, deserves debate as a potential response to negative reciprocity if things turn worse. At the current stage, however, steps such as the introduction of absolute (sectoral) reciprocity requirements or other methods to shut down the European economy to Chinese investment are premature. Not only would they violate European values and interests, they would also require a fundamental overhaul of European treaties. The distortions caused by unequal market access are not yet large and acute enough to warrant such aggressive steps.

(3) Keep national security screenings separate from reciprocity goals. EU leaders and member state officials have repeatedly framed the proposal on investment screening presented by the EU Commission in September 2017 as a tool to level the playing field with China (FMEAE 2017). This is wrong and dangerous. The new Commission proposal is focused on security interests and was not created to address the reciprocity problem. The proposed "enabling framework" might open the door for an expanded definition of strategic assets that allows member states –with the tacit support of Brussels and partners– to scrutinize and potentially block investments for strategic-economic reasons beyond very limited public security and public order concerns. Such an instrumentalization of a security screening framework to achieve economic goals through the backdoor is a slippery slope and would violate Europe's principled openness. Not only will it most likely result in inefficient interventions, but it will also increase the chances of Chinese retaliation, which could lead to substantial economic losses and ignite a global protectionist spiral.

(4) Seek solutions based on existing frameworks and bureaucratic structures. Instead of creating additional layers of bureaucracy across various levels of European governance,

European leaders should seek solutions that can be implemented through existing structures, and that do not require a fundamental overhaul of processes or legal frameworks.

(5) Cooperate with like-minded market economies. The EU would benefit from ramping up international coordination with like-minded economies. OECD economies are affected to Chinese behavior in different ways, but, fundamentally, they all share the goal of getting China back on track to convergence with market-oriented economic principles.

A Policy Package for Europe

Based on these principles, we have identified a set of policies that the EU and its member states should pursue to address reciprocity concerns:

(1) Push for a robust bilateral investment treaty. Europe's current approach to achieving greater FDI reciprocity with China is centered on getting China to agree to a bilateral treaty that defines investment market access based on a negative list. Negotiations of a Comprehensive Agreement on Investment (CAI) between China and the EU started in 2013 and assume that China has self-interest in further opening up to sustain inflows as well as openness for Chinese investors in the European market.

A robust CAI with China would be the most elegant solution to address current reciprocity gaps. However, for it to be robust, any agreement will need to go beyond existing templates such as the FDI chapter in the Vietnam-EU FTA. European negotiators need to develop innovative solutions to address different channels of party-state influence in China's corporate realities. They will also need to devise transparency and regulatory standards as a basis for sophisticated dispute settlement mechanisms. Given these complexities and fundamental differences about how extensive the FDI negative list should be, it is uncertain that CAI negotiations are going to produce tangible results any time soon. EU leaders need to prepare for a scenario in which CAI negotiations go nowhere.

(2) Build an efficient, focused, and transparent European framework for security screenings. The starting point for EU efforts to address reciprocity concerns must be the creation of a transparent and efficient process for screening foreign investment for national security concerns. A robust European framework is a prerequisite for keeping up public support for economic engagement with China, despite its authoritarian regime and increasingly aggressive geopolitical posture. An efficient security screening regime is also important because it would draw a clear line between security interests and purely economic goals.

The recent proposal for a pan-European EU investment screening regime, which operates with an updated understanding of what constitutes the European defense-relevant industrial base, is a step in the right direction. More transparency and a more coordinated, up-to-date approach to protect critical infrastructures, strategic assets, and critical (enabling) technologies are sensible, and are long overdue.[8] However, in our view, the current proposal still lacks teeth and requires fine-tuning before it can become the foundation of a more coordinated European effort. European legislators need to make sure that "enabling technologies" are properly defined to not evoke national debates about "strategic sectors"; establish ways for expanding the coverage of investment types and lower thresholds (currently screening only applies to FDI); and align dual-use technologies, data, and information security with the export control regime.

(3) Explore new avenues for EU competition policy to address China-specific concerns. In its search for instruments to identify and mitigate economic risks from Chinese

8 See our long-standing views and recommendations, for example in: https://www.merics.org/en/papers-on-china.

investment, Europe must consider competition policy. The EU has in the past adjusted its competition policy to new challenges (most recently from US technology companies), and the emergence of Chinese companies as global players presents such a novel challenge. European merger control has already shifted towards a more encompassing assessment of Chinese corporate networks and control in horizontally and vertically related markets (Baket McKenzie 2016). While this is an important first step, it needs to be expanded beyond SOE s and formal aspects of state-holding. Going further, new avenues for competition policy could address many concerns related to Chinese practices, but European policy makers need to start this modernization process now.

Potential areas for modernization include:

- Treating the lack of two-way investment openness in innovative sectors and future industries as a potential barrier to market entry and participation when assessing mergers;
- Enabling public authorities to prioritize the availability of EU or OECD supply chains under limited circumstances (for instance by redefining what "substitutability" for relevant product and geographical markets means when assessing market shares);
- Allowing for more national leeway in defining legitimate public interest concerns depending on a EU member state's innovation environment and its secure supply (not control) of enabling technologies;
- Strengthening the external grip of the EU's state-aid regime for assessing market-distorting subsidies to cover investment-related activities of non-OECD foreign enterprises, for instance by defining domestic market protection as an implicit subsidy; and
- Strengthening the linkages of competition policy with intellectual property protection and standard setting

policies to tackle technology appropriation more comprehensively.

Moving towards some of these suggested revisions will not be an easy task and might require fundamental changes, including of European treaties. It is also clear, however, that the EU needs to step up its game for a new phase of global competition in which FDI, innovation and standard-setting by state-influenced economies such as China's will become a dominant force in global markets.

(4) Push for reciprocal market access where the EU has leverage. Access to European government procurement as well as European financial and digital markets can be used to create leverage *vis-à-vis* Beijing. China has so far shunned the notion of clean procurement processes and still has not joined the international Government Procurement Agreement. European governments need to align behind the EU Commission's proposals to introduce an international procurement instrument (or IPI) that could potentially tackle some of the reciprocity issues in investment relations with China. The EU also could condition future Chinese activities in European financial and digital markets through coordinated low key regulatory measures (for instance through transparency and privacy requirements or data security certification). The Chinese response to such measures will indicate how serious Beijing is about making changes, and how quickly Europe may have to consider worst case scenarios.

(5) Build coalitions with like-minded countries. OECD countries are in the same boat, yet there is relatively little coordination among them as to a joint strategy toward China. OECD members are, on the contrary, likely to enter into a race to the bottom in which certain countries will seek special treatment for their own investments in China at the expense of a collective approach. Several areas of cooperation should be prioritized:

- First, large OECD members need to agree on a basic set of demands and timetables. This coalition should coordinate its assessment of which sectors it considers security relevant or legitimately critical for developmental purposes. Officials from these countries should then ask for a clear timetable to open all sectors that are not on those lists, with milestones and measures to hold Beijing accountable. OEDC countries should not wait with their demands for liberalizing these sectors until Chinese state-supported enterprises already dominate the domestic market, preventing a reasonable participation of foreign actors. One particularly relevant framework of coordination would be US-EU exchanges on BIT-negotiations with China (despite different interests and approaches on both sides of the Atlantic).
- Second, OECD countries need to intensify information sharing on persisting problems. Only then can policy debates about the lack of reciprocity with China and potential remedies be linked up more meaningfully. Placing these themes on the research and policy agendas of international financial institutions could generate additional input and add legitimacy to European requests.
- Finally, it will be critical to create incentives for Beijing to raise its standards through exclusive trade, data/privacy, and investment agreements. Putting TPP and TTIP back on the table, or possibly moving forward with a more minimalist transatlantic approach (for instance on services) could go a long way toward inducing Beijing to converge. An agreement on privacy, localization, and cyber standards as well as relatively free data flows among a club of OECD members could also create leverage for reciprocal market access on European terms.

Not all of these efforts need to exclude China. On the contrary, Beijing should, for instance, be pulled much more forcefully into the orbit of OECD coverage and related policy exchanges, which would require equipping the institution with the necessary resources to expand its facilitating role and peer-pressure function. While designing a genuine multilateral approach to investment regulation together with China remains a longer term ambition, the G20 investment agenda deserves continuous support and clear direction by European leaders.

How to level the playing field and establish greater reciprocity in economic relations with China has become a major question in many capitals. As a major force in global FDI flows and an important destination of Chinese capital, Europe should not sit on the sidelines and let the take the lead. Europe is well positioned to help the world deal with Chinese investment without creating damage to productive Chinese capital or the global investment environment.

References

Asia Society and Rhodium Group. 2018. "The China Dashboard. Tracking China's Economic Reform Program". *Asia Society* and *Rhodium Group*. In: https://chinadashboard.asiasociety.org/china-dashboard/

Baker McKenzie. 2016. "EU merger decisión shines light on state-owned enterprises". *Baker McKenzie*, in: https://www.internationallawoffice.com/Newsletters/Competition-Antitrust/European-Union/Baker-McKenzie-LLP/EU-merger-decision-shines-light-on-state-owned-enterprises.

CEBR (Center for Economic Business Research). 2018. *World Economic League Tables*. London: CEBR.

Chilton, Adam, Helen Milner, and Dustin Tingley. 2017. "Reciprocity and Public Opposition to Foreign Direct Investment". *British Journal of Political Science*, pp. 1-25.

FMEAE (Federal Ministry for Economic Affairs and Energy). 2017. "EU proposal on investment vetting is an important step towards level playing field in Europe and better protection in case of corporate acquisitions. Joint press reléase by Germany, France, Italy". Brussels: FMEAE.

Judgement of the Court. 2007. "Judgement of the Court (Grand Chamber) in Case C-101-05". In: http://curia.europa.eu/juris/showPdf.jsf;jsessionid=C874FF90920F631AA75072CC2A9B1570?text=&docid=71748&pageIndex=0&doclang=EN&mode=lst&dir=&occ=first&part=1&cid=526707.

He, Liu. 2018. "More reform and opening up policies will be implemented in China. World Economic Forum 2018". CGTN January 24th, in: https://www.youtube.com/watch?v=2tDoVv0GPOE.

Keohane, Robert O. 1986. "Reciprocity in International Relations". *International Organization*, 40(1), pp, 1-27.

MOFCOM (Ministry of Commerce). 2017/a. In: http://wzs.mofcom.gov.cn/article/n/201712/20171202691805.shtml

MOFCOM. 2017/b. In: http://www.mofcom.gov.cn/article/ae/ai/201708/20170802627851.shtml

MOFCOM. 2018. In: http://www.mofcom.gov.cn/article/b/c/201707/20170702617581.shtml.

OECD (Organisation for Economic Co-Operation and Development). 2018. OECD *Code of Liberalisation of Capital Movements*. Paris: OECD.

Stevenson, Alexandra. 2017. "Wilbur Ross, Fresh from China Visit, Warns of ´Lopsided´ Trade Relationship". *The New York Times*, September 27.

The European Chamber of Commerce in China. 2018. In: http://www.europeanchamber.com.cn/en/publications-archive.

The State Council of the People´s Republic of China. 2017. In: http://www.gov.cn/xinwen/2017-11/17/content_5240376.htm

USTR (United States Trade Representative). 2017. "USTR Announces Initiation of Section 301 Investigation of China". Washington D.C.: USTR. In: https://ustr.gov/about-us/policy-offices/press-office/press-releases/2017/august/ustr-announces-initiation-section.

USTR. 2018. 2017 Report to Congress On China's WTO Compliance. Washington D.C.: USTR.

Wübbeke, Jost, Mirjam Meissner, Max J. Zenglein, Jaqueline Ives, and Björn Cornrad. 2016. "Made in China 2025: The making of a high-tech superpower and consequences for industrial countries". MERICS *Papers on China* 2, pp. 1-76.

Xinhua. 2017. In http://www.xinhuanet.com/politics/2017-07/17/c_1121333722.htm.
XYZ. 2017/a. In: http://www.gov.cn/zhengce/content/2017-12/22/content_5249525.htm.
XYZ. 2017/b. In: http://www.gov.cn/zhengce/content/2017-01/17/content_5160624.htm.
XYZ. 2018. In: http://www.gov.cn/zhengce/content/2018-01/09/content_5254764.htm.

CHINESE OFDI IN AFRICA

Linda Calabrese

Introduction

The relationship between China and Africa is longstanding but recent historical and economic developments have brought China and Africa closer together. China is now Africa's largest trading partner, and one of its largest investors. African countries have found in China a new partner that can, under the right conditions, support their development objectives.

The narrative around China-Africa looks at the effects of the recent strengthening of commercial and political relationships. This chapter focuses on Chinese investment in Africa and its potential impacts, benefits and challenges. First, it describes the status and trends of Chinese investment in Africa. Secondly, it examines the main features of this investment as outlined by the current literature. In particular, it looks at China's role in building infrastructure, investing in natural resources, and creating jobs in Africa. Thirdly, it analyses African agency as part of the relationship and finally, it offers some conclusions.

Overview of Chinese OFDI in Africa

Global foreign direct investment (FDI) stocks into Africa have increased from US$ 150 billion in 2000 to more than 800 billion in 2016, growing at an average 10% a year (UNCTAD 2018). Chinese outward investment in Africa has also increased, though at a faster pace compared to the global average. Data collected by the John Hopkins University China-Africa Research Initiative shows that Chinese outward FDI (OFDI) stocks in Africa have increased from less than US$ 500 million in 2003 to almost US$ 40 billion in 2016, growing at an average 29% a year, or three times faster than global investment (China-Africa Research Initiative, 2018). The highest Chinese investment stocks were found in South Africa (US$ 4.7 million, or 13.6% of the total stock of Chinese OFDI in Africa), the Democratic Republic of Congo (US$ 3.2 million, or 9.6% of total) and Algeria (US$ 2.7 million, of 7.3% of total) (see Figure 1; China-Africa Research Initiative 2018).

Figure 1. Chinese OFDI into Africa, Stock (million US$, current prices)

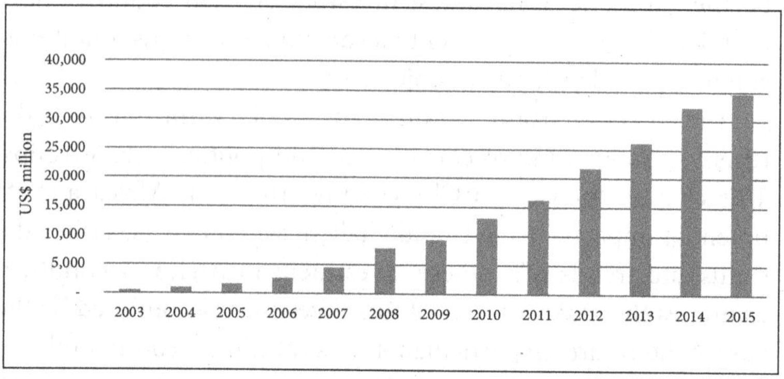

Source: author´s elaboration based on China-Africa Research Initiative (2018).

Chinese investment flows into Africa grew considerably since 2003, peaking in 2008. Figures for the latest years show a more stable trend, with investment flows stabilizing at around US$ 3 billion per year (see Figure 2; China-Africa Research Initiative 2018).

Figure 2. Chinese Investment into Africa, Flows (million US$, current prices)

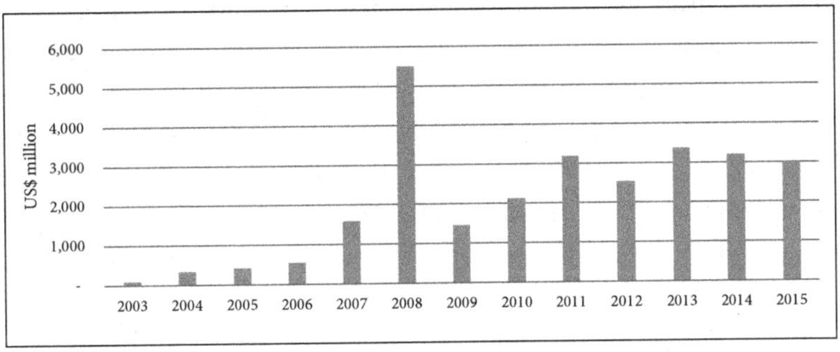

Source: author´s elaboration based on China-Africa Research Initiative (2018).

The most recent available data show that China is still behind the United States, the United Kingdom, and France in terms of investment stock in Africa. However, while the other major investors have barely increased their stock in the 2011-2016 period, China is still investing and catching up quickly (see Figure 3).

Figure 3. Top 10 Investors in Economies in Africa by FDI Stock (billion 3)

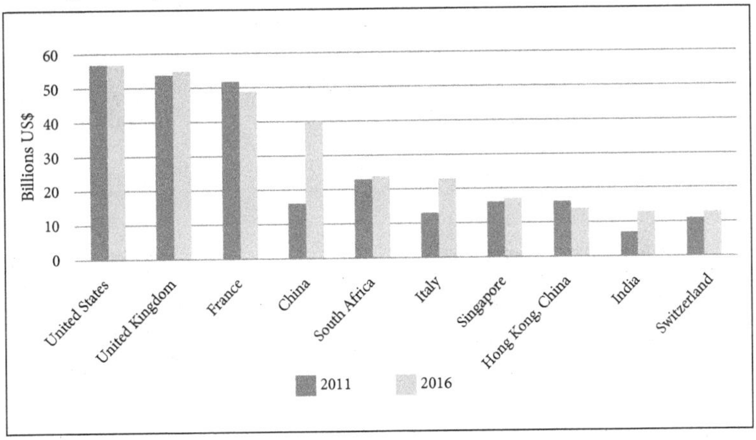

Source: author´s elaboration based on UNCTAD (2018).

Investments by the United States, the United Kingdom, and France to Africa target the extractives sector and financial services. Chinese investment is quite different: while mining and financial services receive some investment, they are much less prominent compared to the other countries. Construction and manufacturing constitute 40% of Chinese investment stocks in Africa.

This is not a negligible difference, especially considering African countries' renewed interest in industrialisation and job creation. Construction and manufacturing can be labor-intensive, manufacturing allows domestic value addition and diversification of exports, and construction of infrastructure unlocks potential growth for many other sectors. Given their sectoral composition, Chinese investment in Africa has more potential to kickstart economic transformation than the investments from traditional partners (see Figure 4).

Figure 4. FDI Stock in Africa by Investment Source and Sector

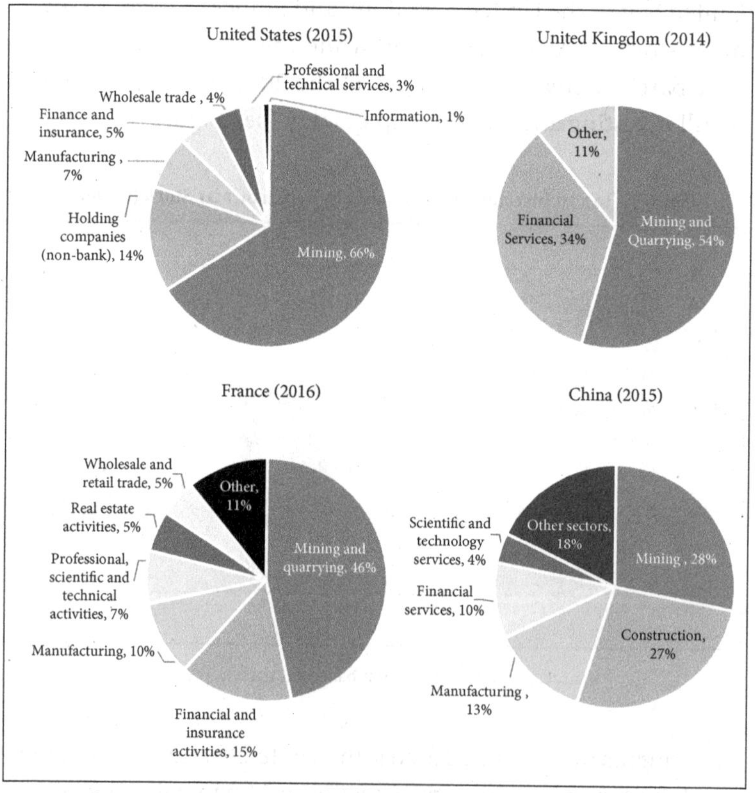

Sources: author's elaboration based on data for the United States and China comes from Eom et al. (2017); data for the United Kingdom comes from the Office for National Statistics (2016); data for France comes from the Banque de France (2018).

As much as China is an important investor for Africa, Africa is less prominent for China. Investment stock in Africa constituted less than 4% of Chinese outward investment in 2014 –less than what China had invested in the United States alone (US$ 32 billion versus 38 billion) (see Figure 5; Dollar 2016).

Figure 5. Chinese Outward FDI Stocks by Destination, 2017

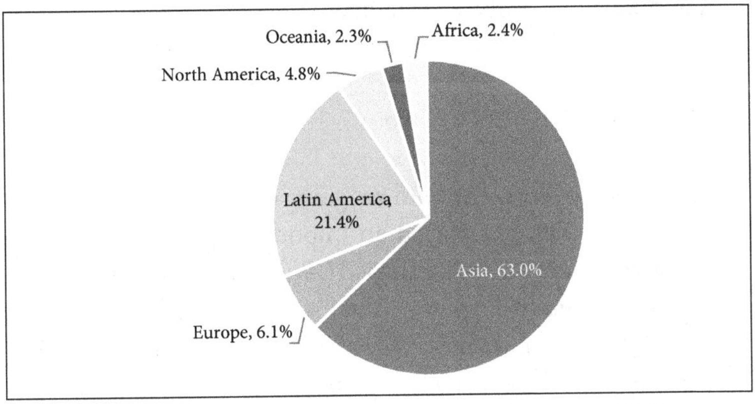

Source: author´s elaboration based on Ministry of Commerce (2017).

Box 1: What are the sources of information on Chinese investment in Africa?

Data on Chinese investment in Africa, especially if disaggregated by country and by sector, is difficult to obtain. Data collected by the United Nations Conference on Trade and Development (UNCTAD) at UNCTADStat provides disaggregated information by country but not by sector. Similarly, data by the Chinese Ministry of Commerce (MOFCOM) does not disaggregate enough by country and by sector, and only provides information on the largest investment destination.

A few datasets provide disaggregated data by country and sector. One is produced by the China-Africa Research Initiative combining data from China Statistical Yearbooks and Statistical Bulletins of China's Outward Foreign Direct Investment of various years (China-Africa Research Initiative, 2018).

The American Enterprise Institute and Heritage Foundation collect firm-level data at firm level for transactions larger than US$ 100 million (American Enterprise Institute & The Heritage Foundation, undated). However, this database does not include the smaller transactions which are likely to be prevalent in the manufacturing space, and only tracks commitment rather than actual spent. This is a common challenge for many datasets, including sources like FDIntelligence.

A Profile of Chinese Companies Investing in Africa

The Chinese government, with its "going out strategy" (*zou chu qu*) launched in 1999, has played an important role in encouraging Chinese companies to invest abroad (*Zhongguo Renmin Gongheguo Zhongyang Renmin Zhengfu* [The Central People's Government of the People's Republic of China], 2006). The Chinese government has been instrumental in directing state-led investment towards sectors of strategic interest in Africa. However, the Chinese private sector has also been heavily involved. Several studies have shown that Chinese companies investing in Africa are very diverse, ranging from last State-Owned Enterprises (SOEs) to small private companies. In 2011, 45% of total Chinese OFDI was coming from the Chinese private sector (Shen 2015).

Gu (2009) notes that between the 1950s and the 1980s, Chinese investment in Africa was dominated by companies implementing development assistance and by large SOEs. From the mid-1990s, acting independently from the government, Chinese private companies started investing in Africa and have continued to do so until now. The motivation behind this private interest is based on the domestic conditions in China, in particular the intensified domestic competition and surplus production. Most of these firms started in Africa as trading companies, and gradually moved into production. Private companies are generally small and medium-sized companies, and they are the driving force behind investment in African manufacturing (Gu 2009).

Shen (2015) notes that prior to 2000, MOFCOM did not record any private Chinese investment to Africa, but in 2013 its databased listed 1,217 projects, or 53% of the total investment projects in Africa. While state-led Chinese investment focus on construction and extractives, private investors (many of whom are doing business outside China for the first time) preferred manufacturing of garments, shoes, leather goods, food products, and trade and logistics (Gu 2009; Shen 2015). MOFCOM reports that by the end of 2015, a little less than 3,000 Chinese enterprises, or 9.6% of the total Chinese enterprises abroad, had set up shop in Africa. Chinese firms were present in all African countries and regions, except for a handful (Ministry of Commerce 2016)[1].

Box 2: How many Chinese companies are operating in Africa?

Many have attempted to estimate the number of Chinese businesses in Africa, but these estimates vary widely. Using MOFCOM data, Chen et al. (2015) estimates the presence of around 2,000 Chinese enterprises in Africa. A more recent study by McKinsey suggest there are about 10,000 Chinese firms in Africa (I. Y. Sun, Jayaram, & Kassiri, 2017), but the way this estimation is computed is not clear. Their figure seems to include both 'standard' FDI (companies with a head office in China) and 'entrepreneurial' FDI, where the firm has been set up by Chinese nationals who moved to an African country (Lin and Xu 2016; Xu, Gelb, Li, and Zhao 2017).

Why is it so difficult to estimate the number of Chinese firms operating in Africa? It has to do with the quality of the data held by the Chinese and the African counterparts. An example of this challenge is provide by Chen and Landry (2016) in their study on Chinese enterprises in Madagascar. They find that data from MOFCOM only records the larger companies

1 Among the countries and regions not hosting Chinese enterprises are Burkina Faso, La Reunion, Somalia, Swaziland, and Western Sahara (Ministry of Commerce 2015).

or those which seek assistance and permission from the government when investing abroad. The MOFCOM lists may also include investments approved by the Chinese government but not materialized in country. Investment data provided by host countries' investment agencies, on the other hand, often include closed or non-operational investments, as well as approved or pledged investment that was never realized. In addition, there may be firms that are not present in either list and have thus escaped the official headcount.

Drivers behind Chinese Investment in Africa

Why are Chinese companies investing in Africa? The reasons vary according to the sector, country and type of company undertaking the investment. Surveys conducted among Chinese companies investing in Africa found that the main drivers were divided into two main types of factors.

The first are push factors that encourage Chinese companies to invest outside China. These include the intense competition experienced in China, and the desire to export excess domestic capacity. The push factors are a response to China's domestic context, including rising wages and increased domestic competition as well as the desire to re-orient the Chinese economy towards more high-value industries and shed the excess capacity in low value industries (Gu 2009; Hou, Gelb and Calabrese 2017).

The second category includes pull factors that attract investors to Africa, such as the desire to access the local market and take advantage of Africa's trade agreements and preferential market access to export to third countries (W. Chen et al. 2015; Gu 2009:577; Shen 2015). Pull factors include the availability of labor and the quality and reliability of infrastructure in the host countries (Calabrese, Gelb and Hou 2017). Pull factors also determine which countries will host the investment. Countries like Nigeria and Ethiopia are attractive investment destinations due to their large domestic markets (Shen 2015). Many African countries also have preferential access to export to selected markets. For example, the African Growth and Opportunity Act (AGOA) allows selected African countries to export more than 6,000 tariff lines duty-free and quota-free to the United States. Chinese companies have established textile and garment operations in these countries to produce and export apparel to the United States (Traub-Merz and Jauch 2006).

The availability of resources is also an important driver for Chinese investment into Africa. Natural resources should be viewed in the broader sense, to include any sort of natural endowment of a country. Shen (2015), for example, finds that Chinese companies producing wood furniture and footwear set up shop in Ethiopia due to the availability of timber and leather.

Chinese Infrastructure Projects in Africa

African countries face an infrastructure gap across all main dimensions, including transport and logistics, energy, water, and sanitation, and information and telecommunication (ITC) (Dollar 2016). African countries fare poorly in terms of energy, logistics, and telecommunications even when compared with other developing regions (Calabrese et al. 2017).

In the 1970s and 1980s, traditional donors financed several infrastructure projects in Africa, but these financial streams dried out. Private funding was also not widely available to finance large-scale projects (Dollar 2016).

China's investment in infrastructure therefore takes place in this context of intense need combined with lack of financial resources. Infrastructure development has been critical for China's own development path, and therefore the Chinese government recognizes the important of infrastructure for developing countries. In recent years, China has become a large funder of infrastructure in Africa (Sautman and Yan 2008), effectively filling a gap left by others[2].

2 However, official development finance and foreign private financing remain larger than Chinese funding in Africa. China only provides about a sixth of the US$ 30 billion that African countries receive every year to fund their infrastructure (Dollar 2016).

The role China plays in Africa's infrastructure is very much enshrined in the official China-Africa relationship. The Forum of China-Africa Cooperation (FOCAC) regularly highlights infrastructure as a strategic area of cooperation between China and Africa (see Box 5), and in 2015 a Memorandum of Understanding on collaboration on infrastructure development was signed between China and the African Union (Xinhuanet 2015).

China's role does not only revolve around financing the infrastructure, but also around constructing it. Very often (but not always) loans from China have been tied to the use of Chinese goods and services (Brautigam and Gallagher 2014; Brautigam and Hwang 2016).

Chinese funds mostly go towards transportation and power projects. In the period 2000-2014, the two main sectors receiving Chinese loans in Africa were transport (28% of total) and energy (20%) (Brautigam & Hwang, 2016; Dollar, 2016). Examples include the ports (such as Bagamoyo in Tanzania and Lamu in Kenya), railways (the Standard Gauge Railway in Kenya and the Ethiopia-Djibouti railway) and hydropower projects (the Karuma plant in Uganda).

Box 3: The Belt and Road Initiative in Africa

As a major flagship project of the Chinese government, the Belt and Road Initiative (BRI) has implications for Africa. BRI links China to the eastern coast of Africa through the "21st Century Maritime Silk Road," the sea route of the BRI. Originally targeting Kenya, Djibouti and Egypt, the scope of this inclusive initiative is expanding to include other countries such as Ethiopia, Tanzania and South Africa.

Africa was not part of the Belt and Road when this was first launched in 2013 (H. Chen 2016). Former World Bank Chief Economist Justin Yifu Lin first proposed Africa's inclusion in the BRI, and his proposal was backed by many in Africa and China (Y. Sun 2015a).

From the Standard Gauge Railway and the Lamu port in Kenya, to the port of Bagamoyo in Tanzania, many BRI-linked infrastructure projects in Africa have benefitted from China's construction capacity and financial contributions. China is also involved in the construction of industrial parks and special economic zones in Africa (see Box 4).

African countries are also borrowing considerable amounts to finance infrastructure projects, including from China. Most of the Chinese financing is provided at commercial rates by the China Export Import (Exim) Bank, and increasingly also by commercial banks (Brautigam and Hwang 2016).

Angola is the largest recipient of Chinese loans (with US$ 21.2 billion in 2000-2014), followed by Ethiopia (US$ 12.3 billion over the same period), Sudan (US$ 5.6 billion), Kenya (US$ 5.2. billion) and Democratic Republic of Congo (DRC)(US$ 4.9 billion) (Brautigam and Hwang 2016). Three of these five countries (Ethiopia, Kenya, DRC) are also among the top borrowers from the World Bank, suggesting that China and the World Bank might have similar lending criteria (Onjala 2018). In contrast to traditional donors like the International Monetary Fund and the World Bank, China's loans are unconditional. According to some experts, this may promote a less cautious behavior on the borrowers' side, which could increase the risk of debt distress (Onjala 2018).

In general, the question of debt sustainability is heavily present in this debate. Countries like Kenya, for example, have seen their loans from China increasing dramatically since 2014 (Onjala 2018). However, there is little evidence that this challenge is uniquely linked to financing from China. For example, Eom et al. (2018) look at 17 African countries which received financing from China, and find that Chinese loans are a source of risk in three countries, while the other six countries that borrowed heavily from China also did so from other financiers (Eom et al. 2018).

In some cases, Chinese loans follow a resource-backed model, using future resources revenues to guarantee the loans. Chinese financial institutions started using resource-backed finance in the 1990s, but the trend accelerated in 2003-2004. Resource-backed loans offer the potential to make use of existing natural resources to access much-needed finance, and they allow the parties to avoid conducting multiple transactions in US dollars (Brautigam and Hwang 2016). These loans have been used widely by European countries (Halland and Canuto 2013).

In 2016, around a third of total Chinese finance to Africa comes in the form of resource-backed loans (Brautigam and Hwang 2016). While oil is predominantly used to guarantee these loans, other commodities such as minerals and agricultural products like cocoa beans have also been used (Brautigam and Hwang 2016).

The resource-backed model also presents some challenges. First, it is subject to fluctuations of commodity prices and it shifts most of the risk on to the borrower. Secondly, it restricts the borrower's ability to manage the future revenue streams from the resources committed as guarantee. Other issues concern the competition and transparency of the process, in particular concerning the way the repayment is designed (Brautigam 2009). Despite these challenges, this model is widely used and often encouraged (Songwe, 2013). Examples of Chinese loans using this model include a US$6 billion deal in the DRC, guaranteed by a copper and cobalt mining joint venture (Brautigam 2009). Brautigam and Hwang (2016) provide a comprehensive list of such deals in East, West and Southern Africa.

Chinese Investment and African Natural Resources

China is relatively resource-scarce, and its recent economic growth has prompted Chinese firms to increasingly seek access to natural resources (Dollar, 2016). Africa on the other hand is resource-abundant. This imbalance is reflected in China-Africa trade patterns, with African countries exporting mineral fuels and other commodities to China in exchange for manufactured goods (Dollar 2016).

Many studies use panel data or look at the broader trading relationships to provide evidence that one of the main factors driving Chinese investments in Africa is the host countries' natural resources endowment (Biggeri and Sanfilippo 2009; Chen et al. 2015; Sanfilippo 2010; Schiere 2010).

This claim requires two main qualifications. First, some argue that the strong natural resources orientation was characteristic of the earlier China-Africa relationship, especially in the early 2000s. In recent years these flows have evolved in response to changing domestic conditions in China, increasingly focusing on services and manufacturing, among others (Dollar, 2016). Moreover, as discussed earlier, there are differences among Chinese companies. Large SOE s in Africa are more likely to be interested in natural resources than small or medium-sized private companies (Shen, 2015). Secondly, this is not unique to Chinese companies, as many other countries have sought access African natural resources (Alden and Alves 2009; Moyo 2012; Yao 2008).

Chinese investment in African natural resources presents challenges and opportunities. The opportunities are linked to the potential to support economic growth and improve livelihoods. The challenges refer to potential negative social and environmental impacts, especially in the informal economy, where safeguards are more limited (Weng 2015).

A series of studies by the International Institute for Environment and Development investigated the short- and long-term effects of Chinese investment in the African rural informal economy. The studies highlight positive short-term effects on the rural communities: Chinese investment enabled the rural populations to be involved in global value chains and to receive financial benefits, either by being directly employed or by selling products to Chinese traders.

In the longer term, however, the effects are less clear-cut. Extensive exploitation of natural resources can pose risks for the environment, such as biodiversity losses, soil depletion and pollution, and can endanger the ability of these resources to provide benefits over a longer period of time. This is especially true in informal settings, where environmental safeguards may not be present, or may not be strictly implemented (Weng 2015). However, the environmental and social concerns emerging in the case studies are not unique to Chinese businesses but rather pertain to all foreign and domestic investors alike. The main challenge stems from the fact that host countries have limited ability to establish and enforce safeguards to protect their resources in the long term.

Chinese Investment and African Labor Markets

While some African countries may have experienced periods of growth, this has not been accompanied by job creation. This "joblessness" has limited the poverty-reduction potential of growth (African Development Bank 2018). African countries are still facing high rates of unemployment and underemployment with potentially damaging consequences for poverty levels and social stability.

In recent years Chinese investment has been instrumental in creating significant numbers of jobs for Africans. Chinese companies invest heavily in sectors with large employment creation potential, such as construction and labor-intensive manufacturing.

Although there is no total estimate of the number of jobs created by Chinese enterprises in Africa, the country and sectoral evidence confirms that job creation takes place, often on a significant scale. The numbers range from a few dozen jobs in small Chinese-run mines in Tanzania (Schoneveld et al. 2018), to 9,000 jobs in a special economic zone in Zambia (Brautigam and Tang 2014). The Nigeria investment promotion agency reported that Chinese firms generated 69,000 jobs, the Ethiopian government reported 35,000 regular jobs and 40,000 seasonal ones, and Liberia and Rwanda reported 3,000 (Shen 2015:93-94). In addition to the direct jobs generated, investment also creates employment through contractual or sales arrangements, such as in the cotton sector in Zambia and Zimbabwe, where Chinese companies had contracted 40,000 and 30,000 cotton farmers respectively (Kabwe et al. 2018).

While the job creation of Chinese investment is undisputed, doubt still lingers about the number of African versus Chinese workers. The claim that Chinese companies mostly employ

Chinese workers has persisted for a long time, despite being repeatedly disproven (Sautman & Yan 2008).

Several studies have been conducted on the localization of workforce in Chinese firms in Africa, covering manufacturing, construction, extractives and other sectors. These show that African employees in Chinese firms range from 50% to 90% of the total workforce, sometimes reaching as high as 97% (Brautigam 2009; Broadman 2006; Chen, Goldstein and Orr 2009; Sautman and Yan 2015; Schoneveld et al. 2018). Chinese factories often employ a small pool of Chinese workers, especially for technical tasks, but hire African for the majority of jobs (Brautigam 2009; Mohan and Lampert 2013; Sun et al. 2017).

When possible, Chinese companies prefer to employ local staff to save on expensive expatriate salaries and work permits. Chinese companies tend to bring in workers from China only when necessary to perform technical or managerial skills that cannot be immediately developed in country. Many studies confirm that African workers are mostly employed in unskilled and low-skilled positions, while managerial roles are mostly reserved for Chinese individuals (Chen et al. 2009; Sun et al. 2017). In many cases, Chinese workers occupy only 10% of the positions but they may actually account for a much larger share of the payroll of the company.

However, research suggests that Chinese companies that have been established in African countries for longer tend to employ more local staff, as they gradually replace their foreign experts with domestic experts from the cheaper local workforce (Tang 2010). Mohan and Lampert (2013) also note that while management is often Chinese, companies typically rely upon a few trusted domestic employees to navigate the country's administrative and political environment and deal with the workforce and with subcontractors.

Box 4: Chinese Special Economic Zones in Africa

Special Economic Zones (SEZs) and industrial parks created in China during the economic reform period played an important role in the country's rapid development process (Zeng 2010). China has transferred this model abroad. In 2006, China initiated an Overseas Zone Program, to build SEZs in selected African and Asian countries. Six zones were built in Zambia, Ethiopia, Mauritius, Nigeria, and Egypt (Brautigam and Tang 2014).

These zones have created employment in the target areas, although most of them are behind targets. Beyond employment creation, evidence of technology transfer and clustering are still limited. A major obstacle to realize the zones' potential is the difference in views and objectives between the African and Chinese actors, which has caused considerable delays in the implementation of the zones. These differences raise questions about the replicability in an African context of the Chinese model, which is strongly government-led (Brautigam and Tang 2014). In recent years, Chinese private industrial parks have also emerged in Africa, such as the Liao Shen Industrial Park in Uganda.

Knowledge Transfers and Chinese Investment

In recent years, some of the China-Africa literature has explored the topic of Chinese investment and knowledge transfers in Africa. Beyond the immediate benefit of job creation, the positive impact of foreign investment is maximized when foreign firms transfer some of their productivity-enhancing knowledge, skills, and technology into the host country's markets.

Chinese firms often provide trainings to their employees (Bashir 2015; Sun et al. 2017). So far, formal and informal trainings have been the main mode of knowledge transfer from Chinese companies to host countries. Other forms of technology transfers, for example through the introduction of new machinery and equipment and new production and organizational processes, have taken place but their impact has been limited (Chen and Landry 2016; Chen, Sun, Ukaejiofo, Tang and Brautigam, 2016; Calabrese 2017).

Sun et al (2017) found that Chinese firms prompted innovations. Half of them brought a new product or service, and one third introduced new technologies. However, the outcomes of these transfers in terms of higher productivity, output and growth are not yet clear. Compared to the most immediate employment results, benefits accruing from knowledge transfers may take longer to materialize.

From China in Africa to Africa-China: Shifting the Focus on African Agency

The China-Africa relationship is often described by a narrative in which the Chinese dominate the agenda and African countries are a "passive space" receiving China's interventions. This narrative underplays the role of African stakeholders in the relationship. A recent strand of the literature has focused on "reinserting African agency into China-Africa relationships" (Mohan and Lampert 2013). By looking at how African stakeholders react to and negotiate the presence of Chinese actors in their own countries, this literature highlights the importance of understanding the African side of the story.

Mohan and Lampert (2013) quote several interesting examples of how African businessmen were pivotal in facilitating the access of Chinese traders and investors to Africa. For example, they reveal that Ghanaian and Nigerian traders played key roles in attracting Chinese traders first and later companies into West Africa. These traders travelled to China in the mid-1990s to import Chinese products. This alerted Chinese traders about the presence of a promising market in West Africa. Ghanaian and Nigerian entrepreneurs also brought in Chinese capital goods, workers, and business partners from China, thus paving the way for Chinese migration to Africa. Many African traders acted as "local patrons" for Chinese businesses in West Africa, allowing them to thrive (Mohan and Lampert 2013).

In addition to facilitating trade and migration flows, African actors are also active in mobilizing in favor of or against Chinese businesses. For example, a Chinese-Nigerian venture in Lagos under the name of "Chinatown" generated resistance from local entrepreneurs, whose protests led to the center being shut down for a few months. The project never recovered (Mohan and Lampert 2013). Similar examples of strong opposition to Chinese businesses can be found across Africa.

Box 5: The Forum on China-Africa Cooperation (FOCAC)

The Forum on China-Africa Cooperation (FOCAC) brings together China and the African countries with which China has a diplomatic relationship (in 2018, this included all but Swaziland) in addition to the African Union. The FOCAC is a forum to discuss matters of political and economic cooperation. Established in 2000, the Forum holds a summit every three years –the latest being in Beijing in 2018.

During the Summit, the Chinese government makes some commitments or pledges towards African development. These commitments have increased massively over the years, from US$5 billion in 2006, to US$10 billion in 2009, to US$20 billion in 2012, finally reaching US$60 billion in 2015 and in 2018, distributed in various funds and financial instruments.

The summit also establishes the main areas of cooperation between China and African countries for the following three years. In 2018, eight areas were identified: industrial promotion, infrastructure connectivity, trade facilitation, green development, capacity building, health, people-to-people exchanges, and peace and security.

Sources: Kai (2015); Sun (2015b); Xinhuanet (2018).

African agency is not only manifested in Africa's relationship with China but also in how this relationship is leveraged with other partners. African countries exercise their agency as donor recipients, especially in light of the emergence of China as the largest non-traditional donor (Prizzon, Greenhill and Mustapha, 2016). A study on Ghana finds that the Ghanaian government is partially able to leverage the entry of China as a donor to negotiate its requests towards traditional donors. The study reveals that the Ghanaian government has not yet exercised its negotiation power to the maximum extent but nonetheless it is an active part in the negotiation process (Zeitz 2015).

Conclusions

This chapter has looked at Chinese investment in Africa and at some of the issues raised by those investments as identified in the literature.

Investment in infrastructure and in manufacturing is crucial to promote Africa's economic transformation. Traditional investors in Africa are less interested in these areas. China has filled a gap, and many observers are hopeful that this will catalyze economic transformation.

The chapter has shown that Chinese investment comes with opportunities and challenges. The opportunities refer to infrastructure financing, gains from natural resources, employment generation and creation of linkages with the global economy. The challenges lie in how the relationship is managed. Many factors shape the outcomes of these investment, including their interaction with the domestic context. The regulations and practices that African countries put in place to scrutinize and benefits from these investments will contribute to determine their impact on the countries' development objectives. In this sense, African agency is crucial to understanding China-Africa relationship, and to shaping them for the development of African countries.

While China's FDI flows to Africa have not increased in recent years, these remain an important factor in Africa's economic development. For the next few years, African countries should focus not only on increasing the quantity of Chinese investment, but also increasing their quality by directing them towards sectors that they believe to be important for their own growth objectives. In particular, African countries should ensure that these investments help the continent diversify its export basket and move it away from extractives and raw materials towards more high-value added products that increase the share of total value remaining in Africa. In particular, African countries should seek to leverage Chinese investment to ensure that they, the African countries, become part of global value chains. Many African leaders have shown this ability by actively attracting Chinese investment in sectors of choice.

Another priority in the China-Africa relationship is for African countries to ensure that their borrowing is healthy and sustainable, both in terms of quantities borrowed and in terms of projects financed. This not only refers to Chinese investment but to all the finance borrowed by African governments.

References

African Development Bank. 2018. *African Economic Outlook 2018.* African Development Bank.

Alden, Chris, and Alves, Ana Carolina. 2009. China and Africa's natural resources: The challenges and implications for development and governance. SAIIA Occasional Paper 41. Johannesburg: SAIIA.

American Enterprise Institute, & The Heritage Foundation. (undated). *China Global Investment Tracker.* Retrieved from: http://www.aei.org/china-global-investment-tracker/

Banque de France. 2018. *Foreign Direct Investment Position – Geographical and industrial breakdown – Annual data (2000 - 2017) (2017 annual report).* Paris: Banque de France

Bashir, Sajitha. 2015. *The Imperative of Skills Development for the Structural Transformation of Sub-Saharan Africa.* Washington, DC: World Bank Publications.

Biggeri, Mario, and Sanfilippo, Marco. 2009. Understanding China's move into Africa: an empirical analysis. *Journal of Chinese Economic and Business Studies, 7*(1), 31-54. doi:10.1080/14765280802604714

Brautigam, Deborah. 2009. *The dragon's gift: the real story of China in Africa.* Oxford: Oxford University Press.

Brautigam, Deborah , and Gallagher, Kevin P. 2014. Bartering Globalization: China's Commodity-backed Finance in Africa and Latin America. *Global Policy,* 5(3), 346-352.

Brautigam, Deborah and Hwang, Jyhjong. 2016. Eastern promises: New data on Chinese loans in Africa, 2000 to 2014. *China Africa Research Initiative Working Paper No. 4*. Washington, DC: SAIS CARI.

Brautigam, Deborah and Tang, Xiaoyang. 2014. "Going Global in Groups": Structural Transformation and China's Special Economic Zones Overseas. *World Development, 63*, 78-91.

Broadman, Harry G. 2006. *Africa's silk road: China and India's new economic frontier*. Washington, DC: The World Bank.

Calabrese, Linda. 2017. *Chinese investment and knowledge transfer in Africa*. London: DFID-ESRC Growth Research Programme.

Calabrese, Linda, Gelb, Stephen and Hou, Jun. 2017. *What drives Chinese outward manufacturing investment? A review of enabling factors in Africa and Asia: Background paper*. Supporting Economic Transformation programme. London: Overseas Development Institute.

Chen, Chuan, Goldstein, Andrea and Orr, Ryan J. 2009. Local Operations of Chinese Construction Firms in Africa: An Empirical Survey. *International Journal of Construction Management,* 9(2), 75-89. doi:10.1080/15623599.2009.10773131

Chen, Huiping (2016). China's 'One Belt, One Road' initiative and its implications for Sino-African investment relations. *Transnational Corporations Review,* 8(3), 178-182. doi:10.1080/19186444.2016.1233722

Chen, Wenjie, Dollar, David, and Tang, Heiwai. 2015. Why Is China Investing in Africa? Evidence from the Firm Level. *The World Bank Economic Review*, lhw049-lhw049. doi:10.1093/wber/lhw049

Chen, Yunnan, and Landry, David G. 2016. *Where Africa meets Asia: Chinese agricultural and manufacturing investment in Madagascar*. Washington, DC: SAIS CARI.

Chen, Yunnan, Sun, Irene Yuan, Ukaejiofo, Rex Uzonna, Tang, Xiaoyang and Brautigam, Deborah. 2016. *Learning from China?: Manufacturing, investment, and technology transfer in Nigeria*. Washington, DC: SAIS CARI.China-Africa Research Initiative. 2018. *Chinese FDI Stock in African Countries*. Retrieved from: http://www.sais-cari.org/chinese-investment-in-africa

Dollar, David. 2016. *China's engagement with Africa: From natural resources to human resources*. Washington, DC: The Brookings Institution.

Eom, Janet, Brautigam, Deborah and Benabdallah, Lina. 2018. *The Path Ahead: The 7th Forum on China-Africa Cooperation*. Washington, DC: SAIS CARI.

Eom, Janet, Hwang, Jyhjong, Atkins, Lucas, Chen, Yunnan and Zhou, Siqi. 2017. *The United States and China in Africa: What does the data say?* Washington, DC: SAIS CARI.

Gu, Jing. 2009. China's Private Enterprises in Africa and the Implications for African Development. *The European Journal of Development Research, 21*(4), 570-587. doi:10.1057/ejdr.2009.21

Halland, Havard, and Canuto, Otaviano. 2013. Resource-Backed Investment Finance in Least Developed Countries. *World Bank Economic Premise* (123). Washington, DC: The World Bank.

Hou, Jun, Gelb, Stephen, and Calabrese, Linda. 2017. *The shift of manufacturing employment in China*. Supporting Economic Transformation Programme. London: Overseas Development Institute.

Kabwe, Stephen, Mutambara, Jackqeline, Mujeyi, Kingstone, Blackmore, Emma, Vorley, Bill, and Weng, Xiaoxue. 2018. *Contract farming and informality: drivers and governance responses in Zambia and Zimbabwe*. London: International Institute for Environment and Development.

Kai, Xue. 2015. FOCAC 2015: Making sense of the numbers. Retrieved from https://chinaafricaproject.com/focac-2015-making-sense-of-the-numbers/

Lin, Justin Yifu and Xu, Jiajun. 2016. *Applying the Growth Identification and Facilitation Framework to the Least Developed Countries: The Case of Uganda*. New York: United Nations Department of Economic and Social Affairs.

Ministry of Commerce. various years. *Statistical Bulletin of China's Outward Foreign Direct Investment.* Beijing: Ministry of Commerce.

Mohan, Giles, & Lampert, Ben. 2013. Negotiating China: Reinserting African Agency into China-Africa Relations. *African Affairs, 112*(446), 92-110.

Moyo, Dambisa. 2012. *Winner take all: China's race for resources and what it means for the world.* New York: Basic Books.

Office for National Statistics. 2016. *The UK's trade and investment relationship with Africa: 2016.* London: Office for National Statistics.

Onjala, Joseph. 2018. China's Development Loans and the threat of Debt Crisis in Kenya. *Development Policy Review,* 1-19.

Prizzon, Annalisa, Greenhill, Romilly and Mustapha, Shakira. 2016. *An age of choice for development finance: evidence from country case studies. Synthesis Report.* London: Overseas Development Institute.

Sanfilippo, Marco 2010. Chinese FDI to Africa: What Is the Nexus with Foreign Economic Cooperation? *African Development Review, 22*(s1), 599-614. doi:doi:10.1111/j.1467-8268.2010.00261.x

Sautman, Barry and Yan, Hairong. 2008. The Forest for the Trees: Trade, Investment and the China-in-Africa Discourse. *Pacific Affairs, 81*(1), 9-29.

Sautman, Barry and Yan, Hairong. 2015. *Localizing Chinese enterprises in Africa: From myths to policies.* HKUST IEMS Thought Leadership Brief Series. Hong Kong: HKUST.

Schiere, Richard. 2010. Building Complementarities in Africa between Different Development Cooperation Modalities of Traditional Development Partners and China. *African Development Review, 22*(s1), 615-628. doi:doi:10.1111/j.1467-8268.2010.00262.x

Schoneveld, George, Chacha, Maisory, Njau, Maria, Jønsson, Jesper, Cerutti, Paolo and Weng, Xiaoxue. 2018. *The new face of informality in the Tanzanian mineral economy: Transforming artisanal mining through foreign investment?* London: International Institute for Environment and Development.

Shen, Xiaofang 2015. Private Chinese investment in Africa: Myths and realities. *Development Policy Review, 33*(1), 83-106.

Songwe, Vera. 2013. From Bottom Billion to Top Trillion: Using Commodity-Backed Securities to Support the Future of Africa's Resource Economies. *Op-ed.* Washington, DC: Brookings Institute.

Sun, Irene Yuan, Jayaram, Kartik and Kassiri, Omid. 2017. *Dance of the lions and dragons: How are Africa and China engaging, and how will the partnership evolve?* McKinsey Global Institute.

Sun, Yun. 2015a. Inserting Africa into China's One Belt, One Road strategy: A new opportunity for jobs and infrastructure? *Africa in focus.* Washington, DC: Brookings Institute.

Sun, Yun. 2015b. *Xi and the 6th Forum on China-Africa Cooperation: Major commitments, but with questions.* Washington, DC: Brookings Institute.

Tang, Xiaoyang. 2010. Bulldozer or Locomotive? The Impact of Chinese Enterprises on the Local Employment in Angola and the DRC. *Journal of Asian and African Studies, 45*(3), 350-368. doi:10.1177/0021909610364777

Traub-Merz, Rudolf and Jauch, Herbert. 2006. The African Textile and Clothing Industry: From Import Substitution to Export Orientation. *The Future of the Clothing Industry in Sub-Saharan Africa.* Bonn: Friedrich-Ebert-Stiftung.

United Nations Conference on Trade and Development (UNCTAD). 2018. *World Investment Report.* Geneva: UNCTAD.

Weng, Xiaoxue. 2015. *The rural informal economy: Understanding drivers and livelihood impacts in agriculture, timber and mining.* London: International Institute for Environment and Development.

Xinhuanet. 2015 (25 January). AU, China to cooperate on infrastructure, industrialization. *Xinhuanet.* Retrieved from http://www.xinhuanet.com/english/africa/2015-01/27/c_127428344.htm

Xinhuanet. 2018. Full text of Chinese President Xi Jinping's speech at opening ceremony of 2018 FOCAC Beijing Summit. Retrieved from http://www.xinhuanet.com/english/2018-09/03/c_129946189.htm

Xu, Jiajun, Gelb, Stephen, Li, Jiewei, and Zhao, Zuoxiang. 2017. *Adjusting to rising costs in Chinese light manufacturing*. Supporting Economic Transformation Programme. London: Overseas Development Institute.

Yao, GM. 2008. Africa: A promising land for Chinese enterprises to invest. *Africa Investment, 1*(3), 17.

Zeitz, Alexandra. 2015. *The changing political economy of international development assistance. The Ghanaian case.* GEG Working Paper. Oxford: University of Oxford.

Zeng, Douglas Zhihua. 2010. *Building engines for growth and competitiveness in China: Experience with special economic zones and industrial clusters.* Washington, DC: The World Bank.

Zhongguo Renmin Gongheguo Zhongyang and Renmin Zhengfu [The Central People's Government of the People's Republic of China]. (2006). *Geng Hao de Shishi "Zou Chu Qu" Zhanlve* [Better implementation of the "Going Out" Strategy]. Retrieved from http://www.gov.cn/node_11140/2006-03/15/content_227686.htm

CHINESE INVESTMENT IN AUSTRALIA

SUSTAINABLE DIVERSIFICATION?

Adrian H. Hearn[1]

Chinese overseas foreign direct investment (OFDI) is as controversial in Australia as it is in Latin America. A deep ambivalence has characterized public debate about the balance of national interest, community benefit, and the motives of Chinese enterprises. When Chinese OFDI exceeded $10 billion in 2012,[2] the leader of the opposition Liberal-National Party, Tony Abbott, stated that "It would rarely be in Australia's national interest to allow a foreign government or its agencies to control an Australian business" (Grigg 2012). His party simultaneously published a pre-election Policy Paper on Foreign Investment in Australian Agricultural Land and Agribusiness. The paper expressed concern that "the creeping cumulative acquisition of agricultural land... may be inconsistent with both the national interest and the interests of local communities," and that if elected, the Liberal-National Party would "investigate options to strengthen the rules governing the sale of agricultural land and agribusinesses to foreign entities," including through the introduction of a land registry system (Liberal National Party of Australia 2012:3-4).

Victorious in the election, Abbott's tone changed in 2014 when he told a business convention that, "We now appreciate that most

1 I thank the Australian Research Council for supporting this work.

2 Figures are presented in U.S. dollars unless otherwise indicated.

Chinese state-owned enterprises have a highly commercial culture... They're not the nationalized industries that we used to have in Australia" (quoted in Kenny and Wen 2014). The identity and agendas of Chinese investors, who have typically been affiliated with the Chinese state, remain divisive. In this context, it is noteworthy that the proportion of OFDI from private Chinese sources is growing. As discussed below, Chinese private finance grew to a record 60% of Chinese OFDI into Australia for the year of 2017.

Regardless of its source, investment into Australia's agriculture sector has been especially sensitive. On the one hand, land acquisition by foreign entities has generated tensions over foreign ownership of national territory; on the other, appropriately managed foreign investment is recognized as a possible pathway to initiatives that align more closely with community interests. Such opportunities are growing as the public becomes more conscious of the need for food systems reform, nutritional health, and environmental sustainability.

The chapter begins by outlining the political economy of Chinese OFDI in Australia, drawing parallels with its reception among other resource-exporting nations. It then considers investment data from the KPMG/University of Sydney *Demystifying Chinese Investment* series, the United Nations Commodity Trade Database, and the annual Lowy Institute Poll. Chinese OFDI in Australia, whether from state or private sources, has the potential to generate national benefits, but to do so emerging strategies –including the Belt and Road Initiative– will need to engage with local level actors, particularly in Australia's food and agriculture sector.

Overview of China-Australia Relations

As in the Americas, public debate in Australia reflects concerns that investing Chinese firms do not act independently but rather in the service of the Chinese state, and therefore cannot be trusted to respect the rules of market competition. Whether or not such trepidations are justified is disputed in the public sphere and by scholars and politicians. Some argue that the Chinese state, coherent in structure and unified in purpose, is the commanding actor behind front-line Chinese investors. This concern is evident in the United States, where a Congressional report by the China Economic and Security Review Commission emphasizes the resulting threat to national businesses:

> Investments made by Chinese state-owned or -controlled companies can also pose economic security threats. The Chinese government provides significant financial and logistical support. This puts U.S. firms, which receive no such support, at a competitive disadvantage. When Chinese SOEs invest abroad, they do not necessarily seek profit and may instead pursue government goals such as resource acquisition or technology transfer....[G]aps exist in the U.S. government's ability to address the competitive challenges posed by SOEs (USCC 2013:106).

In Brazil, the Chairman of the China-Brazil Business Council, Sergio Amaral, has voiced similar preoccupations: "Sometimes you don't know whether the investments are looking for Brazil as a market or whether they correspond to strategic purposes of the Chinese government" (quoted in Pyne 2010). It is noteworthy that these comments, as with Tony Abbott's in Australia, coincided with a sudden influx of Chinese OFDI. As the *Monitor of Chinese OFDI in Latin America and the Caribbean* specifies, in 2010 Chinese OFDI in Brazil reached an unprecedented $12.9 billion, contributing to the nation's standing as Latin America's largest recipient of Chinese OFDI ($48 billion) by 2017 (Dussel Peters 2018:6).

Others contend that Chinese firms, including SOEs, are independent actors that pursue their own agendas. Researchers have found that some Chinese SOEs in the minerals sector exercise a high degree of operational discretion and in some cases –such as the Shougang Hierro iron ore mine in Peru– come into conflict with administrators in China (Gonzalez-Vicente 2012; Guo et al. 2012). Scholars of Sino-Latin American relations have explored the implications of Chinese state ownership for more than a decade and found that rising primary exports have generated a range of social and economic consequences but Chinese domination is generally not among the outcomes (Hearn and Manríquez, 2011; Myers and Wise, 2016; Strauss and Armony, 2012; Trápaga Delfín 2015, 2017). As Thomas Narins writes, "The interests, activities, and actions typically associated with control and ownership of Latin American industrial sectors are more often associated with US, EU, and Brazilian actors than those originating in China" (2016:35).

Figure 1. Top Ten Investors in Australia (including direct and portfolio investment) in billions of USD, 2015-2017

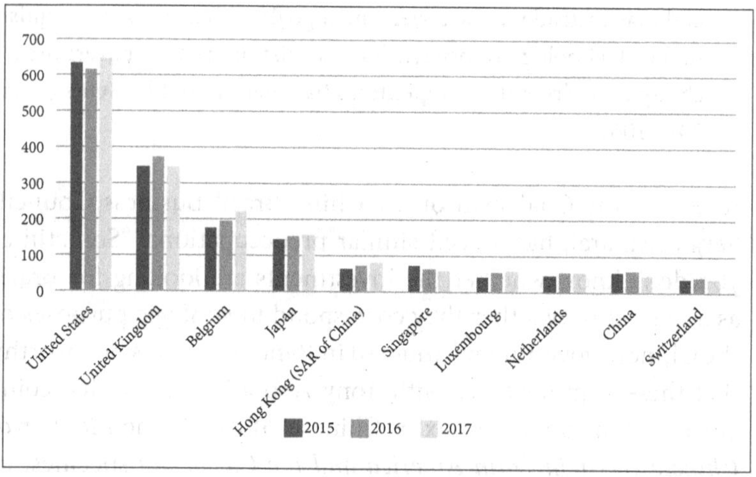

Source: author´s elaboration based on DFAT (2018).

In Europe, former European Commissioner for Competition Policy, Joaquín Almunia, has tried to lower the heat in the dispute over Chinese SOE independence by focusing on the implications for competition rather than the identities of actors:

> We look carefully at whether, through the State, companies in the same sector act as one or different entities. This is not because they are foreign or we have a prejudice against State control, but because it is a relevant aspect for assessing if competition will be significantly reduced or not (Amunia 2011).

In Australia, the annual Lowy Institute Poll, which canvasses public opinion on a range of issues facing the nation, shows discomfort with Chinese OFDI. In 2014, 56% of respondents agreed with the statement that the Australian government is "allowing too much investment from China," and by 2018 the number had grown to 72% (Lowy Institute 2018:10). Of primary concern is Chinese OFDI in agriculture, residential real estate, and critical infrastructure such as ports and airports. It is not surprising in this environment that the Australian federal government has blocked several significant Chinese deals in recent years as they gained public notoriety, and subsequently approved some of these when media attention subsided. These include the 2015 prohibition of a 99-year lease of the Darwin port facility to Chinese firm Landbridge (approved later that year), the 2015 denial of permission to sell the 10 million hectare Kidman cattle empire to Shanghai Pengxin (approved in 2016 as a joint venture), and a 2016 block on the sale of electricity provider Ausgrid to a consortium of Chinese state-owned and Hong Kong corporations. In August 2018 the federal government banned a joint bid from Huawei and ZTE for contracts in the lucrative 5G mobile phone network, reasoning that "Vendors…subject to extrajudicial directions from a foreign government that conflict with Australian law, may risk failure by the carrier to adequately protect a 5G network from unauthorised access or interference" (quoted in Smith 2018). But as former Australian ambassador to China Geoff Raby points out, "What matters is whether there is any nuance allowing Huawei to participate in some form" (quoted in Grigg and Murray 2018).

Agriculture has been no less contentious than other sectors, with 87 percent of respondents to the 2016 Lowy Poll saying they were against "the Australian government allowing foreign companies to buy Australian farmland" (Lowy Institute 2016). Reflecting these concerns, in 2018 the Foreign Investment Review Board (FIRB) issued new guidelines requiring scrutiny of investment in agricultural land by all foreign governments and by private individuals whose cumulative holdings exceed AUD $15 million (FIRB 2018:1). While these conditions reflect public unease toward Chinese OFDI, the Australian Tax Office's *Register of Foreign*

Ownership of Agricultural Land finds that only 2.5% of Australian agricultural land is owned by Chinese investors, compared to 2.6% by those from the United Kingdom and 0.7% by those from the United States (ATO 2017:8).

The relatively small proportion of land held by Chinese entities is rising quickly while holdings attributed to other nations are declining. Between the 2015-16 and 2016-17 financial years, the ATO registered noteworthy changes in the category "area of land with foreign interests." In this period, the area of land attributed to the United Kingdom fell from 27.5 million hectares to 16.4 million and the area for the United States from 7.7 million hectares to 2.7 million. While the significant reduction of registered U.S. holdings may reflect a change in ATO methodology, there is no question that holdings with Chinese interests increased rapidly in this period from 1.5 million hectares to 14.4 million (ATO 2017:8). As noted, the 2016 sale of the Kidman Cattle station accounts for much of this sudden increase.

As Chinese OFDI expands into agriculture it is generating concerns, both in Australia and Latin America, not seen with mining, gas, oil, and other extractive activities (Hearn 2013). Noting parallels with Australia, the China-Brazil Business Council (CBBC) perceives an emerging regulatory challenge in this increasingly global phenomenon:

> This issue is controversial in Brazil and other countries (Canada and Australia, particularly) and has led governments to take action. In this respect, it seems that a consensus is being formed: countries need strong legislation and institutions which can clearly distinguish and characterize opportunities and threats arising from the sale of land to foreign groups (CBBC 2011:26).

A broader set of objections to foreign investment in agriculture results from the loss of crop diversity in rural and peri-urban zones, intensification of chemical inputs, and associated environmental impacts. These concerns are intertwined with demand-side suspicion of safety standards, unhealthy processed foods, and personal disconnection with the productive process (Altieri 2009, Baptista da Costa et al. 2017). Objections such as these relate to the expansion of industrial agriculture in general, regardless of the investor, but as the data presented in the next section shows, Chinese finance is becoming more prominent.

Impact of Chinese OFDI in Australia

Chinese OFDI in Australia should be understood in the context of the bilateral trade relationship. As Australia's number one trade partner since 2009, China has underpinned the expansion of the nation's resources sectors. As seen in figure 2, Australia has consistently achieved significant annual surpluses with China. These are underpinned by commodities trade, which represents approximately 79% of Australia's exports to China (60% to the world). By comparison, commodities represent approximately 90% of Latin America's exports to China (40% to the world). Like many Latin American countries, Australia has become dependent on Chinese demand for its natural resources, to great extent explaining the interest of Chinese investors in these sectors. And as in Latin America, Chinese OFDI in Australia has diversified

Figure 2. Australian Imports from and Exports to China as Reported by Australia (in USD).

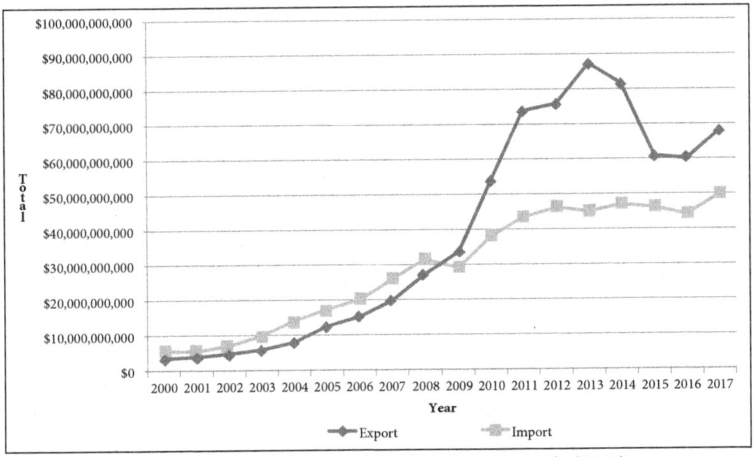

Source: author's elaboration based on UN-Comtrade (2018).

beyond raw materials into manufacturing and services to the domestic economy (Dussel Peters 2018:5).

The analysis below draws on KPMG/University of Sydney datasets, which combine statistics from commercial databases, corporate information, the Australian Bureau of Statistics, the Australian Foreign Investment Review Board, and the Chinese Ministry of Commerce (MOFCOM). The *Demystifying Chinese Investment in Australia* reports produced since 2011 enable year-on-year comparisons, capturing deals at the point that they become legally binding and secure necessary approvals from Australia's Foreign Investment Review Board (FIRB) and the Chinese government (KPMG 2018). The data does not include portfolio investments, such as the purchase of stocks and bonds or deals valued below $5 million.

In 2017 Chinese OFDI declined by 35% into the United States, by 17% into the European Union, by 11% into Australia, and by 29% in general (Dussel Peters 2018:2). The decline is logical given the high outflows of 2016, amounting to $46 billion into the United States alone. Australia maintains its position as the second largest worldwide recipient of Chinese OFDI after the United States, with $99 billion since 2008. Year-on-year volatility in dollar terms is magnified by the large size of some individual deals, for instance Yancoal's 2017 purchase of Rio Tinto's Mount Thawley Warkworth and Hunter Valley thermal coal mine assets for $2.7 billion. The deal was executed in partnership with another Chinese-owned mining giant, Glencore, with Yancoal taking 51% ownership and Glencore 49%.

Mining was the most significant sector for Chinese investment in 2017 with 35% of total OFDI, totaling $3.3 billion that year, mainly in the Yancoal deal but also in lithium operations. Tianqi Lithium, for instance, invested $450 million to develop a processing plant and double the capacity of its Greenbushes mine, which supplies approximately 40% of the world's lithium. Mining projects are labor intensive during the construction phase and less so when they come into operation, which has become increasingly mechanized. Yancoal's acquisition of an existing facility will therefore not in itself generate significant new employment, while Tianqi's expansion of the Greenbushes is more likely to do so.

While the economic dynamics of mining are well known in Australia, a more controversial target of Chinese investment is real estate. The sector accounted for 33% of Chinese OFDI into Australia in 2017, amounting to $3.2 billion. With generally higher returns that comparable real estate markets, Australia has been a target for Chinese property investors for over a decade. The resulting upward pressure on residential property prices particularly in Sydney and Melbourne has generated discontent over housing affordability as many citizens –particularly first home buyers– are squeezed out of the market. As the title of a recent article in *The Diplomat* puts it, "Australians fret as Chinese investment in property market surges" (Chazan 2017). In 2017 the FIRB introduced new application fees for foreign property investors, which together with the Chinese government's recent OFDI capital controls, saw foreign real estate development approvals drop from $53.1 billion in 2015-2016 to $18.5 billion in 2016-2017 (Rogers 2018).

A rapidly rising sector for Chinese OFDI in Australia is healthcare, amounting to $4.1 billion between 2015 and 2017, a sum equivalent to Chinese OFDI into U.S. healthcare over the same period. More than half of this investment is in the Australian supplement industry, which is internationally well regarded for developing and testing high-end products, though it has been slow to reach international markets. Australian free trade agreements (including with China) and government support for the industry provide a promising environment for expanding exports, thus strengthening the sector's appeal to Chinese investors. The largest investment in recent years was undertaken by Biostime, a Chinese probiotics and infant formula giant, which acquired Swisse Wellness in 2015-2016 for $1.2 billion.

As discussed above, a perennially controversial sector for Chinese investment is food and agribusiness, which accounted for 8% ($800 million) in 2017. Dairy, beef, and seafood have been targeted by Chinese investors to help supply their nation's growing middle class with trustworthy high-protein products. Conscious of tensions over foreign land ownership, investors have increasingly targeted higher value chain opportunities in this sector, such as processing and packaging, rather than primary production. Furthermore, they increasingly pursue joint ventures, retain Australian management, and reflect a growing proportion of private investment. In 2017 Chinese private investors accounted for 60% of total deal value while finance from Chinese SOEs into Australia dropped for the first time since 2014.

Agriculture demonstrates the range of consequences brought by Chinese demand: the primarization associated with reliance on unprocessed commodity exports has been accompanied by the increasing industrialization of food systems. While export-oriented development has generated macro-economic benefits for Australia and Latin America, it has also incurred micro-level costs. These include contamination of crops and groundwater with pesticides, displacement of young people from rural communities to cities, and the replacement of family farms by broadacre plantations producing soybeans in Latin America, wheat in Australia, and livestock in both. These consequences constitute an opportunity for Chinese investors to improve on past practices in the agriculture sector. Sensitivity to environmental concerns through projects that demonstrably contribute to ecological balance and sustainable food production is likely to become more important.

Conclusions and Policy Suggestions

The demand for metals, energy, and food generated by China's growing cities has sustained Australia through the global economic turbulence of the past two decades. Like many Latin Americans, Australians recognize the benefits of trading with China, and that Chinese OFDI can strengthen economic performance. And like Latin Americans, Australians worry about several aspects of Chinese OFDI, from uncompetitive practices to ecological impacts. As a recent study of Chinese infrastructure projects in Latin America finds, Chinese firms "do not usually seek the highest labor, safety, and environmental standards" (Armony, Dussel Peters, and Cui 2018:x). Australians have expressed concerns about China's domestic record, noting in a survey by the newspaper *Sydney Morning Herald*: "China has polluted its waters, air and soil. They have no respect to their own motherland. Why would they care about the environment of Australia?" (quoted in Bachelard 2018).

There is no single pathway for Chinese enterprises to establish themselves as environmentally responsible actors overseas, but the Belt and Road Initiative (BRI) provides an opportunity. BRI's statement of "Vision and Proposed Actions" commits to "conserving eco-environment, protecting biodiversity, and tackling climate change" (China Daily 2015). An important step in doing so will be to formulate guidelines for investors, potentially drawing on the Ministry of Commerce and Ministry of Environment 2013 joint declaration on the responsibilities of Chinese enterprises overseas (Ministry of Commerce 2013). The Environment and Social Framework developed by the Asian Infrastructure Investment Bank (AIIB) to assist partner countries in fulfilling their commitments under the Paris Agreement provides further precedent. Uncertainty about BRI's environmental impact will persist until such guidelines are formulated and become evident on the ground. As the subtitle of a recent article in China Dialogue asks, "Will the Belt and Road Initiative bring environmental devastation or a new era of Chinese global resource stewardship?" (Pike 2017).

Seventy countries have signed Belt and Road Cooperation Agreements. Australia has yet to sign such an agreement, but it is well placed to formulate strategies for environmental engagement with BRI, given its deep integration with Chinese trade and investment. One Chinese renewable energy investor, Goldwind, established offices in Sydney and Melbourne in 2009 and currently employs 130 people across Australia. Its 2017 purchase of the Stockyard Hill Wind Farm in the state of Victoria for $81 million, driven by Australia's steadily growing electricity demand, may spearhead further investments in the rapidly expanding renewables sector. A Belt and Road Cooperation Agreement to deepen engagement in wind and solar power generation would be a logical step for both nations.

Agriculture could also provide a platform for investment in ecologically sustainable projects. Chinese vertical greenhouse technology, developed by the Center for Protected Agriculture and Environmental Engineering, and the Liuzhou Forest City initiative are good examples of smart infrastructure innovations relevant to Australia. Such projects would resonate with Australian preferences for locally grown produce and, if scaled up, could also service Chinese demand for "clean and green" premium products. To integrate these and other projects into BRI would require Chinese enterprises to build relationships not only with the Australian federal government, but also with partners at the state and municipal levels. Sub-national actors are generally more attune to local environmental concerns, and working with them could help Chinese enterprises to stay abreast of public preferences and opinions.

Food systems innovations in organic production, waste reduction, employment, land protection, and ecological sustainability are typically led by divisions within local governments. The Council of Moreland in metropolitan Melbourne, for instance, recently became the nation's first municipal government to finance a Food Systems Strategy (see Rose and Hearn 2018). Moreland and other local governments would benefit from dialogue with China's expanding organic food movement, in which large-scale projects like Shared Harvest in Beijing are already establishing international networks. Facilitating technical exchanges to improve operational dynamics could extend these networks to Australia and build BRI's reputation as an environmentally and socially engaged initiative.

Chinese OFDI in Australia has demonstrated its impact on sectors from healthcare and housing to mining and agriculture. Whether targeting infrastructure or extractives, it has generated controversy around its competitive (and potentially anti-competitive) impact. Concerns about the motives of Chinese state-affiliated capital have given rise to intense debates over the protection of Australian national interests, especially in relation to foreign ownership of farmland. Against this divisive backdrop it is important to recall the Australian Tax Office's finding that Chinese investors have interests in only 2.5% of national agricultural land, and in many cases are the minority partners in joint ventures. Nevertheless, policymakers should evaluate the broader implications of land use transformation to service China's growing demand for food, not least because agricultural adaptations have contributed to broader public discomfort with the influx of Chinese capital. OFDI in infrastructure to promote sustainable food production and trade would align with widely shared Australian and Chinese interests, providing an opportunity to strengthen bilateral cooperation.

References

Almunia, Joaquín. 2011. *Recent developments and future priorities in EU competition policy*. Speech to the International Competition Law Forum, St. Gallen, 8 April; available at: http://papers.ssrn.com/sol3/papers.cfm?abstract_id=2214853

Altieri, Miguel A. 2009. "Agroecology, Small Farms, and Food Sovereignty." *Monthly Review*, vol.61, no.3, https://monthlyreview.org/2009/07/01/agroecology-small-farms-and-food-sovereignty/

Armony, Ariel C., Enrique Dussel Peters, and Cui Shoujun. 2018. "Introduction." In Armony, Dussel Peters, and Cui (eds) *Building Development for a New Era: China's Infrastructure Projects in Latin America and the Caribbean*, pp.ix-xi. Pittsburgh: University of Pittsburgh Asian Studies Center and Center for International Studies.

Ascensão, Fernando; Lenore Fahrig; Anthony P. Clevenger; Richard T. Corlett; Jochen A. G. Jaeger; William F. Laurance, and Henrique M. Pereira. 2018. "Environmental challenges for the Belt and Road Initiative." *Nature Sustainability* volume 1, pp.206-209.

Australian Tax Office (ATO). 2017. *Register of Foreign Ownership of Agricultural Land.*

https://cdn.tspace.gov.au/uploads/sites/79/2017/09/Register_of_Foreign_ownership_of_Agricultural_Land_2017.pdf

Bachelard, Michael. 2018. "Readers respond: Should Australia support China's Belt and Road Initiative." *The Sydney Morning Herald*, 26th June.

www.smh.com.au/world/asia/readers-respond-should-australia-support-china-s-belt-and-road-initiative-20180625-p4znna.html

Baptista da Costa, Manoel B.; Monique Souza, Vilmar Müller Júnior, Jucinei José Comin, and Paulo Emílio Lovato. 2017. "Agroecology development in Brazil between 1970 and 2015." *Agroecology and Sustainable Food Systems* 41(3-4): 276-295.

Chazan, Yigal. 2017. "Australians fret as Chinese investment in property market surges." *The Diplomat*, 10th June.

https://thediplomat.com/2017/06/australians-fret-as-chinese-investment-in-property-market-surges/

China Daily. 2015. "One Belt One Road Plan."

http://language.chinadaily.com.cn/2015-03/30/content_19950951.htm

China-Brazil Business Council (CBBC). 2011. *Chinese investments in Brazil: A new phase in the China-Brazil relationship*. Rio de Janeiro: CBBC.

Department of Foreign Affairs and Trade (DFAT). 2018. Foreign Investment Statistics: Statistics on who invests in Australia.

https://dfat.gov.au/trade/resources/investment-statistics/Pages/statistics-on-who-invests-in-australia.aspx

Dussel Peters, Enrique. 2018. Monitor of Chinese OFDI in Latin America and the Caribbean 2018. Mexico City: Academic Network of Latin America and the Caribbean.

www.redalc-china.org/monitor/

Foreign Investment Review Board (FIRB). 2018. "Agricultural Land Investments", Guidance Note 17, 27 February. http://firb.gov.au/resources/guidance/gn17/

Gonzalez-Vicente, Ruben. 2012. "Mapping Chinese mining investment in Latin America: Politics or market?" *China Quarterly* 209: 3558.

Grigg, Angus. 2012. "Abbott warns China on takeovers." *Australian Financial Review*, July 24.

www.afr.com/news/policy/foreign-affairs/abbott-warns-china-on-takeovers-20120724-j2750

Grigg, Angus and Lisa Murray. 2018. "Federal government bans Huawei, ZTE from 5G on security concerns." *The Australian Financial Review*, 23rd August. www.afr.com/business/telecommunications/federal-government-bans-huawei-zte-from-5g-on-security-concerns-20180822-h14cv0

Guo, Yingjie, Shumei Hou, Graeme Smith, and Selene Martinez Pacheco. 2012. "Chinese outward direct investment: Case studies of SOEs going global". In, J. Garrick (ed.), *Law and policy for China's market socialism*. New York: Routledge: 131-143.

Hearn, Adrian H. 2013. "China and Brazil: Searching for Sustainable Complementarity." *Policy paper for the Europe China Research and Advice Network (ECRAN)*. The European Commission. London: ECRAN.

Hearn, Adrian H. and José Luis León Manríquez (eds.). 2011. *China Engages Latin America: Tracing the Trajectory*. Boulder: Lynne Rienner Publishers.

Kenny, Mark and Philip Wen. 2014. "Tony Abbott briefs Xi Jinping on search for MH370" *The Sydney Morning Herald*, 11th April.
www.smh.com.au/federal-politics/political-news/tony-abbott-briefs-xi-jinping-on-search-for-mh370-20140411-zqtnj.html

KPMG. 2018. *Demystifying Chinese Investment in Australia*. Sydney: KPMG and the University of Sydney.

Liberal National Party of Australia. 2012. *The Coalition's Policy Discussion Paper on Foreign Investment in Australian Agricultural Land and Agribusiness*, Canberra: LNP.

Lowy Institute for International Policy. 2018. Lowy Poll 2016.
www.lowyinstitute.org/publications/lowy-institute-poll-2016.

Lowy Institute for International Policy. 2018. Lowy Poll 2018.
www.lowyinstitute.org/publications/2018-lowy-institute-poll

Ministry of Commerce. 2013. "MOFCOM and MEP Jointly Issued Guidance on Environmental Protection in Foreign Investment and Cooperation."
http://english.mofcom.gov.cn/article/newsrelease/significantnews/201303/20130300043146.shtml

Myers, Margaret and Carol Wise. (eds). 2016. *The Political Economy of China-Latin America Relations in the New Millennium: Brave New World*. New York: Routledge.

Narins, Thomas P. 2016. "Are Chinese economic actors poised to dominate Latin American economies?: A view from Bolivia and Chile." *The Global Studies Journal* 9(4):19-39.

Pike, Lili. 2017. "Explainer: Will China's new Silk Road be green?" 11th June.

www.chinadialogue.net/blog/9775-Explainer-Will-China-s-new-Silk-Road-be-green-/en

Pyne, Solana. 2010. "China's Brazilian shopping spree." *Global Post*, 22 November.

www.globalpost.com/dispatch/brazil/101118/china-foreign-investment-trade

Rogers, Dallas. 2018. "Australia's foreign real estate investment boom looks to be over. Here are five things we learned." *The Conversation*, 31st May. https://theconversation.com/australias-foreign-real-estate-investment-boom-looks-to-be-over-here-are-five-things-we-learned-97460

Rose, Nick and Adrian H. Hearn. 2017. *Food Systems and the Role of Local Government*, Melbourne: SUSTAIN. www.circlesoffood.org/2016/04/18/food-governance-taskforce/

Smith, Michael. 2018. "Chinese media describe Peter Dutton as a 'low version of Trump.'" *The Australian Financial Review*, 23rd August. https://www.afr.com/news/policy/foreign-affairs/chinese-media-describe-peter-dutton-a-low-version-of-trump-20180823-h14dfg

Strauss, Julia C., and Ariel C. Armony (eds.) 2012. *From the Great Wall to the New World: China and Latin America in the 21st Century*. Cambridge: Cambridge University Press.

Trápaga Delfín, Yolanda (ed.) 2015. *América Latina y el Caribe y China: Recursos Naturales y Medio Ambiente 2015*, Mexico City: Unión de Universidades de América Latina y el Caribe.

Trápaga Delfín, Yolanda (ed.) 2017. *América Latina y el Caribe y China: Recursos naturales y medio ambiente 2017*, Mexico City: Unión de Universidades de América Latina y el Caribe.

UN-COMTRADE. 2018. United Nations commodity trade statistics database. http://comtrade.un.org

USCC (United States-China Economic and Security Review Commission). 2013. *USCC 2013 Annual Report*. http://www.uscc.gov

SECTION II.

CHINA'S OFDI IN LATIN AMERICA AND THE CARIBBEAN

CHINA'S OFDI IN LATIN AMERICA AND THE CARIBBEAN (2000-2018)

DEBATES AND GENERAL TENDENCIES

Enrique Dussel Peters

Introduction

The relationship between Latin America and the Caribbean (LAC) and China has grown substantially since the beginning of the 21st century and moved well beyond economics to include culture, bilateral and regional political relations, and other areas like education and language. This qualitatively new and complex relationship has generated important opportunities and massive challenges for the region in each of the fields mentioned above.

This document will focus on China's outbound or overseas foreign direct investment (OFDI) and consider the increasing systematization of China's recent socioeconomic presence in LAC in the fields of trade, financing, OFDI, and infrastructure projects (Dussel Peters, Armony, and Cui 2018; Salazar-Xirinachs, Dussel Peters and Armony 2018). The analysis will highlight the main features and characteristics of China's OFDI in the region during 2000-2018.

This chapter will first briefly examine a group of authors and institutions that have analyzed China's OFDI in LAC with the goal of highlighting debates and discussions on China's OFDI in the region. The chapter will then lay out the main tendencies of China's OFDI in LAC during 2000-2018 in terms of its macroeconomic relevance and generation of employment, as well as by country of destination, ownership, and sector, among other characteristics. Finally, chapter will provide a set of suggestions for policy-makers and future researchers.

Recent Debates on China's OFDI in LAC

Surprisingly, there is very little detailed analysis on China's OFDI in LAC as a region. The China-LAC relationship in general has been the subject of many authors and institutions in LAC, China, and in the US, including think-tanks, but the massive, albeit insufficient, literature on China's OFDI in LAC has not garnered much attention.[1]

In China, the Ministry of Commerce (MOFCOM) reports annually on China's OFDI in the world and in LAC (see next section) and its analysis of MOFCOM in 2015 (MOFCOM et. al 2015) is, to date, the most accurate and thorough existing overview. The analysis was based on visits to companies, interviews with nearly 50 multinational companies, dozens of meetings, and a questionnaire with more than 60 questions answered by 254 companies. Among the most significant results of the report is the observation that labor issues in LAC are the greatest risk for Chinese companies, followed by the political and regulatory setting. Worker safety issues and cultural differences were the main challenges in labor relations, as well as a lack of understanding of local culture and habits.[2]

1 See, for example, the Atlantic Council (Avendaño, Melguizo, and Miner 2017; González 2018), the Brookings Institution (Dollar 2017) and the Inter-American Dialogue (Myers and Barrios 2018), among others. Reviews of existing literature in China and in LAC on the respective issues are practically non-existent or insufficient. The lack of knowledge and integration of the literature, especially in LAC and China, on methodological issues, case studies, and analysis of the respective issues for specific countries, of public, private and academic institutions not only limits the learning process but also reflects the poor conclusions and policy proposals and the repetitive nature of the overall conversation.

2 Other Chinese authors such as Jiang (2017) have also contributed to understanding China's OFDI in LAC, particularly regarding the respective policies in the last decades.

Internationally the IISD (2016), Koleski and Blivas (2018) and the work of Kevin Gallagher at the Global Economic Governance Initiative (GEGI) (Ray, Gallagher, López and Sanborn 2017) have made important contributions to the understanding of China's OFDI in LAC. The IISD notes the significant economic impact of Chinese OFDI in general, ranging from from economic development to local industry linkages and technology and skills transfers, while Koleski and Blivas (2018) highlight the increasing quantitative importance of China's OFDI in LAC, particularly in countries such as Brazil, Peru and Argentina to meet China's rising demand for "raw materials." Ray et. al (2017), as well as other authors (Garzón 2018) emphasize that China's increasing presence in LAC in general, and specifically their OFDI, has so far had a negative impact on LAC´s environment as a result of the lack of policy guidelines for China's OFDI and their firms but also because of institutional weaknesses in the region.

Within LAC there is an increasing complexity in the analysis at the bilateral and regional level regarding China's OFDI in LAC. Business organizations such as the China-Brazil Business Council (CEBC 2018), as well as academic efforts in Argentina, Brazil, Mexico, and Peru have brought an increasing depth to the understanding of China's OFDI in LAC (Blanchard 2016). The work of the Academic Network of Latin America and the Caribbean on China (Red ALC-China) has been especially relevant, with dozens of analyses in the last decade on China's OFDI in particular countries and sectors. The overview of ten Chinese firms in LAC (Dussel Peters 2014) indicates that Chinese firms still lack experience and information on LAC for investing, in specific fields such as suppliers, clients, labor and environmental laws, etc. and that LAC countries have so far not been able to provide support to Chinese firms because of a limited understanding of Chinese firms. In general, Chinese firms require long periods for adapting and learning in LAC, which brings important ramifications in terms of costs and the time to begin successful operations and turn a profit. This process, however, is changing quickly as the increasing presence of Chinese OFDI in LAC is also generating a learning process within Chinese firms. Chinese firms present a wide heterogeneity and ability to generate backward and forward linkages, depending on the legal framework and concrete options provided by the respective public and private sectors in LAC. This topic is of critical relevance for the discussion on the potential impact of China's OFDI on LAC's development.

China's OFDI in LAC (2000-2018)

The most recent official analysis of FDI for LAC (ECLAC 2018), with information up to 2017, confirms the downward trend in the reception of FDI in the region since 2014, due to the drop in international prices of raw materials and the economic recession of 2015 and 2016, particularly in Brazil. From a longer term perspective, FDI in LAC has been increasingly concentrated in manufacturing and services. Beyond FDI in raw materials and extractive sectors, it is important to highlight the drop in the average profitability of FDI in LAC: from levels close to 9% in 2008 and 2011 to less than 5% in 2017 (ECLAC 2018:34-35).

Figure 1. Statistical Disfferences in China's OFDI to LAC According to Different Sources (2004-2018) (in USD million)

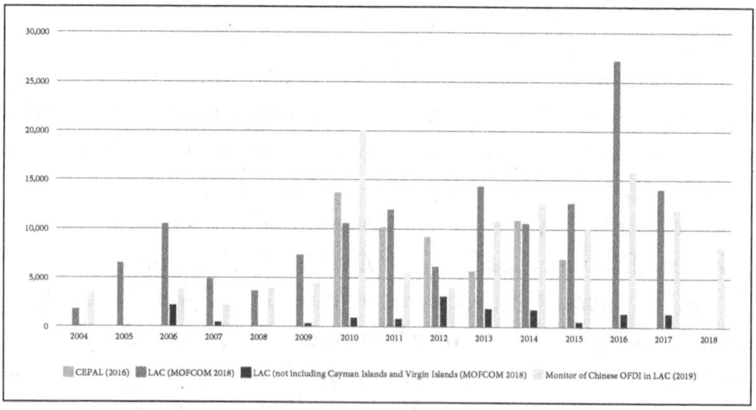

Source: author's elaboration based on ECLAC (2016) MOFCOM (2018/a) and Dussel Peters (2019).

The *Monitor of Chinese* OFDI *in Latin America and the Caribbean* has stressed the relevance of different methodological approaches for measuring and recording OFDI in recent years (Ortiz Velásquez 2016). Statistical records diverge significantly (see Figure 1), with implications for academic, business, and public policy analysis. Most of international institutions and authors analyzing China's OFDI in LAC have not understood the methodological differences that result in substantial statistical differences.

Although the differences among data from ECLAC, MOFCOM, and the *Monitor of Chinese* OFDI *in Latin America and the Caribbean* for the entire 2010-2015 appear small –US$ 56.7 billion, US$ 66.2 billion, and US$ 63.2 billion– they are in fact truly important (see Figure 1). MOFCOM information, for example, includes two financial centers representing 86.34% FDI to LAC for the period. By excluding the Virgin Islands and Cayman Islands during the 2010-2015 period, Chinese OFDI is reduced to US$ 9 (or 13.65% of the amount recorded by the *Monitor* in 2019 for the 2010-2015 period). Although the difference between the information from ECLAC and the *Monitor* is barely US$ 6.5 billion, each year the differences are greater than 50%. For 2012, for example, ECLAC reports US$ 9.2 billion and the *Monitor* 2019 reports barely US$ 4 billion.[3]

Two additional general aspects of Chinese OFDI are relevant. First, Chinese OFDI in 2018 recovered slightly to reach US$ 129.830 million and a growth rate of 4.2% over 2017. With this, China managed to overcome the drastic drop of Chinese OFDI in 2017, -36.5% and the first in more than a decade (see Dussel Peters 2019) but was still below the maximum levels reached in 2016 and 2010.[4] If during 2015 and 2016, Chinese OFDI had for the first time surpassed its FDI, in 2018 the OFDI/FDI ratio was 96.17%. Second,

3 These record differences are further exacerbated by country. In the case of Mexico, for example, the Mexican authorities still differentiate between the Chinese and Hong Kong OFDI flows. The differences between the Mexican and Chinese authorities' records in 2006 and 2015 are notable, i.e., Chinese authorities (MOFCOM) registered a negative OFDI (Dussel Peters 2019).

4 However, in specific markets such as the US, Chinese OFDI fell between 60 and 80%, particularly in the last quarter of 2018 (Miller 2019).

total Chinese OFDI employs around 4.92 million Chinese abroad and contracted by -3.0 percent in 2018 (MOFCOM 2019/a/b).

Main Trends of Chinese OFDI in LAC (2000-2018)[5]

During the 2000-2018 period, Chinese companies carried out 402 transactions in LAC countries, representing US$ 8.2 billion in 2018 with a growth rate of -31.8% with respect to 2017. In 2018, Chinese OFDI represented 51.66% of 2016 (see Table 1). The fall in employment generated by Chinese OFDI in 2018 was even more pronounced, at -66.3% for the year.[6] As a result of these trends since 2017 and again in 2018, the amount per transaction decreased to US$ 178 million. If the 2018 Monitor showed three phases of Chinese OFDI in LAC, from 2017 onwards a fourth phase with a dynamism significantly lower than that of 2010-2016 can be seen: in the short and medium term a relative stagnation is expected at relatively low levels of OFDI and particularly compared with the dynamism of the previous phase (see Table 1).

By type of investment Table 1 also shows that:

a) In 2018, mergers and acquisitions became the main type of Chinese OFDI, accounting for 74.76% and 67.98% of the amount and employment generated by Chinese OFDI, respectively.
b) As a result, Chinese OFDI mergers and acquisitions in LAC have become the most significant, accounting for 62.35% of the OFDI total and 60.66% of employment during 2000-2018, respectively.

5 For a full analysis see: Dussel Peters (2019) and http://www.redalc-china.org/monitor/.

6 For an analysis of the quantity and quality of employment generated by China in LAC, with four national studies and respective case studies, see: Salazar-Xirinachs et. al (2018).

Table 1. LAC: Chinese OFDI and Employment (2000-2018)

	Transactions (number)	Amount (million USD)	Employment (number of workers)	Amount / transaction (million USD)	Amount / workers (million USD)	Employment / transaction (number of workers)
Total Chinese OFDI						
2000-2005	16	4,444	13,905	277.73	0.32	869
2006-2009	58	15,825	33,023	272.85	0.48	569
2010-2018	238	101,429	277,168	426.17	0.37	1,165
2000-2018	402	121,698	324,096	302.73	0.38	806
2015	35	10,182	29,554	290.91	0.34	844
2016	38	15,879	48,523	417.87	0.33	1,277
2017	59	12,018	71,984	203.70	0.17	1,220
2018	46	8,203	24,240	178.32	0.34	527
Mergers and acquisitions						
2000-2005	3	570	5,950	190.00	0.10	1,983
2006-2009	22	4,466	16,750	203.00	0.27	761
2010-2018	120	70,841	173,893	590.34	0.41	1,449
2000-2018	145	75,877	196,593	523.29	0.39	1,356
2015	7	7,381	17,670	1054.44	0.42	2,524
2016	17	14,323	39,258	842.53	0.36	2,309
2017	27	8,682	54,839	321.55	0.16	2,031
2018	23	6,132	16,478	266.61	0.37	716
New investments						
2000-2005	13	3,874	7,955	297.97	0.49	612
2006-2009	36	11,360	16,273	315.54	0.70	452
2010-2018	208	30,588	101,275	147.06	0.30	487
2000-2018	257	45,821	125503	178.29	0.37	488
2015	28	2,801	11,884	100.03	0.24	424
2016	21	1,556	9,265	74.09	0.17	441
2017	32	3,336	17,145	104.26	0.19	536
2018	22	2,031	7,562	92.31	0.27	344

Source: author´s elaboration based on Dussel Peters (2019).

As a result of previous trends, the share of Chinese OFDI with respect to total FDI in LAC, as well as its gross fixed capital formation, declined in 2018 and fell to its lowest level since 2012, at 6.28% and 0.63%, respectively (see Figure 2).

Figure 2. LAC: Chinese OFDI in Relationship to Total FDI and Gross Fixed Capital Formation (2000-2018)(percentage)

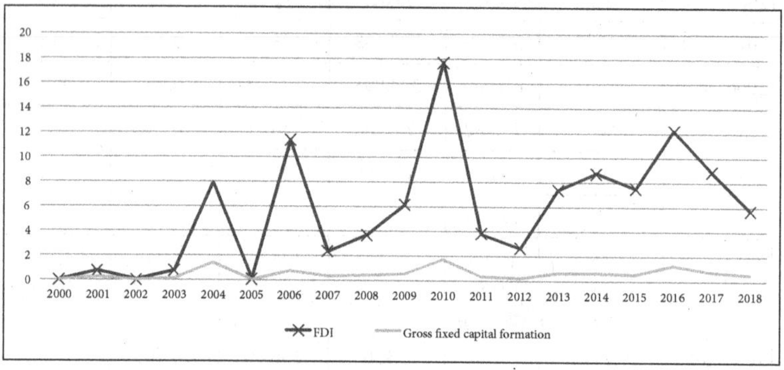

Sources: author's elaboration with information of CEPAL an MOFCOM.

Chinese OFDI by Destination Country (2000-2018)

Chinese OFDI continues to diversify in LAC. The countries with the largest share of Chinese OFDI in LAC, Brazil and Argentina, saw their reception decline, while Chile and Peru became by far the most important countries in this regard, receiving 63.03% and 16.31% of Chinese OFDI in LAC in 2018, respectively. Beyond the collapse of Chinese OFDI in Brazil and Argentina, the decline of Chinese OFDI in Mexico in 2018 and over the previous year is also notable (see Table 2).

Table 2. LAC: Chinese OFDI by Main Countries (2000-2018)

	2000-2005	2006	2007	2008	2009	2010	2011	2012	2013	2014	2015	2016	2017	2018	2000-2018
Argentina															
Number of Transactions	0	0	1	0	0	3	1	0	5	3	0	3	5	6	27
Amount (million USD)	0	0	4	0	0	5,597	330	0	3,919	523	0	215	1,413	513	12,512
Employment	0	0	200	0	0	2,601	1,600	0	1,785	480	0	670	4,824	3,451	15,611
Brazil															
Number of Transactions	6	2	4	1	2	10	12	3	6	13	19	16	17	11	122
Amount (million USD)	3,565	30	152	60	425	12,867	2,919	3,232	902	1,747	5,319	13,903	3,017	421	48,557
Employment	6,303	2,111	4,174	61	61	15,208	15,748	1,200	2,551	7,128	13,950	37,163	34,220	5,756	145,634
Chile															
Number of Transactions	0	0	0	2	2	1	1	3	3	2	1	3	4	6	28
Amount (million USD)	0	0	0	39	2,450	18	11	227	45	36	286	215	2,764	5,170	11,261
Employment	0	0	0	78	250	0	55	64	81	43	175	4,284	5,691	6,515	17,236
Ecuador															
Number of Transactions	2	1	0	2	1	2	1	0	1	0	0	1	0	2	13
Amount (million USD)	162	100	0	1,400	33	672	610	0	11	0	0	3	0	32	3,023
Employment	248	450	0	533	21	1,041	22,000	0	11	0	0	150	0	276	24,730
Mexico															
Number of Transactions	4	2	3	4	1	4	6	1	1	10	9	4	23	9	81
Amount (million USD)	563	45	109	331	40	84	39	70	8	1,140	1,001	81	2,733	398	6,643
Employment	6,354	103	1,409	3,654	1,000	478	1,106	144	3	2,470	4,915	1,455	18,099	2,628	43,818
Peru															
Number of Transactions	0	3	4	3	2	4	1	2	5	5	1	1	3	2	36
Amount (million USD)	0	289	228	3,760	124	582	50	61	1,338	7,778	4	150	3,985	3,985	22,333
Employment	0	1,542	1,575	6,365	98	3,946	57	56	3,497	5,631	23	1,500	9,800	850	34,940
Venezuela															
Number of Transactions	2	1	0	2	1	2	1	0	1	0	0	1	0	2	13
Amount (million USD)	162	100	0	1,430	33	672	610	0	11	0	0	3	0	31	3,052
Employment	248	450	0	533	21	1,041	22,000	0	11	0	0	150	0	276	24,730

Source: own elaboration based on Dussel Peters (2019).

Chinese OFDI by Destination of Economic Activity (2000-2018)

During 2000-2018, Chinese OFDI amounts have been concentrated in three activities: raw materials (60.02%); manufacturing (8.62%); and services and domestic market (30.76%) (see Table 3):

a) The diversification of Chinese OFDI in LAC by sector has been one of the most notable developments in the last five years. If during 2000-2010 the share of raw materials in OFDI and in the employment generated was by far the most significant, since then its presence has become more varied. By 2018 it accounted for only 53.39% of the amount of Chinese OFDI in LAC and 35.99% of employment by 2018, respectively.
b) In recent years, Chinese OFDI has focused on manufacturing and particularly on services, the latter accounting for 36.21% and 34.88% of the amount of OFDI and employment during 2010-2018, respectively.
c) The purchase of technology in LAC by the Chinese OFDI has been a secondary factor. For the entire period 2000-2018, four cases worth US$ 395 million were recorded, generating almost 2,500 jobs throughout the region.

Chinese OFDI in LAC by Type of Firm Ownership (2000-2018)

One of the most striking features of Chinese OFDI is the very high public sector share. During 2000-2018, participation in the amount of OFDI and employment generated in LAC was 70.2% and 49.1%, respectively (see Table 4). This tendency is changing rapidly. In 2018, for example, participation of public firms in Chinese OFDI was only 6.3 percent.

Public sector transactions are much more capital-intensive with respect to employment and employment per transaction. For

Table 3. LAC: Chinese OFDI by Sector (2000-2018)

	2000-2005	2006-2009	2010-2018	2000-2018	2015	2016	2017	2018
Raw materials								
Transactions	7	39	78	124	4	9	8	12
Amount (million USD)	3,795	15,097	54,152	73,045	6,953	4,505	2,807	6,467
Employment	7,048	23,815	99,757	130,620	4,498	13,111	13,081	6,423
Amount / Transaction (million USD)	542.20	387.11	694.26	589.07	1,738.18	500.51	350.85	538.88
Amount / Employment (million USD)	0.54	0.63	0.54	0.56	1.55	0.34	0.21	1.01
Employment / Transaction	1,006.86	610.64	1,278.94	1,053.39	1,124.50	1,456.78	1,635.13	535.25
Manufacturing								
Transactions	4	11	121	136	17	14	29	9
Amount (million USD)	118	540	9,831	10,489	2,012	484	4,497	454
Employment	954	6,576	73,860	81,390	22,000	7,007	20,144	4,486
Amount / Transaction (million USD)	29.55	49.08	81.25	77.12	118.36	34.56	155.08	50.42
Amount / Employment (million USD)	0.12	0.08	0.13	0.13	0.09	0.07	0.22	0.10
Employment / Transaction	238.50	597.82	610.41	598.46	1,294.12	500.50	694.62	498.44
Services and Domestic Market								
Transactions	5	8	120	133	11	15	20	20
Amount (million USD)	530	188	36,726	37,444	1,146	10,890	4,460	788
Employment	5,903	2,632	96,671	105,206	2,306	28,405	37,084	7,876
Amount / Transaction (million USD)	106.00	23.50	306.05	281.53	104.15	726.03	223.00	39.41
Amount / Employment (million USD)	0.09	0.07	0.38	0.36	0.50	0.38	0.12	0.10
Employment / Transaction	1,180.60	329.00	805.59	791.02	209.64	1,893.67	1,854.20	393.80
Purchase of Technology								
Transactions	0	0	9	9	3	0	2	4
Amount (million USD)	0	0	720	720	71	0	254	395
Employment	0	0	4,880	4,880	750	0	1,675	2,455
Amount / Transaction (million USD)	0	0	542	542	250	0	838	614
Amount / Employment (million USD)	0.00	0.00	0.15	0.15	0.10	0.00	0.15	0.16
Employment / Transaction	0.00	0.00	542.22	542.22	250.00	0.00	837.50	613.75

Source: own elaboration based on Monitor of Chinese OFDI in LAC 2019.

Table 4. LAC: China's FDI by Type of Property (2000-2018)

	2000-2005	2006-2009	2010-2018	2000-2018	2015	2016	2017	2018
TOTAL								
Transactions	16	58	328	402	35	38	59	44
Amount ($US millions)	4,444	15,825	101,429	121,698	10,182	15,879	12,018	8,103
Employment	13,905	33,023	275,168	322,096	29,554	48,523	71,984	21,240
Amount / Transaction ($US millions)	277.73	272.85	309.23	302.73	290.91	417.87	203.70	184.16
Amount / Employment ($US millions)	0.32	0.48	0.37	0.38	0.34	0.33	0.17	0.38
Employment / Transaction	869.06	569.36	838.93	801.23	844.40	1276.92	1220.07	482.73
Public Firms								
Transactions	8	30	121	159	9	19	14	10
Amount ($US millions)	3,869	11,190	70,401	85,460	4,974	13,378	6,892	507
Employment	7,839	16,418	133,751	158,008	7,239	35,832	25,851	2,862
Amount / Transaction ($US millions)	483.58	373.00	581.83	537.48	552.68	704.12	492.32	50.70
Amount / Employment ($US millions)	0.49	0.68	0.53	0.54	0.69	0.37	0.27	0.18
Employment / Transaction	979.88	547.27	1105.38	993.76	804.33	1885.89	1846.50	286.20
Private Firms								
Transactions	8	28	207	243	26	19	45	35
Amount ($US millions)	575	4,635	31,027	36,238	5,208	2,501	5,126	7,596
Employment	6,066	16,605	141,417	164,088	22,315	12,691	46,133	18,378
Amount / Transaction ($US millions)	71.88	165.55	149.89	149.13	200.30	131.61	113.91	217.03
Amount / Employment ($US millions)	0.09	0.28	0.22	0.22	0.23	0.20	0.11	0.41
Employment / Transaction	758.25	593.04	683.17	675.26	858.27	667.95	1025.18	525.09
	PERCENTAGE (TOTAL = 100)							
Public Firms								
Transactions	50.00	51.72	36.89	39.55	25.71	50.00	23.73	22.73
Amount ($US millions)	87.06	70.71	69.41	70.22	48.85	84.25	57.35	6.26
Employment	56.38	49.72	48.61	49.06	24.49	73.85	35.91	13.47
Amount / Transaction (compared to private firms, percentage)	174.12	136.71	188.15	177.55	189.98	168.50	241.69	27.53
Amount / employment (compared to private firms, percentage)	154.43	142.23	142.80	143.15	199.45	114.09	159.69	46.43
Employment / transaction (compared to private firms, percentage)	112.75	96.12	131.76	124.03	95.26	147.69	151.34	59.29

Source: own elaboration based on Monitor of Chinese OFDI in LAC 2019.

2000-2018, for example, the ratio of amount per transaction was US$ 538 million and only US$ 149 million for private enterprises.

Conclusions

China's OFDI in LAC has been, so far, a rather recent development and is part of China's increasing presence in a group of cultural, political and socioeconomic factors. China's OFDI has been increasing substantially since 2006-2007 and reached its highest point in 2010, accounting for 17.64% of LAC´s total FDI and 1.71% of gross fixed capital formation, respectively.

Although there has been insufficient analysis on China's OFDI in LAC, the first section reviews a group of recent analysis regarding China's sectorial specialization and its impact on the environment, backward and forward linkages, as well as in general on development. The existing literature suggests that, in general, China's OFDI has generated diverse and heterogeneous results and that the respective counterparts in LAC, particularly the public sector, plays an important role to understand the impact of China's OFDI, also in terms of learning processes of Chinese firms in LAC.

It is in the context of these discussions that the more recent trends of China's LAC are most significant. It is indispensable to understand the methodology of registration of the respective data sources, both national and international, since potential analysts do not otherwise understand the substantial differences in their volume and trends, as discussed in the second section; Firm-level registration, as presented in the *Monitor of Chinese OFDI in Latin America and the Caribbean* is a valuable contribution because [add explanation here]. In general, China's OFDI in LAC has diversified significantly in the last years. Considering the reviewed debates, China's OFDI has moved well beyond raw materials or extractivism, and is increasingly focused on manufacturing and services in LAC. This diversification is reflected in the number of new countries receiving Chinese OFDI and the increase in the number of Chinese private firms active in the region. In 2017 and 2018 China's OFDI fell substantially, making it impossible to argue that China's OFDI in LAC will grow "exponentially" over time. This is also why the respective chapters of these book are so relevant, i.e. in terms of deepening and extending the specific activities, sectors, firms, and particularities of China's OFDI in the respective countries.

Research and analysis of Chinese OFDI needs to extend and deepen the existing data produced by public, private, and academic institutions in LAC and China. Studies of specific global value chains like oil and energy, minerals, as well as manufacturing and services (related to electronics, the auto industry, telecommunications, ports, etc.) in LAC would be important to understand Chinese OFDI, as well as firm-level analysis of Chinese activity in the region. The systematization of existing analysis of bilateral OFDI, particularly in cases such as Argentina, Brazil, Mexico, and Peru, among others, should improve in the future, both from a Chinese and LAC perspectives. Better data and analysis would improve policies in terms of the impact of Chinese OFDI on the environment, technological upgrading, backward and forward linkages, as well as on development in general.

References

Avendaño, Ricardo, Ángel Melguizo, and Sean Miner. 2017. *Chinese FDI in Latin America: New Trends with Global Implications.* Washington, D.C. and Paris: Atlantic Council and OECD.

Blanchard, Jean-Marc. 2016. "Special Issue. The Political Economy of China-Latin America Investment Relations". *Asian Perspective* 50(4), pp. 553-674.

CEBC (Conselho Empresarial Brasil-China). 2018. *China. Direcoes Globais de Investimentos 2018.* CEBC: Sao Paulo.

Dollar, David. 2017. "China's Investment in Latin America". *Geoeconomics and Global Issues* (Paper 4), pp. 1-24.

Dussel Peters, Enrique (coord.). 2014. *La inversión extranjera directa de China en América Latina: 10 estudios de caso.* México: Red ALC-China, UDUAL y UNAM/Cechimex.

Dussel Peters, Enrique. 2019. *Monitor of Chinese* OFDI *in Latin America and the Caribbean 2018.* Red ALC-China: Mexico.

Dussel Peters, Enrique, Ariel C. Armony and Shoujun Cui (coord.). 2018. *Building Development for a New Era. China's Infrastructure Projects in Latin America.* Mexico: Red ALC-China and University of Pittsburgh.

2018. *La inversión extranjera directa en América Latina y el Caribe 2017.* Santiago de Chile: ECLAC.

ECLAC (Economic Commission for Latin America and the Caribbean). 2016. *Relaciones económicas entre América Latina y el Caribe y China. Oporetunidades y desafíos.* Santiago de Chile: ECLAC.

Garzón, Paolina. 2018. *Handbook on Chinese Environmental and Social Guidelines for Foreign Loans and Investments.* China-Latin America Sustainable Investments Initiative (CLASII): Washington, D.C.

IISD (International Institute for Sustainable Development). 2016. *Sustainability Imapcts of Chinese Outward Direct Investment: A Review of the Literature.* Winnipeg: IISD.

Jiang, Shixue. 2017. "La inversión China en América latina: características, mitos y propectos". In, Pastrana Buelvas, Eduardo, and Hubert Gehring (edits.*). La proyección de China en América Latina y el Caribe.* Editorial Javeriana: Bogotá, pp. 267-292.

Koleski, Katherine, and Alec Blivas. 2018. *China's Engagement with Latin America and the Caribbean.* Washington D.C.: U.S.-China Economic and Security Review Commission.

MOFCOM (Ministry of Commerce). 2018/a. China FTA Network. At: http://fta.mofcom.gov.cn/english/index.shtml.

MOFCOM. 2018/b. 2017. *Statistical Bulletin Foreign Direct Investment.* MOFCOM: Pekín.

MOFCOM. 2019/a. *China Monthly Economic Indicators 2019.1. The Latest Monthly Statistics.* MOFCOM: Beijing.

MOFCOM. 2019/b. *Yearly Overview* XXI *for Commerce Work in 2018. Outward Investment and Cooperation: Steadily, Orderly and Healthily, and Achieve Mutual Benefit and Win-Win.* February 2nd. MOFCOM: Beijing.

MOFCOM, State-owned Assets Supervision and Administration Commission of the State Council) and UNDP (United Nations Development Programme China). *2015. Report on the Sustainable Development of Chinese Enterprises Overseas.* Mofcom: Beijing.

Myers, Margaret and Ricardo Barrios. 2018. *What Do China's New Investment Guidelines Mean for Latin America?* Washington, D.C.: Inter-American Dialogue.

Ortiz Velásquez, Samuel. 2016. *Methodological Differences in Chinese OFDI. Monitor de la OFDI China in LAC.* Red ALC-China: Mexico.

Ray, Rebecca, Kevin P. Gallagher, Andrés López and Cynthia Sanborn. 2017. *China and Sustainable Development in Latin America: The Social and Environmental Dimension.* Anthem Press: London and New York.

Salazar-Xirinachs, José Manuel, Enrique Dussel Peters, and Ariel C. Armony (edits). *Efectos de China en la cantidad y calidad del empleo en América Latina (2000-2018).* Lima: OIT.

CHINA'S OFDI IN ARGENTINA

Leonardo E. Stanley

Introduction

Argentina and the People´s Republic of China's (PRC) bilateral relations date from March 1972. The relationship grew steadily thereafter, becoming economically significant after 2003 when Chinese demand induced a soybean boom in the Pampas and permitted the South American country to recover from its worst economic crisis.

Despite growing commercial links and the financial assistance provided by China after the Argentine crisis, bilateral relations have not been exempt from tensions (Uriburu Quintana 2009; López and Ramos 2009; Hua 2017). The latest example of these tensions irrupted on March 16th, 2016, after the sinking of a Chinese trawler for illegal fishing in Argentine territorial waters. Overall, tensions and frictions might be unmasking the substantial environmental and social costs imposed by the new structural growth model (Fabinyi and Liu 2014; Sharma 2014; Ray et al. 2017). In any case, discordancy did not alter the bilateral but uneven commercial relationship between partners. Argentine economic dependence on China may increase enlarging as local authorities become reliant upon Beijing for financial support. So indeed, Argentina´s urgencies represent an opportunity for China, always obsessed with the idea of food (Veeck 2013; Kuteleva 2016; Zhou

2016) and energy security (Zweig and Jianbai 2005; Downs 2007; Kong 2011; Jiang and Sinton 2011; de Graaf 2014). Argentina's actual macroeconomic circumstances (low asset prices, recession, and local private firms in trouble) offer Chinese firms a golden opportunity at bargain prices (and cheap bargaining) for gaining a foothold in the natural resource value chain (ECC 2018). The next paragraphs will elucidate the relationship between the two sovereigns, but mainly assess the relevance of Chinese OFDI in the economy of Argentina.

The Argentina chapter contains three sections. It first introduces a brief analysis of the bilateral relationship and describes trade and services flows along with the financial assistance provided by China after the global financial crisis. The second and largest section introduces Chinese OFDI in Argentina. At the very start, it briefly discusses methodological issues, describing the main traditional asset-liability approach and the so-called directional approach to FDI assessment. Next, it brings a short and concise map, illustrating the principal locations for Chinese OFDI. Then, it discusses the sectoral composition of Chinese OFDI in Argentina. The last section brings some ideas for the debate.

The Chinese Relationship with Argentina (2000-2017)

The emergence of China as an insatiable purchaser of commodities reimposed the natural resource export-led growth model trade pattern of 19th and early 20th century in Latin America. For Argentina, the result was an increase in a few agricultural exports in contrast to the importation of more than 5,000 goods coming from China. Only three products account for 85% of Argentine exports to the Middle Kingdom: soybeans (56.2%), soybean oil (13.4%), and crude oil (15.0%). The bilateral trade balance turned favorable to China after 2008, whose rise not only displaced old Argentine partners but reconfigured the country's export basket.

Figure 1. Argentina - China Bilateral Trade (2008-2017)

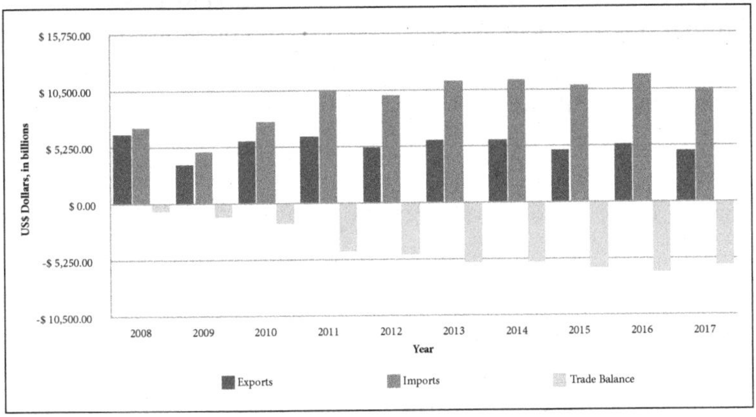

Source: author's elaboration based on Oviedo (2016) and indec

Chinese firms have also become very active in infrastructure-related projects (Stanley 2018; Uriburu Quintana 2018; Madhavan et al. 2018). Beijing has promoted the internationalization of national firms through these projects, and Argentina, which has been desperately searching for new funding sources, has welcomed them. The quest led by President Mauricio Macri for membership in the Asian International Investment Bank (AIIB), as to enthusiastically endorse for the Belt and Road Initiative (BRI) enlargement in Latin America. Meanwhile, Xi Jinping promised to provide Argentina with a US$ 17 billion credit line for infrastructure-related investments (Myers 2018).

Chinese influence in the financial realm is also expanding and benefits Argentina through preferential loans or swaps agreements. On the heels of the global financial crisis, the People's Bank of China (PBC) and the Central Bank of Argentina (BCRA) signed their first swap agreement in June 2009 (BCRA 2009), which has been renewed twice by former president Cristina Fernández de Kirchner (first during 2014, a complementary agreement in 2015) and two more times by current president Mauricio Macri. The original agreement objective was to strengthen Argentina's currency reserves but during the political transition, the funds were used to stabilize the exchange rate. Following the recent currency crisis, the Argentine government once again initiated talks with China and asked Beijing to participate in providing a package of support from foreign lenders. Argentine authorities obtained a three year extension in 2017 and recently agreed to an enlargement of the swap agreement (Reuters 2018b).

Impact of Chinese OFDI in Argentina (2000-2017)

The arrival of Chinese investors to Argentina was limited before 2003 and then increased and peaked in 2010 (Sevares 2016). According to Ernesto Taboada, CEO of the Chinese Argentine Chamber of Commerce, China OFDI during 2017 totaled US$ 12 billion. That optimistic vision is shared by Diego R. Guelar, the Argentine Ambassador to China, who has suggested that the Middle Kingdom was Argentina's principal investor in 2017 (Nuevos Papeles 2017). Official statistics, however, suggest a slightly different picture.

Two key concepts should be considered when evaluating whether an operation should be classified as FDI or not: country of residence and the investor´s long-term interests or influence over the enterprise (UNCTAD 2009). According to these criteria, an investment undertaken by a Chinese citizen who is a resident of Argentina should not qualify as a direct investment. For example, when a Chinese citizen (foreigner but resident in the country) obtains a fishing license or owns and manages a supermarket in Buenos Aires, an increasingly common practice, their activities do not represent FDI. Likewise, a foreign citizen who maintains a minority stake in an Argentine firm and is not involved in the firm's administration is likewise not engaged in FDI. The foreigner has to acquire a lasting interest of more than 10% in an enterprise for it to qualify as such, according to IMF standards (IMF 1993). The OECD guidelines, on the other hand, treat a direct investment as "a category of cross-border investment made by a resident entity in one economy (the direct investor) with the objective of establishing a lasting interest in an enterprise (the direct investment enterprise) that is resident in an economy other than that of the direct investor" (OECD 2008). In contrast to the former definition, the OECD view also considers minority shareholders who maintain an active voice in management to be FDI, independently of any threshold. China's perspective situates it at the other extreme, with MOFCON FDI guidelines establishing a 25% threshold to identify and report investment as FDI (Vicek 2010).

Table 1. China's OFDI in Argentina, BCRA official figures (information on FDI in local companies, $USD)

Date	China	Bermudas	Hong Kong	Cayman Islands	Virgin Islands	Total
December 2004	13	908	29	2,059	966	3,974
June 2005	11	997	29	2,131	1,068	4,235
December 2005	10	826	37	1,980	462	3,315
June 2006	20	955	39	2,042	415	3,472
December 2006	44	1,001	35	2,088	429	3,596
June 2007	71	1,062	41	2,090	431	3,695
December 2007	89	1,164	43	2,099	449	3,844
June 2008	117	955	85	2,070	494	3,721
December 2008	110	845	52	2,297	447	3,752
June 2009	105	873	33	1,753	459	3,223
December 2009	124	920	35	1,198	511	2,787
June 2010	143	1,249	33	1,908	508	3,842
December 2010	191	1,530	48	1,766	612	4,146
June 2011	224	1,845	70	2,474	572	5,185
December 2011	239	1,611	134	2,450	724	5,158
June 2012	221	2,032	111	2,196	795	5,356
December 2012	575	1,959	59	1,590	697	4,880
June 2013	652	2,043	77	1,581	581	4,935
December 2013	607	1,690	74	1,423	552	4,344
June 2014	621	1,569	93	991	500	3,773
December 2014	726	1,003	105	1,221	619	3,674
June 2015	758	1,127	85	1,173	722	3,865
December 2015	661	716	68	1,034	516	2,994
June 2016	628	786	93	1,021	512	3,039
December 2016	618	802	123	1,158	556	3,256

Source: author's elaboration based on BCRA.

The traditional asset-liabilities approach, however, does not adequately reflect the realities of today's economy. The OECD has also proposed an alternative method: the so-called directional one, which qualifies flows and stocks according to the ultimate investing country (OECD 2008; Ortíz Velásquez 2016). The directional principle also permits a differentiation of FDI inflows into four different types: greenfield investments, merger and acquisitions (M&A), extension of capital (additional new venture), and financial restructuring. The directional approach more accurately delineates the role played by Chinese investors in Argentina.

Tracking M&A operations would be helpful in tracking inward FDI according to investing country, especially after globalization altered the market for corporative control dynamics. In recent years, Chinese firms become highly active in the M&A global market, acquiring leading technology firms in Europe and elsewhere. However, Chinese firms´ merger & acquisition spree has grown beyond tech firms to include TNCs participating in energy, mining, and other natural resources industries. Deals like those involving agri-business subsidiaries like Syngenta or Nidera have altered asset ownership around the world and in Argentina, including. Likewise, the current wave of mergers in the mining sector is transforming the industry globally and permitting China to participate in the Argentine lithium boom.

In some cases, direct investments are too unclear to assess. Redirecting FDI flows from offshore centers (round tripping capital if capital is going to tax havens and then eventually back to China) has become one of the leading practices for emerging market economies firms going global (Vicek 2010; Shuterland et al. 2010; Qiu 2014; Buckley et al. 2015) and has been extensively observed with respect to Chinese OFDI.1 Offshore centers as hubs for capital intermediation have altered patterns of business investments and traditional accounting practices (Kolstad and Wiig 2012; Buckley et al. 2015) and caused a distortion in figures that misrepresents the role of Chinese firms in the Argentine economy. A significant

1 According to unofficial figures, around 69-87% of annual Chinese OFDI was direct to offshore and tax havens during 2003-2011 period and concentrated in three locations: Cayman Islands, Hong Kong, and the British Virgin Islands (Buckley et al. 2015).

amount of Chinese flows come from societies legally settled at offshore centers locations in the Caribbean (especially the Cayman Islands and the British Virgin Islands) and therefore remain unaccounted for in Argentina's official records, which are based on the traditional asset-liabilities criteria. "Identifying the country of origin of FDI flows from national accounts tends to be imprecise as this shows only the immediate bilateral background of funds, and does not identify transactions conducted through third-party markets" (ECLAC 2018). To accurately assess the source of the investment, and to avoid misunderstandings originating from round-tripping practices, OECD guidelines suggest evaluated FDI according to the directional principle (OECD 2008).

Despite the increasing relevance of China in the Argentine economy, China is not even mentioned in the Central Bank direct investment annual report (BCRA 2016). According to official figures, by the end of December 2016 the gross liability position of Chinese FDI in Argentina (classified by first-rate investor country) totaled $618 million, with the financial sector receiving most of the flows (BCRA, online statistics). Chinese investors are not reported in ECLAC statistics either, at least not among countries listed as the primary source of FDI flows arriving in the country during the 2007-2016 period (ECLAC 2018). Underreporting is also observed in MOFCON statistics which, by the end of December 2016, estimated Chinese FDI in Argentina at US$ 181,52 million. Official figures do not take into account M&A operations settled abroad; even when they have societal consequences on local markets their ultimate origin –for example through offshore centers located in the Caribbean– is not considered.

A series of deals recently made by Chinese investors were unreported in the previous edition of the Red ALC-China dataset. The ICBC takeover of Standard Bank (US$ 600 millions) is the most substantial unreported investment. Official records (and Red ALC-China until now) have also overlooked Chinese activity in the mining sector (US$ 370,8 millions), which might be due to the fact that most lithium-related deals take place abroad (mainly Canada), but positively affecting lasting control rights over Argentine societies. Chinese investments in the fisheries sector ($ 91,3 millions)

Table 2. Chinese OFDI in Argentina at company level (2000-2017)
(transactions not included by Red ALC-China in 2018)

Date	Investing Company	Target company	Destination city	Destination sector	Project Type	Employment (number of workers)	Investment (millions of dollars)	Natural Resources = 0, Manufacturing =1, Services=2, Technological Acquisition =3
2005	Ambassador		Tierra del Fuego	Electronics	M&A		1.5	2.0
2012	Lenovo	Newsan	Tierra del Fuego	Electronics	JV		6.0	1.0
2010	TCL	Radio Victoria Argentina SA	Tierra del Fuego	Electronics	JV		60.0	1.0
2011	ZTE	BGH	Tierra del Fuego	Electronics	JV		1.0	1.0
	CHEMCHINA - SYNGENTA	COFCO NIDERA Seeds	NATIONAL	Agro-food sector	M&A	400	3.0	1.0
APRIL 2014	Shanghai Fisheries Group Co. (SFGC)	ALTAMARE	Chubut	Foods - Fisheries	M&A		21.5	0.0
JULY 2017	Dalian Huafeng Aquatic Products.	ARBUMASA	Santa Cruz	Foods - Fisheries	M&A		54.8	0.0
May 2018	R&J Globe Investments		Chubut	Foods - Fisheries	New	300	10.0	0.0
	FOBAO Food Company Argentina	Centauro	Buenos Aires	Foods - Fisheries	M&A	50 - 100	5.0	0.0
2011	ICBC		NATIONAL	Financial	M&A		600.0	2.0
2018	Nextview	Lithium x	Salta	Mining	M&A		265.0	0.0
2018	Mariana Lithium Company	International Lithium Corp (ILC)	Salta	Mining	JV		17.0	0.0
2018	Ganfeng Lithium & Lithium America	Minera Exar	Jujuy	Mining	M&A		87.5	0.0
2018	Chengdu Chemphys Chemical Industry Co. Ltd	NRG Metals Inc	Salta & Catamarca	Mining	M&A		1.3	0.0

Source: author´s elaboration based on Academic Network of Latin America and the Caribbean on China (2019).

have also remained unnoticed but are becoming significant in local ports. A series of takeovers has given Chinese firms control over a group of Spanish fisheries firms operating in Argentina. Lastly, a series of investments made by well-known electronics firms in the Tierra del Fuego free trade zone ($ 68,5 millions), correlate to joint-venture deals with local firms (see Table 2).

To the total amount of Chinese OFDI in Argentina originally reported in the Red ALC-China Table ($ 11.870 millions), we are adding $ 1.133,6 million for a new total of $ 13.003,6. Chinese investments in Argentina, differentiated by sector, are the following: natural resources, $ 7.967,1; manufacturing, $ 407,7; and services, $ 4.628,5.

Geographical Map

In geographical terms, Chinese firms have spread to every corner of Argentina but some provinces have received more attention given their good fortune with respect to natural resources. Brine reserves in the northern provinces of Jujuy, Salta or Catamarca are attracting an increasing number of Chinese investors. Oil and gas initially brought investors to the San Jorge basin at Chubut, although now they are turning their attention toward the Vaca Muerta shale gas basin located at Neuquén. Argentine sea fisheries, especially those with squid and pelagic varieties, have generated considerable interest in China. An increasing number of Chinese investors and fishing firms are landing in the Argentine ports of Buenos Aires, Chubut, and Santa Cruz. Food security also drives the latest merger and acquisitions movements made by Chinese conglomerates in the agribusiness sector. For companies like Chemchina or COFCO, operations are national but located mainly on the Central Region (Buenos Aires, La Pampa, Santa Fe, and Córdoba). Those investing in the meatpacking sector follow a similar geographical pattern. Chinese electronics firms typically settle on Tierra del Fuego, as investments on the island historically benefitted from tax breaks and industrial subsidies.

Sectoral Map

In sectoral terms, most Chinese investments established in Argentina follow a resource-seeking pattern, with the exception of some atypical participation in manufactures and services. Investments are mainly found in the following sectors: oil and gas, mining, agribusiness, beef, and fisheries.

Once a significant exporter, after 2013 China transformed into the world's largest net importer of petroleum and other liquid fuels –importing 8.4 million barrels per day (b/d) during 2017. To match its growing energy demands and to secure access at the point of supply, Chinese national oil companies (NOCs) began to go global in the late 1990s. The objective has drawn them to the Argentine oil and gas sector, which hosts two of the Chinese leading energy firms since the beginning of the present decade: China National Offshore Oil Company (CNOOC) and China Petrochemical Corporation (SINOPEC) (López and Ramos 2014).[2]

CNOOC is the largest producer of offshore crude oil and natural gas in China and one of the largest independent oil and gas exploration and production companies in the world. Regionally the company operates in Brazil, Colombia, Mexico, Guyana, and Trinidad and Tobago. CNOOC entered Argentina after paying US$ 3.1 billion for a 50% stake at Bridas at March 2010, a deal that transformed CNOOC as BP partner at PAE.[3] Two years later Bridas (CNOOC and Bulgheroni) acquired ExxonMobil's assets in Argentina, Uruguay, and Paraguay, giving birth to Axion Energy group. Finally, during 2017, PAE merged with Axion Energy to become PAE Group (or simply PAEG). PAEG is one of the main hydrocarbon companies in the country (983 MMBOE of proven oil

2 A more small energy company intended to join this energy delegation, but its ambitious project in Tierra del Fuego never came to life. The proposal was initially presented by "*Tierra del Fuego Energía & Química-TDFEQ*," and consisted in the construction of a US$ 650 million urea plant near the Río Grande at Tierra del Fuego Province. As the company failed to meet with royalties payments, the project stalled and eventually failed.

3 In 1997, the Bulgheroni family (BRIDAS) and British Petroleum (BP) created Pan American Energy (PAE).

& gas reserves in 2015[4]), with operations in Argentina in four central hydrocarbon basins (Golfo San Jorge, Neuquén, Noreste, and Marina Austral) and interests in Vaca Muerta shale. Between 2001 and 2016, PAE invested more than US$ 14 billion in hydrocarbon exploration and production in the country. During that same period, PAE increased its gas production by 76% and its oil production by 27% and today accounts for 18% of the consolidated market in the country. In sum, PAEG ranks as the first oil private company and one of the leading Argentine producers and exporters of crude oil.

Sinopec Group is the largest oil and petrochemical products suppliers and the second largest oil and gas producer in China, the largest refining company and the second largest chemical company in the world, ranking 3rd on Fortune's Global 500 List in 2017. SINOPEC is already present in the regional market (Ecuador, Colombia, and Brazil), and entered the local market in 2010 when it acquired Argentine subsidiary of US Occidental Petroleum Company (OXY) (a US$ 2.45 billion operation). Occidental has obtained 23 different concessions with the probe and probable reserves totaling 393 millions of barrels per day (b/d) and with operations at Santa Cruz and Chubut (both at San Jorge basin) as well at Mendoza. In addition to original value miscalculation pitfalls made at the time of the deal (FT 2016b), SINOPEC suffered from more significant than expected costs and disputes with labor unions, all of which made the Chinese firm to look for alternatives, including selling (Paraskova 2017). However, with the prospect of increasing oil prices, the company decided to remain (Revista Petroquímica 2017). Following nine months of negotiations with trade unions, the company chose to restart operations in four oilfields in Santa Cruz Province (US$ 70 million in investments and 240 new jobs) (Revista Petroquímica 2018).

4 PAE maintains the highest reserve replacement ratio in Argentina: 150% between 2001 and 2015 (https://www.pan-energy.com/sites/en/Prensa/Paginas/Comunicados/Bridas-and-BP-agree-to-integrate-PAE-and-Axion-Energy.aspx).

Table 3 shows Argentina´s oil & gas market structure, in which the presence of Chinese firm keeps growing: PAEG (5.6 millions of m3 of production) comes in behind the market leader whereas SINOPEC obtains the fourth place (1.4 million of m3). In natural gas production, PAEG has a 12% market share which places it third (after YPF and Total), whereas SINOPEC comes in 10th place.

Table 3. Argentina's oil and gas market, primary producers (2017)

OIL		
Operator	m3	Market Share
Ypf S.a.	12,566,149.0	45.18%
Pan American Energy (Sucursal Argentina) Llc	5,644,640.7	20.29%
Pluspetrol S.A.	1,719,727.7	6.18%
Sinopec Argentina Exploration Inc	1,459,749.4	5.25%
Tecpetrol S.A.	707,501.6	2.54%
First 5	**22,097,768.3**	**79.45%**
Others	**5,716,117.1**	**20.55%**
TOTAL	**27,813,885.4**	**100.00%**

NATURAL GAS		
Operator	Mm3	Market Share
Ypf S.a.	15,012,753.44	33.66%
Total Austral S.A.	11,907,555.15	26.70%
Pan American Energy (Sucursal Argentina) Llc	5,497,747.70	12.33%
Pampa Energia S.A.	1,667,238.48	3.74%
Tecpetrol S.A.	1,537,651.19	3.45%
Ysur Energía Argentina S.R.L.	1,343,058.87	3.01%
Pluspetrol S.A.	1,099,274.94	2.46%
Compañía General De Combustibles S.A.	1,073,531.72	2.41%
Enap Sipetrol Argentina S.A.	803,871.36	1.80%
Sinopec Argentina Exploration Inc	753,590.64	1.69%
First 10	**40,696,273.49**	**91.26%**
Others	**3,899,139.14**	**8.74%**
TOTAL	**44,595,412.63**	**100.00%**

Source: author's elaboration based on Academic Network of LatinAmerica and the Caribbean on China (2019).

Recent investment inflows are also impacting agribusiness, as food security remains a crucial priority for officials at Beijing. Back in 2008, the Ministry of Agriculture formulated a program of "outward agricultural investment, including a possible strategy of overseas land purchase and leasing" (Myers and Jie 2015:3). The plan laid out the ambitious attempt made by China to buy land for crop production in Argentina, although few deals were ultimately concluded. Two initiatives initiated by the Chongqing Grain Group (CGG): one in Chaco province (130.000 hectares, for US$ 420 million) for soybean production and another in Cordoba (10.000 hectares, US$ 1.2 billion), both aimed at soybean and (in association with Molino Cañuelas, a local producer of vegetable oils and flour) dairy farming. Heilongjiang Beidahuang Nongken Group Co., another Chinese firm, purchased 300.000 hectares (US$ 1.5 billion) in Rio Negro province for soybean, corn and wheat production. The entry of foreign investors generated resentment among small and medium farmers and eventually forced national authorities to introduce a new bill restricting the purchase of land by foreigners.[5]

As opposition to land grabbing mounted, authorities in Beijing turned to a new strategy. Chinese efforts shifted towards the control of the main distribution channels to ensure reliable transportation infrastructure. The state-owned Chinese giant Cereals, Oils, and Foodstuffs Company (COFCO) undertook the initiative, buying majority stakes in both the Dutch seed and trading company Nidera and Hong Kong-based agribusiness Noble Group, both of which have an extensive historical presence in Argentina and Brazil.[6] South America has become COFCO's most crucial business unit, a region where the company maintains 60% of their global

5 The new law "Ley de Protección al Dominio Nacional sobre Propiedad, Posesión o Tenencia de Tierras Rurales" was passed by Congress on December 22, 2011.

6 Nidera arrived in Argentina in 1930 and, actually has two crushing plants (at Buenos Aires and Santa Fe provinces) totalizing 11.000 tons/day of crushing capacity (around 8% of Argentina total installed crushing facilities). The Noble group arrived in the year 2000, after which it established both a crushing plant in Rosario (8.200 tons/day) and a port grain terminal at Timbues, both located in Santa Fe province.

assets.[7] Both acquisitions were undertaken in 2014, with COFCO paying US$ 1.2 billion for a 51% stake in Nidera and US$ 1.5 billion for a similar take in Noble Group. Two years later COFCO bought the remaining 49% stake in Nidera (US$ 750 million), completing a full takeover of the Dutch grain trader and further expanding its global footprint (FT 2016). The commercial operation seems to signal Chinese interest in gaining independence from the world's largest grain traders (ADM, Bunge, Cargill, and Dreyfus). In sum, COFCO Argentina has 12.8% of the country crushing capacity but also controls a significant portion of Argentine soy feed, oil, and grain exports (Williamson et al. 2015:15). The latest statistics place China as the central market for Argentine grains (6.4 million tons, a 13% of total exports) and chief buyer of soybean (6,357.046 tons, roughly 87% of the country total exports) (BCR, 2018). In terms of market structure, COFCO has moved into the leading cohort of Argentine exporters of grain and by-products (see Table 4).

Table 4. Argentina: Exports of Grains and By-products by Firms (2017) (values in tons)

FIRM	Grains	Oilmeals	Vegetable Oil	Total	Market Share
Cargill	7.307.003	3.606.009	670.286	11.583.298	14,14%
COFCO	8.209.158	2.538.423	258.982	11.006.563	13,43%
Bunge	4.626.331	3.661.432	459.041	8.746.804	10,67%
Dreyfus	4.547.498	3.063.472	332.405	7.943.375	9,69%
AGD	1.717.388	4.929.001	684.407	7.330.796	8,95%
Vicentin	1.534.239	4.585.758	852.952	6.972.949	8,51%
ADM	5.354.489	7.240	12.250	5.373.979	6,56%
Oleaginosa Moreno	1.452.634	3.192.357	688.598	5.333.589	6,51%
ACA	4.032.144	236.000	57.400	4.325.544	5,28%
Molino Agro	470.318	2.748.318	455.371	3.674.007	4,48%
Five main exporters				**46.610.837**	**56,88%**
Ten main exporters				**72.290.904**	**88,22%**
Total				**81.942.246**	**100,00%**

Source: author's elaboration based on BCR Weekly.

7 For further information: https://www.cofcointernational.com/media/1255/cof_factsheet_en_2018-09-04-no.pdf

China's increasing relevance in the global seeds and agri-chemical industry is undeniable. At present, almost 40% of worldwide glyphosate supply and 33% of worldwide exports are coming from China (Haro Sly, 2017). The Chinese government is pushing local firms to rationalize and inducing their big players to go global. In 2014 Huapont Nutrichem bought a 20% stake (US$ 220 million) in Albaught LLC group (controller of Atanor, a chemical group, and Argentina's second largest producer of the herbicide glyphosate) (ECC 2014).[8] In 2016 another Chinese investment would challenge the seed industry in particular: Chinese state-owned ChemChina bought Syngenta to COFCO in 2017 (a US$ 43 billion deal, including US$ 3 billion for the Argentine branch) –worldwide leaders in the seed business along with DuPont/Pioneer and Bayer/Monsanto (Reuters 2017; Cámara de Comercio Suizo-Argentina 2018).

The meat industry, with a long history in Argentina, has also attracted Chinese investors. Beef exports to the Middle Kingdom started slowly in 2012, following the signature of a bilateral agreement permitting frozen boned meat to enter in China. Recently, exports have grown more steadily. A new protocol signed with the China General Administration of Quality Supervision, Inspection, and Quarantine (January 17th, 2018) set forth new and more ambitious sanitary standards for Argentine exports. It permits local producers to enter the Chinese market of higher quality (chilled or frozen beef with bones). At the moment 18 meatpacking firms are allowed to trade with China, a voracious market that absorbed half of the total beef exports in 2017 (121.000 out of 259.0000 tons, and around US$ 456 MM) (Orientar January 2018). The Pampas is becoming a highly appreciated source for Chinese beef and meat processing producers.

FORESUN Group, the giant meat processor part of Heilongjiang-Foresun Agriculture Group, recently bought Brazilian meatpacking Margrif Global Foods' three beef slaughterhouses. In Argentina, Black Bamboo Enterprises (the local division of the

8 The company has three plants, two in Buenos Aires province (Pilar and San Nicolas) and one in Cordoba (Rio Tercero) (more information at https://albaugh.com.ar).

Foresun group) operates a livestock confinement unit located at Hughes in Santa Fe province (formerly Argentina Breeders & Packers (AB&P). Black Bamboo also has two meatpacking plants, one at Vivorata in Buenos Aires (formerly Best Beef) and another at Unquillo in Cordoba (formerly Estancias del Sur). Compañia Central Pampeana, a joint venture formed by the Chinese investor Bao Liu and two Argentineans (Juan Manual Budano Roig and Mario Quinteros), is ranked fifth in Argentine beef exports –three local firms and JBS from Brazil are explaining the closing reduced list (ECC 2017), Black Bamboo Enterprises ranks 11th. Argentine beef exports are expected reach US$ 1.8 billion, implying shipments of a minimum of 4000,000 tons, well above the 200,000 tons shipped during 2017 (MercoPress 2018).

Chinese (mainly indirect) investments are also establishing a foothold in Argentine fisheries and transforming the local industry. China has become a leading player, with the world's largest fleet of deep-sea fishing boats: a new "Armada" of long-distance vessels.[9] Massive (national) governmental fuel subsidies,[10] of course, are behind the rapid fleet growth –without them, the fleet would not be profitable (FT 2018; Greenpeace, 2018). Besides, (local and regional) authorities fund fisheries related to loans facilities, research and development costs, and infrastructure development. International ports are expected to be favored under BRI (an overseas fisheries basis for local and Chinese-led global fleet) (AACPPP 2017; Godfrey 2018). In a nutshell, the industry has become a hot diplomatic issue (Mallony 2013). Because of its rich territorial waters, Argentina often confronts illegal fishing, a practice that affects highly valuable resources like squid (China Dialogue Ocean 2018).

9 Between 2010 and 2016, the number of fishing companies licensed by the Agriculture Ministry to operate abroad reached 162, an increase of 46 percent. These firms had a combined 2,571 vessels in the waters in 2016, up 66% since 2010. Mark Godfrey "China rushing to build global fishing bases before capping its fleet size" January 17, 2018.

10 Fuel represents almost 40% of the boat cost and helps to explain 80% of industry non-operating income. Following an increase in fuel prices, the Ministry of Finance decided to subside the industry in 2006, a practice that it maintained with subsidies increasing in subsequent years. Although massive, fuel subsidies by China (US$ 418 million) are behind those granted by Japan (US$ 841 million) and Spain (2 603 million).

Argentine authorities should expect problems to worsen: the Chinese long-distance fleet is targeting an annual catch of 2.3 m tons in 2020 (FT 2018).[11] Because of international pressure to freeze its distant-water fishing fleet, authorities in Beijing are moving towards an alternative strategy –transfer and place its fleet under a third country flag. This delocalization strategy might imply the presence of a Chinese citizen with residence in Argentina, in this case, who could bid for new permission or buy existing firms with fisheries licenses).

Dalian Huafeng Aquatic Products bought Arbumasa from the Spanish Amasúa Group, proprietor of ten vessels in Argentina: 7 trawlers (shrimp), two jigging (squid), and one factory ship (pelagic and other species). Dalian Huafeng also obtained a factory at Puerto Deseado, in Santa Cruz province. The purchase agreement grants Dalian Huafeng exclusive rights to commercialize Arbumasa products in China (in particular, shrimp). Back in 2014, Shanghai Jinjou Deep Sea Fisheries Co., a subsidiary of Shanghai Fisheries General Corporation (SFGC), bought Altamare (a subsidiary of Spanish Armadora Pereira) for US$ 21.5 million. The Armadora Pereira operation gave this state-owned fishery group from China direct control of shrimp fishing vessels, fishing licenses, and a processing plant in Argentina.[12] SFGC has made much of its strategy to "go global" and buy fishing companies and resources around the world.[13] Fubao Food Company recently bought Centauro, whose plant in Mar del Plata, Buenos Aires province will be refurbished by the Chinese group to process frozen fish and vegetables and is expected to generate 50 to 100 new jobs (US$ 5 MM investment) (Orientar, January 2018). According to official statis-

11 According to independent sources, more than 4,000 Chinese vessels are operating at the 201 mile mark, the border of Argentina territorial waters (SEPRIN-portal de noticias independientes http://seprin.info).

12 Shanghai Fisheries is also the ultimate parent of Shanghai Kaichuang Marine International, which acquired Spanish tuna canner Conservas Albo for €60.99m in cash earlier in the year.

13 As an example of the public-private interconnection, in 2016 Pu Shaohua, Shanghai Fisheries General Corp. President, declared his firm intention to to bring new products into the domestic market through overseas business, in line with the government's One Road, One Belt initiative (Wang Ying "Conquering the seven seas" (China Daily 2016/08/20).

tics, China has become the second export market for Argentina (with purchases valued at US$ 289,6 million in 2017) and is the first external market for both red shrimp and squid (Ministerio de Agroindustria 2017). China is also importing a low volume of high-value commercial species from Argentine coasts like hake and Patagonian toothfish to satisfy the increasing demand for fish (Clarke 2009; Hanson et al. 2011).

Mining remains one of the leading Latin American sectors for Chinese OFDI but is at an incipient stage in Argentina. Shandong Gold Group is an exception, having paid US$ 960 MM for a 50% stake of Valedero gold mining project from Barrick Gold Corporation soon after an environmental accident severely affected the reputation of the Canadian mining group (El Inversor Energético y Minero 2017; Clarin 2017). Located at San Juan province, Veladero has probable reserves for 6,7 mm ounces (3,3 MM proved), and expected to produce as much as 830,000 ounces of gold this year. Shandong Mining and Barrick Gold will also look at options for developing Pascua Lama, an unfinished project that the Canadian firm put on hold in 2013, and joint investments in the gold-rich region straddling the border of Argentina and Chile, located a mere 10 km from Veladero (China Daily 2017).

The abundance of lithium in northern Argentina region is also attracting Chinese investors, primarily through indirect investments and recent deals with lithium-specialized Canadian mining firms. A takeover launched by Beijing and Shanghai -based NEXTVIEW New Energy Lion Hong Kong Company launched a takeover on Lithium X, a Canadian TSX- listed exploration and development company with lithium projects in Argentina. TSX flagship lithium brine project "Sal de Los Angeles" at Salta Province. The recent US$ 265 million deal (US$ 2.61 per share, a 22.5% premium on the closing price at December 15th, 2017) signals the Chinese company's interest in securing the materials for vehicle batteries (Financial Post 2017).14 Mariana Lithium Co Ltd., a subsidiary of Chinese lithium producer Ganfeng Lithium Co.,

14 In early 2017, Sinochem, China's state chemical company, along with several other Chinese companies, placed competing bids to purchase a US$4 billion stake in Chile's SQM, a giant lithium producer (Financial Post 2017).

has teamed up with the Canadian company International Lithium Corp (ILC) to exploit lithium reserves in Salta Province. For the Salta operations, Mariana decided to create a new joint venture company (Litio Minera Argentina S.A.), a private company registered in Argentina in which the Chinese shareholder maintains 83% percent of the shares (up from an original 27% stake) and the remaining 17,246 % remains owned by the ILC company (ILC, 2017). The Mariana field qualifies as one of the more promising salt lakes in the region. Following the decision of Chilean SQM to leave the local market, Ganfeng Lithium & Lithium America acquired a 37.5% stake at Minera Exar (US$ 87,5 MM) (El Inversor Energético y Minero 2018; Reuters 2018), to become a minority partner in the Cauchari-Olaroz project in the Jujuy province project, the majority of which remains under the control of Canadian LAC. The new arrangement brings Ganfeng Lithium a minority stake (37.5%) but equal participation in the company's decision. Chinese investors will provide a US$ 100 million loan to fund the brine project, whose production is expected to start in 2020 (FT 2018b). Chinese high-purity lithium manufacturer Chengdu Chemphys Chemical Industry Co. Ltd has recently made a strategic alliance with Canadian NRG Metals Inc. to advance the exploration and development of the Hombre Muerto North (HMN) Lithium Project –a massive project located in Salta and Catamarca. Under the CAD$ 1.6 million agreement, the Canadian mining company will supply Chemphys its products for the battery and energy markets. With the completion of this private placement and the financial support of warrant and option holders, Chengdu Chemphys is now fully funded to carry out its planned work program on the HMN Project. The lithium triangle made up of Argentina, Bolivia, and Chile holds the bulk of lithium precious brines reserves, a type of mineral much cheaper to produce than Australian hard-rock sources. Argentina is responsible for 16% of the world's lithium supply, but local authorities expect to expand its market share to 45% soon. A new natural resource race is on the way.

Besides natural resources, Chinese investors are also active in manufacturing at Tierra del Fuego (TdF), a regional hub for electronic firms in Argentina (Economist 2016; Carrizo Gorgni

2018). To enter, a couple of Chinese giants, Lenovo, Telephone Communication Limite (TCL), and ZTE, have initiated minor investments alone or in association with local partners. Despite the limited demand for cars in Argentina, a group of Chinese carmakers is beginning to look at the local market. Commercialization started in 2012, and now eleven different brands are selling their cars in the local market (iProfesional 2018). BYD and Dongfeng have also expressed their interest in producing in the country but none of them have sunk capital in the country yet.

Finally, Chinese investors are also venturing into the Argentine services sector. The Industrial and Commercial Bank of China (ICBC) bought a majority stake at Standard Bank Argentina, becoming the first Chinese financial entity to enter in the Argentine banking sector (US$ 600 million).

Conclusions

The Argentina-China relationship has become deeper but undoubtedly more complicated. Once based on a complementary but highly biased pattern of exchanging natural resources for manufactures, the relationship now extends into asymmetries well beyond trade and includes new investments and financing flows. This complexity has also resulted in greater political tensions. With its rising economic influence, Beijing has also brought political leverage to the bilateral agenda, which gives an advantage to Chinese investors. Chinese firms going abroad have an exceptional advantage: funding (Naughton 2007; Shuterland 2009). Funds come in hand with the public character of most of the companies operating in natural resource-related industries.[15] For most of these companies, investment decisions reflect political objectives and not just the profit-maximization of privately owned multinationals from other countries. The Chinese "going out" policy remains alive with the political goal of further advancing in

15 As noted by Neil Wang, global partner and China president of the consulting firm Frost and Sullivan "The Chinese government encourages outbound investment in overseas plants of agricultural products" (China Daily 2016/04/09).

global agri-business industries to secure China's food supply. Chinese agribusiness internationalization is not a new phenomenon; nor is it a spontaneous one (Zhang 2012; Schneider 2016). Greater international involvement by China is beginning to challenge the old geopolitics of trading and "shaping the trajectories of agrarian change" (McKay et al. 2017). In other words, "China agribusiness is subverting the power of leading TNCs by leaving those firms out of the trade picture, and, second, that building a robust domestic agribusiness sector is about enhancing the global competitiveness of Chinese firms as it is about national level development" (Schneider 2016:16). Similar statements could be made regarding energy, fisheries, or mining industries.

Official statistics do not provide answers to the questions these lines might propose, as Most of the flows arriving in Argentina are channeled through third countries –because of the increasing role played by Chinese investors in M&A markets or due to the role played by tax havens and offshore center in mediating the Chinese OFDI. Henceforth, a more detailed statistical analysis is undoubtedly faulting.

How to account for Chinese investment flows as most of them are being intermediate through tax havens and offshore locations? Independently of its legal form, as being a special purpose entity, for most Chinese OFDI the ultimate decision is taken at China. Henceforth, and in virtue of that, more work from local agencies is needed. Mainly due to the relevance Chinese investment has recently gained in Argentina; otherwise, public policies goals might be misleading.

The Red ALC-China figures bring academics and policymakers a broader, and most complete picture of China OFDI in Argentina –often disregarded at official reports. By tracking M&A operations lead by Chinese firms all around the world, the report provides more acute information of its inward FDI position.

References

Buckley, Peter J., Dylan Sutherland, Hinrich Voss, and Ahmad El-Gohari. 2015. "The economic geography of offshore incorporation in tax havens and offshore financial centres: the case of Chinese MNE s." *Journal of economic geography* 15(1), pp. 103-128.

Calzada, Julio. 2018. Who exported grains and by-products in 2017? Which were the destinations? *Bolsa de Comercio de Rosario* - BCR *Weekly Review.*

Carrizo Gorgni, Maria Mercedes. 2018. "La IED de China en Tierra del Fuego a la luz del paradigma ecléctico de John Dunning dentro del período 2005-2015". In, Eduardo Daniel Oviedo (comp.). *Inversiones de China, Corea y Japón en Argentina: Análisis general y estudio de casos.* Rosario: Editorial de la Universidad Nacional de Rosario.

Downs, Erica. 2007. "China's Quest for Overseas Oil". *Far Eastern Economic Review* - September.

Dussel Peters, Enrique. 2011. "La relación económica entre América Latina y China". In, Navarrete, Eduardo (coord.). *La huella global de China: Interacciones internacionales de una potencia mundial.* Universidad Nacional Autónoma de México - Centro de Investigaciones Interdisciplinarias en Ciencias y Humanidades, Mexico, pp. 131-174.

Economic Commission for Latin America and the Caribbean (ECLAC). 2018). *Foreign Direct Investment in Latin America and the Caribbean.* Santiago de Chile: ECLAC.

European Commission. 2017. *Proposal for a Regulation of the European Parliament and the Council establishing a framework for screening of foreign direct investments into the European Union.* Brussels: EC. (available at https://ec.europa.eu/info/law/better-regulation/initiatives/com-2017-487_en).

Fabinyi, Michael and Neng Liu. 2014. "The Chinese policy and governance context for global fisheries". *Ocean & Coastal Management* (96), pp. 198-202.

Gaudreau, Matthew. 2015. "Seeds, Grain Trade and Power Off-land: Chinese Agribusiness in Global Agrarian Change. Land grabbing, conflict, and agrarian - environmental transformations: perspectives from East and Southeast Asia". International Conference, 5-6 June, Chiang Mai University.

Graaf de, Nana. 2014. "Global Networks and the two faces of Chinese National Oil Companies". *Perspectives on Global Development and Techno*logies, Vol. 13, pp. 539-563.

Haro Sly, María José. 2017. "The Argentine portion of the soybean commodity chain". *Palgrave Communications* 3, pp. 1-11.

Hua, Lin. 2017. "Las relaciones económicas y comerciales entre China y Argentina en la era de Mauricio Macri". *Dossier: Evolución de la Política Exterior de China para América Latina.*

International Monetary Fund. 1993. *International Monetary Fund Balance of Payments Manual.* Washington D.C.: IMF.

Kolstad, Ivar and Arne Wiig. 2012. "What determines Chinese outward FDI?" *Journal of World Business* 47, pp. 26-34.

Kong, Bo. 2011. "Governing China's Energy in the Context of Global Governance". *Global Policy* Vol. 2. Special Issue, pp. 51-64.

Kuteleva, Anna. 2016. "China's food security situation: key issues and implications for Canada". *University of Alberta, China Institute. Occasional Paper Series* (3)(1), pp. 1-24.

Jiang, Julie and Jonathan Sinton. 2011. "Overseas Investments by Chinese Oil Companies: Assessing Drivers and Impact." OECD/IEA *Information Paper*, pp. 1-52.

López, Andrés and Daniela Ramos. 2009. "The Argentine Case." In, Jenkins, Rhys and Enrique Dussel Peters (edits.). *China and Latin America: Economic Relations in the Twenty-First Century.* Bonn: German Development Institute, pp. 71-157.

——————————. 2014. "Argentina y China: nuevos encadenamientos mercantiles globales con empresas chinas. Los casos de Huawei, CNOOC y Sinopec". In, Enrique Dussel Peters (coord.). *La inversión extranjera directa de China en América Latina: 10 estudios de caso.* México: Red Académica de América Latina y el Caribe sobre China (Red ALC) and Unión de Universidades de América Latina (UDAL), pp. 13-60.

Madhavan, Ravi, Thomas G. Rawski and Qingfeng Tian. 2018. "Chinese infrastructure projects in advanced industries". In, Dussel Peters, Enrique, Ariel C. Armony and Shoujun Cui (editors). *Building Development for a New Era: China's infrastructure projects in Latin America and the Caribbean.* Mexico: Asian Studies Center, Center for International Studies, University of Pittsburgh, and Red Académica de América Latina y el Caribe sobre China, pp. 102-121.

Mallory, Tabitha Grace. 2013. "China's distant water fishing industry: Evolving policies and implications". *Marine Policy* 38, pp. 99-108.

Myers, Margaret and Guo Jie. 2015. "China's Agricultural Investment in Latin America: A Critical Assessment". *Inter-American Dialogue-China and Latin America Report,* pp. 1-24.

McKay, Ben, Alberto Alonso – Fradejas, Zoe W. Brent, Sergio Sauer, and Yy Xu. 2017. "China and Latin America: towards a new consensus of resource control?" *Third World Thematics: A TWQ Journal* 1(5), pp. 592-611.

Naughton, Barry. 2007. *The Chinese Economy: transitions and growth.* Cambridge Mass: MIT Press.

OECD. 2008. OECD *Benchmark Definition of Foreign Direct Investment.* Fourth Edition. Paris: OECD.

Ortiz Velásquez, Samuel. 2016. *Monitor de la OFDI de Chine en América Latina y el Caribe: Aspectos Metodológicos.* México: Red ALC-China.

Oviedo, Eduardo Daniel. 2016. "Déficit comercial, desequilibrio financiero e inicio de la dependencia argentina del capital chino". En, Moneta, Carlos y Cesarín, Sergio (edits.). *La tentación pragmática - China-Argentina / América Latina: Lo actual, lo próximo y lo distante.* Buenos Aires: Universidad Nacional de Tres de Febrero, pp. 273-298.

Qiu, Dongmei. 2014. "Collecting Unpaid Tax Offshore: Caribbean Tax Havens and Foreign Direct Investment in China". *Bulletin for International Taxation* 12, pp. 648-659.

Ray, Rebecca, Kevin Gallagher, Andrés López and Cynthia Sanborn. 2017. *China and Sustainable Development in Latin America: the Social and Environmental Dimension.* London: Anthem Press.

Schneider, Mindi. 2016. "Dragon Head Enterprises and the State of Agribusiness in China". *Journal of Agrarian Change*, Vol. 17(1), pp, 3-21.

Sevares, Julio. 2016. "Préstamos e inversiones de China en América Latina." In, Moneta, Carlos y Cesarin, Sergio (edits.). *La tentación pragmática - China-Argentina / América Latina: Lo actual, lo próximo y lo distante.* Buenos Aires: Universidad Nacional de Tres de Febrero, pp. 247-269.

Schujovitzky, Lara. 2018. "Capitales Chinos en Argentina. naturaleza y clasificación en base a casos de estudios". In, Eduardo Daniel Oviedo (comp.). *Inversiones de China, Corea y Japón en Argentina: Análisis general y estudio de casos.* Rosario: Editorial de la Universidad Nacional de Rosario, pp. 36-52.

Sutherland, Dylan. 2009. "China's national team business groups in strategic-asset seeking OFDI: Are they important?" *Chinese Management Studies* 3 (1), pp. 11-24.

———————, Ahmad El-Gohari, Peter Buckley and Hinrich Voss. 2010. "The role of Caribbean Tax Havens and Offshore Financial Centres in Chinese Outward Foreign Direct Investment". 2nd Copenhagen Conference on 'Emerging Multinationals': Outward Investment from Emerging and Developing Economies, Copenhagen Business School.

Simonet, Silvia. 2012. "Las empresas chinas en Argentina". In, Moneta, Carlos y Sergio Cesarin (edits.). *Tejiendo Redes - Estrategias de las empresas transnacionales asiáticas en América Latina.* Buenos Aires: Universidad Nacional de Tres de Febrero, pp. 133-162.

Stanley, Leonardo E. 2018. "Argentina´s Infrastructure Gap and Financial Needs". In, Enrique Dussel Peters, Ariel C. Armony and Shoujun Cui (edits.). *Building Development for a New Era: China's infrastructure projects in Latin America and the Caribbean.* Mexico: Asian Studies Center, Center for International Studies, University of Pittsburgh, and Red Académica de América Latina y el Caribe sobre China, pp. 77-101.

Uriburu Quintana, Juan. 2018. "El déficit argentino en infraestructura y el rol de China: grandes proyectos en revisión". In, Eduardo Daniel Oviedo (comp.). *Inversiones de China, Corea y Japón en Argentina: Análisis general y estudio de casos*. Rosario: Editorial de la Universidad Nacional de Rosario, pp. 104-117.

Veeck, Gregory. 2013. "China's food security: past successes and future challenges". *Eurasian Geography and Economics* 54(1), pp. 42-56.

Vlcek, William. 2010. "Byways and Highways of Direct Investment: China and the Offshore World". *Journal of Current Chinese Affairs* 39(4), pp. 111-142.

Wilkinson, John, Valdemar Jao Wesz (Jr.), and Anna Rosa Maria Lopane.2015. "Brazil, the Southern Cone, and China: The Agribusiness Connection". *BRICS Initiative for Critical Agrarian Studies - BRICAS, Working Paper* 16.

Zhang, Hangzhou. 2012. "China's Evolving Fishing Industry: Implications for Regional and Global Maritime Security". *RSIS Working Paper Series* 246

Zhao, Zhongxiu. 2012. "Sino-Argentine Trade Relations: From 2000 to 2010". In, Moneta, Carlos and Sergio Cesarin (edits.). *Tejiendo Redes - Estrategias de las empresas transnacionales asiáticas en América Latina*. Buenos Aires: Universidad Nacional de Tres de Febrero, pp. 103-121.

Zhou, Jiayi. 2016. *China and (world) food security*. Stockholm: Stockholm International Peace Research Institute.

Zweig, David and Bi Jianhai. 2005. "China's Global Hunt for Energy". *Foreign Affairs* 84(5), pp. 25-38.

Other sources

AACPPP. 2017. *El avance de los capitanes chinos en la pesca argentina*. Buenos Aires: Asociación Argentina de Capitanes, Pilotos y Patrones de Pesca.

BCRA. 2009. *The People's Bank of China and the Central Bank of Argentina Established a Currency Swap Arrangement*. Buenos Aires: Banco Central de la República Argentina, Comunicado 49465.

——. 2016. Las Inversiones Directas de Empresas Residentes. Buenos Aires: Banco Central de la República Argentina.

BCRA - online. Information on Direct Investment in Local Companies, Foreign Trade and Exchange Statistics Management - Central Bank of Argentina (http://www.bcra.gob.ar/PublicacionesEstadisticas/Estadisticas_inversiones_directas.asp)

————————. 2018b. "Macri Group under investigation for wind farm purchases" Thursday, March 1st.

China Dialogue Ocean. 2018. Argentina, the next battleground for illegal fishing - Pressure mounts on countries to reform fishing practices in the South Atlantic (https://chinadialogueocean.net/1366-argentinas-battleground-against-illegal-fishing-2/)

Clarín. 2017. "Barrick vendió en US$ 960 millones la mitad de su mina en San Juan" (6/04/2017).

China Daily. 2016. "Foresun buys Latin beef-processing units".

—————. 2017. "Chinese company buys half of Argentine mine from Barrick" (2017/04/07).

ECC. 2014. "Atanor presento un plan de US100 millones de inversion en cinco años". *El Cronista Comercial.* Miércoles 5 de November.

ECC. 2017. "Cinco Frigoríficos concentran el 60% de las exportaciones de carne bovina argentina". *El Cronista Comercial.* Lunes 11 de Setiembre.

ECC. 2018. "Oportunidad para invertir: Gobierno dice que activos locales están baratos". *El Cronista Comercial.* Lunes 1 de octubre.

El Inversor Energético & Minero. 2017. "Barrick le vendió un 50% de Veladero a una firma china". June 2nd.

———————————.2017b. "Empresas chinas buscan proyectos mineros en la Argentina" (21/09/2017).

———————————. 2017c. "Impulsan un acuerdo bilateral para el sector minero que facilite la llegada de inversiones chinas " (25/09/2017).

———————————. 2018. "SQM se retira de Cauchari-Olaroz: conforman unión entre Lithium Americas y Ganfeng Lithium".

Economist. 2016. "The tax haven at the end of the world". July 16th.

Financial Post. 2017. "China's appetite for lithium on display in Canadian takeover " December 19, 2017.

FT. 2016a. "China's COFCO buys remainder of grain trader Nidera". *Financial Times*, August 23.

FT. 2016b. "Sinopec could take $2.5bn Argentinian oilfield hit". *Financial Times*, September 2,

—-. 2017. A bigger catch: China's fishing fleet hunts new ocean targets. *Financial Times.*

—-.2018. "China seeks bigger catch from far-sea fishing fleet". February 18th, *Financial Times.*

-—.2018b. "China's Ganfeng Lithium buys a stake in Argentina lithium project". August 14th, *Financial Times.*

Global Meat News. 2015. "Argentina beef tops China's export courses, but for how long?" By Alex Smith and Charles Newbery, August 12th.

iProfesional (2018). "Los autos chinos se imponen en Argentina: ya hay 11 marcas activas que incluso venden más que las premium" (23/04/2018).

International Lithium Corporation. 2017. "International Lithium Reaches Settlement Agreement With Ganfeng Lithium On Mariana JV, Argentina. Kirill Kip". Thursday 28, December.

MercoPress. 2018. "Argentina's beef exports expected to double this year boosted by China's purchases". August 29th.

Ministerio de Agro-industria. 2017. "Exportaciones Pesqueras: Comportamiento de los Principales Mercados". Dirección Nación de Planificación Pesquera y Dirección de Economía Pesquera. Subsecretaría de Pesca y Acuicultura. Ministerio de Agro-Industria, Presidencia de la Nación.

Nuevos Papeles. 2017. "Guelar: Las inversiones chinas en Argentina "no son una promesa sino proyectos en marcha". *Política*, May 16th, 2017.

Orientar - La Revista de Comercio Exterior para China, una publicación de la Cámara de Comercio Argentina - China (varias ediciones)

PESCARE.COM.AR. 2016. "Ardapez adquiere al menos seis buques fresqueros", March 3rd.

Revista de Petroquímica. 2012. "La petrolera china Sinopec llegó a Neuquén por el auge de los no convencionales". March 27th.

————————. 2018. "Sinopec pondrá en funcionamiento cuatro nuevos pozos en Santa Cruz".

Reuters. 2016. "GE venderá negocio de electrodomésticos a Haier de China por 5.400 mln dlr". January, 15th.

————-. 2017. "China's COFCO sells Latam seeds business to Syngenta". November 6th.

———. 2018. "Chilena SQM vende su parte en proyecto conjunto de litio en Argentina a china Ganfeng Lithium". August 13th

—————. 2018b. "Argentina to nearly double currency swap with China". November 8th.

Sullivan, Bartholomew D. 2017. "Mega-mergers in agribusiness raise concerns about food costs, biodiversity". USA *Today*, August 29.

CHINESE OFDI IN URUGUAY

CONDITIONS, CHALLENGES, AND POLICY PROPOSALS

Gustavo Bittencourt

Introduction

Uruguay's economic performance during the 20th century showed high volatility and strong cyclical fluctuations. The result was very low average growth: GDP *per capita* barely grew more than 1% per year. The military dictatorship that began in 1973 was the last step in almost half a century of introverted growth and the beginning of a gradual opening that continues to this day. After the return to democracy in 1985, and especially after 1990, Uruguayan governments accelerated the economic opening both unilaterally and with the signing of the Mercosur integration treaty. However, the opening still resulted in very poor economic performance in the long run: from 1960-2016 the average GDP growth was 2.2% (*per capita* 1.7%), a slight improvement over the whole of the 20th century but far from convergence with the developed world and nowhere near the momentum that many Asian countries experienced.

Growth in the 21st century shows an upward tendency. From 2000-2017 GDP grew 3.5% annually (3.3% *per capita*), reaching 5.6% annually between 2004 and 2013. This historical change was produced by two fundamental causes: the increase in exports and the jump in the investment rate, led by foreign direct investment (FDI). The emergence of the People's Republic of China (PRC) as a driver of Uruguayan production explains both increases in the export value and the investment rate, at least as a crucial causal factor.

Bilateral trade between Uruguay and China has been significant in the last decade and remains so today. China ranked first in Uruguayan export destinations in 2017, with sales that reached US$ 2.5 billion, including free trade zones. China is also the primary origin of Uruguayan imports, valued at an average of US$ 1.7 billion over the last three years (Uruguay XXI 2018a).

Although Uruguay has received a great deal of foreign investment since 2006, FDI of Chinese origin is very scarce. The Uruguayan export sector captured most of the investments that arrived in that period and China played a very important role in determining the flows of FDI as the main source of the increased external demand for the country.

Dr. Tabaré Vázquez, the President of Uruguay, made an official visit to the PRC in October 2016, during which the Strategic Association Agreement (SAA) was signed between the countries. Negotiations then began for the signing of a Free Trade Agreement (FTA), which raises an important question regarding compatibility within the framework of Mercosur. Will an FTA improve the very modest performance of Chinese OFDI in Uruguay? The chapter of conclusions briefly discusses this subject.

Relationship with Uruguay (2000-2017)

Although trade with China exploded after the year 2000, Uruguay has a long history of commercial relationship with the Asian giant. It has been one of the main destinations of Uruguayan wool exports for several decades. Partly because of these economic ties the Uruguayan government has recognized the People's Republic of China since Uruguay's return to the democracy in 1985 unlike most Latin American countries whose commercial relationship with China began after the year 2000. As seen in Figure 1, between 1985 and 1995 Chinese purchases accounted for 5-10% of Uruguayan foreign sales. After 2005, commercial exchange with China accelerated with China quickly becoming Uruguay's main customer. Exports to China surpassed a quarter of total exports after 2014.

Torres Ledezma (2017) has noted the structural pattern of trade between Uruguay and China according to its technological and factorial intensity. His work shows that Uruguayan exports to China during 2015 were composed by 76% of primary products, 21% of products based on natural resources and 3% of low technology manufactures. The sum of exports of "medium and high technology" manufactures does not even represent 1% of exports flows to China. In contrast, Uruguayan imports from China were concentrated in three groups: low, medium, and high technology manufactures, representing 29%, 42%, and 20% of the total, respectively.

Uruguay XXI 2018a reported that Uruguayan exports of goods totaled 9.1 US$ billions in 2017, including free zones. These implied an increase of 9.2% compared to 2016, the largest growth in Uruguayan exports since 2011. Soybeans, wood, pulp and meat

Figure 1. Uruguay: Chinese Participation in Total Exports, 1984-2016

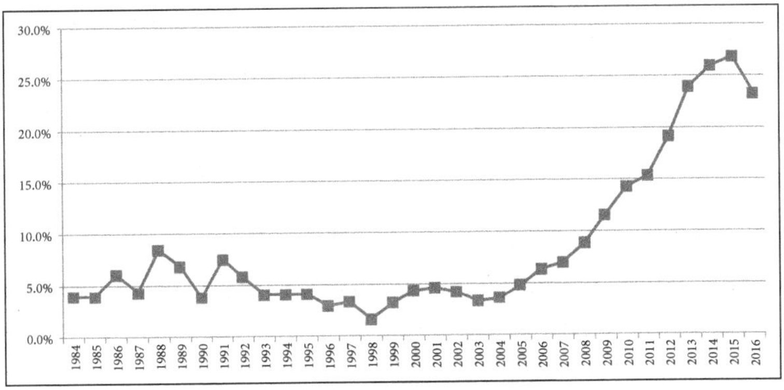

Source: author's elaboration based on COMTRADE.[1]

1 It is difficult to estimate the exact amount of exports to China from Uruguayan Free Trade Zones, and these zones channel soybeans and pulp exports. For this reason I prefer using imports from Uruguay reported by China. The series show figures slightly augmented by Insurance and Freights (CIF vs FOB) but the tendency is the same. While imports reported by China were 27% of Uruguayan exports in 2015 as seen in Figure 1, exports to this destination estimated by Uruguay XXI reached 28% of the total in 2017.

had the greatest positive impact on the total export's growth of 2017. China was the main partner in 2017, with amounts of 2.5 US$ billions, a participation of 28% of Uruguayan exports of goods.

Soybean was the main product exported to China, with a 39% share in the total amount of sales to the Asian giant in 2017. Beef and wood pulp ranked second and third, with a share of 24% and 22% respectively. China was also the main destination for wood exports with a 40% share of Uruguayan external sales. The recovery of exports to China in 2017, up 38% compared to 2016, signaled a recovery after the stagnation 2014-2016, which was driven largely by a reduction in exports to China. China buys a significant share of the soybean and cellulose exports from Uruguay. China also buys an important quantity of meat, although meat exports are more diversified with respect to other markets (Uruguay XXI, 2018 a).

However, recent performance is cause for some concern. Bartesaghi (2018) notes that exports to China fell significantly in the first half of 2018 (down 9%) due to poor soybean sales which declined an extraordinary 62% overall. Uruguay recorded a positive trade balance in goods trade with China in the period, even without exports from free zones. This occurred despite the fact that imports increased (up 2%), especially imports under the temporary admission regime (up 50%), that is, those destined for inputs for the country's exports.

In addition, some signs indicate that established export trade flows have good opportunities to grow. See the following examples from Uruguay XXI (2018):

- At the end of 2017, the XI China LAC 2017 Business Summit was held in Punta del Este, with 2,400 foreign and national businesspeople, trade organizations, authorities and media from China, Latin America and the Caribbean.
- In December 2017, the National Meat Institute (INAC) of Uruguay and the China Certification & Inspection Group (CCIC) signed a commercial traceability agreement. The objective of the agreement is to allow the consumer in China to follow the production processes in Uruguay by reading

a QR code. The goal is to generate greater loyalty among Chinese consumers.
- In October 2016, both countries' delegations signed the phytosanitary requirements protocol for soybeans exported from Uruguay to China. The protocol, already in effect for the 2016/2017 harvest, formally established certain sanitary standards, which along with other links between agricultural R&D institutes in both countries, will allow the export of quality soybeans for human consumption and guarantee improvements in prices.

Regarding financing and infrastructure activities, Chinese banks do not participate in commercial financing on a significant level in Uruguay. There is limited participation by Chinese companies in transport and communications infrastructure (see Table 2). A consortium recently created by the Chinese companies CMEC and SDHS submitted an offer for the new Central Railroad but the Government discarded the proposal for having been incomplete.[2] A few large Chinese companies do have a presence: COFCO in trading companies and the port; ZTE in construction/engineering; and Huawei with commercial representation. These companies have only installed commercial representatives or consultant services, not significant productive investments. Their activities do not change the level of Chinese OFDI.

The establishment of diplomatic relations between the People's Republic of China and the Republic of Uruguay occurred in February 1988, during the government of Dr. Sanguinetti, shortly after the restoration of democracy in Uruguay in 1984. Since then, diplomatic relations have intensified with visits to Uruguay by several Chinese presidents: Mr. Yang Shangkun in 1990, Mr. Hu Jintao in 1994 (before his presidency), Mr. Jiang Zemin in 2001, and another 2001 visit by the former Prime Minister Mr. Zhu Rongji and the President of the National People's Congress of China, Mr. Li Peng.

2 https://www.elpais.com.uy/informacion/politica/gobierno-desestima-empresa-china-tren-upm.html

Since the restructuring of relations in 1988, all Uruguayan presidents and their respective foreign ministers, along with numerous official and private delegations, have visited the PRC. China and Uruguay signed a Strategic Association Agreement (SAA) during President Tabaré Vázquez's last visit to China in 2016.

Chinese Foreign Minister Wang Yi visited Uruguay in January 2018 to commemorate the deepening of bilateral relations in the last 30 years. Mr. Wang and the Uruguayan Foreign Minister Nin Novoa expressed the desire to move towards an integral strategic partnership, which implies a step beyond the SAA. Chinese President Xi Jinping sent a letter to Uruguayan President Tabaré Vázquez at the time: "As intimate friends and great partners, our bilateral ties have made rapid progress as a result of the formalization of relations 30 years ago, and, above all, since October 2016, when the strategic partnership was established." Xi Jinping also expressed his willingness to visit Uruguay in the same letter.[3]

According to local newspapers, Mr. Nin Novoa noted that the Foreign Ministry will push for agreement with the rest of its regional integration bloc regarding the FTA with China.[4] The solidification of a commercial agreement with China would also entail the formation of a free market with clear rules and in the company of the other Mercosur countries. "If the Uruguay Free Trade Agreement with China means the rupture of Mercosur... we will not issue its death certificate," said Nin Novoa. This position slowed internal debate within Uruguay over the signing of the FTA, which had given rise to divisions with the governing party (the Frente Amplio).

3 https://www.elobservador.com.uy/la-carta-que-el-presidente-chino-envio-tabare-vazquez-y-su-deseo-visitar-uruguay-n1168624

4 https://negocios.elpais.com.uy/noticias/tlc-china-nin-mantiene-apuesta-unir-mercosur.html o https://www.elpais.com.uy/informacion/politica/nin-novoa-mercosur-minutos-uruguay.html

Impact of Chinese OFDI in Uruguay (2000-2017)

Official FDI figures published by the Banco Central de Uruguay (BCU) do not identify flows or stocks of OFDI received from China. Through the list of companies with FDI available from Uruguay XXI, supplemented with press information and informal consultations with companies, we arrive at an approximation of the companies present in Uruguay that have Chinese OFDI (Table 1)[5]. These companies carry out productive activities, managing

Table 1. Companies with Chinese OFDI in Uruguay 2018
(US$ millions)

International Group	Identification Uruguay	ISIC	Entry year	COMAP 2006-2016	Place	OFDI prox.	Employment Prox. (workers)
HeZhong Xian Group	CLADEMAR SA /Frig. Florida	10112 Meat processing plants	2018	6.1	Florida	3.0	100
Sundiro Holding	LORSINAL SA	10112 Meat processing plants	2016	4.6	Montevideo	36.0	350
Sundiro Holding	RONDATEL S.A. /Frig. Rosario	10112 Meat processing plants	2015	0.6	Colonia	40.0	350
Big Plastic Corporation	Big Plastic Corporation S.A.	22209 Other plastic products	2012	10.8	Canelones	30.0	200
ChongQing Lifan	Besiney S.A	29100 Automotive manufacturing	2012	4.1	San José	12.0	125
ChongQing Lifan	ANIKTO S.A	29300 Auto parts	2012	1.8	San José	10.0	(included in Besiney)
Chery Automobile	CHERY SOCMA S.A.	29100 Automotive manufacturing (now Importers and wholesale automotive)	2007	12.1	Montevideo	12	

Source: author's elaboration with Uruguay XXI Firms Database

5 The Monitor of Chinese OFDI in Latin America and the Caribbean computes data from companies reported by private analysts: "(FDI Markets, Thomson-Reuters, Bloomberg, Capital IQ, China Global Investment Tracker (CGIT) and investment announcements reported by the trade press" (Dussel Peters 2018). OFDI values are not the financial flows recorded in the respective balance of payments statistics of the host economies.

plants that produce goods or services, not just commercial offices. I especially thank Uruguay XXI, the national agency in charge of investment and export promotion, for providing me this information.

The information presented in Table 1 shows that the Chinese presence in Uruguay through OFDI is very small and concentrated in four Chinese economic groups. Two of them invested in beef exporters, another in plastics, and the last one in the automotive sector. The investments barely exceed US$ 100 million but do create a significant number of jobs, employing about 1200 workers.

For this study, I identified companies with Chinese OFDI in Uruguay in three sectors of activity: a) meat processing; b) plastics; c) the automotive industry.

a) In the case of meat processing, the purchase of pre-existing plants was very recent, and accompanied growing beef exports to China. The Sondiro Holding group, an international food retailer, controls the two most consolidated businesses. These are two plants acquired in 2015 and 2016: 100% of the Frigorífico Rosario (Rondatel SA) in the department of Colonia and 50% of Lorsinal SA in Montevideo, a meat processing plant acquired from the company Ottonello (a well-known maker of pork sausages for the Uruguayan domestic market) with a local investment group. International press mentions a business cost of about US$ 80 million in the purchase of both plants, which employ around 700 people. The group owns three more meat plants in Argentina and one in Australia.[6] The group does not appear to have invested much in improvements, according to the low value of investment projects presented for tax exemptions in the Investment Law (the amount that appears in the COMAP

6 https://rurales.elpais.com.uy/empresas/sundiro-holding-apunta-a-comprar-mas-frigorificos

2006-2016[7] column of Table 1). The third operation was the Clademar SA plant, purchased in 2018 by the Hezhong Xian Group in the department of Florida. The group bought 51% of the shares of the company (previously owned by a Venezuelan group, named Zambrano) and although the plant was ready to resume activity, by mid-2018 it was still closed.

b) Chinese investment in the recycling of plastic materials seems to be the most significant industrial investment, via a plant installed with Chinese capital in 2012 in the department of Canelones, the metropolitan area of the capital Montevideo. Although the press mentions investments for an amount of US$ 30 million,[8] the value presented for approval by COMAP was US$ 10.8 million, so the amount of investment was likely slightly lower than what was declared publicly. Nonetheless, an important plant in this sector is functioning under Chinese ownership and directions.

c) The third sector with important investments is automotive manufacturing, in which the Lifan group is the only firm actually engaged in production. Chery retired from production several years ago and now only maintains its distribution center in Uruguay. This group made some investments before it pulled production, in a plant that today does not assembly for their brand. As we explained in Bittencourt and Reig (2014), Chery upgraded an older plant they were renting, so it was a particular kind of OFDI –they did not install a productive plant or buy a preexisting installation; rather they amplified the productive capacities of a rented plant. The ChongQing Lifan Group was partner of the

7 COMAP (Comisión de Aplicación) is the Investment Law Enforcement Commission, a multi-ministerial body that studies and approves tax exemptions for investment projects. It is important to take into account that since these exonerations can reach up to 60% of the amount invested, and are relatively easy to access, they account for practically the total gross capital formation of the country. In other words, if we do not find an investment amount for this regime, it is very rare that this capital increase has been made, with the exception of the investments made in Free Trade Zones, for which this regime does not apply.

8 http://www.comunacanaria.gub.uy/noticias/empresa-china-invertira-30-millones-de-dolares-en-la-fabricacion-de-fibras-artificiales-en-pando

local group Besiney SA since 2010, providing licenses and auto parts, without making direct investment. The local authorities of the company did not make the investments required to export these automobiles from Uruguay to Brazil. Then, the Lifan Group took control of Besiney SA in 2012 and decided to install an engine manufacturing plant in 2014, under the company name Anikto SA. The difficulties of access to Argentina and then Brazil caused the plant to alternate between closures and openings in the last three years. This plant today employs 125 workers, down from more than 300 workers in 2013, with very little stability. Since 2016, Lifan's managers in Uruguay have discussed the production of electric vehicles as a viable future that would take advantage of national policies, associated with Uruguay's energy transformation in the last decade, to promote this type of vehicles, as well as benefits granted by the departmental government of Montevideo for the public transport fleet based on electricity. This sector, which relies upon on intensive importation, does not seem to lead to successful industrial development, as it does not result in an increase in purchases from local suppliers, which in turn would stimulate the greater industrial density needed for a dynamic sector in the medium term (Bittencourt and Reig 2014).

There are also some companies, with few physical capital investments, managing logistical facilities of a certain magnitude or carrying out commercial activities of significance for the country. Although many of these firms are in the database of Uruguay XXI, these kind of investments fall outside OFDI's definition and therefore, they are reviewed separately from the information presented in Table 2. In the list of companies with Chinese participation collected by Uruguay XXI, the following cases appear:

These cases are not example of OFDI for different reasons. The Chinese automaker GEELY produces in alliance with a local group, in a plant owned by that group, so Geely did not make significant investments in the production line. The Chinese COFCO, related

Table 2. Companies with Chinese Participation Not Qualified as OFDI, in Uruguay 2018

International Group	Business Name in Uruguay	International Standard Industrial Clasification (ISIC)	Entry year	COMAP 2006-2016 (US$ millions)
GEELY International	FEWIN SA	Manufacture of motor vehicles		3.1
China National Chemical Corporation (ChemChina)	Syngenta Agro Uruguay SA	Wholesale agrochemicals	2017	1
COFCO International	NIDERA Uruguaya sa	Wholesale trade grains and oilseeds	2014	6.5
COFCO International	Terminales Graneleras Uruguayas SA	Secondary services to water transport	2014	0.4
China Ocean Shipping Company (COSCO)	COSCO URUGUAY S A	Shipping agents	1996	0
HUAWEI	HUAWEI Technologies (Uruguay) S.A	Wholesale trade computers and software	2005	0
ZTE Corporation	ZTE Corporation Ssucursal Uruguay	Construction of service infrastructure	2008	0
AXION (50% propiedad de BCNOOC LTD.)	ESSO Standard Oil co Uruguay SA	Wholesale fuel trade	2012	0

Source: Author's elaboration with Uruguay XXI Firms Database.

to port activity and logistics for the export of cereals, only deals with part of the logistics of soybean exports to China. Cofco acquired 51% of the share capital of Nidera in the world in 2014, and completed the acquisition in 2017. NIDERA is a traditional grain trading company, with presence in Uruguayan foreign trade since 1944, which carried out export operations close to 50 million dollars in 2016. COSCO is another Chinese company involved in soybean exports that also offers transport services related to Uruguayan imports from China. Huawei and ZTE are also important providers for the companies that operate in the country´s mobile telephone market, in which the public firm ANTEL is the main operator, competing with América Móvil (a Mexican company) and Telefónica (Spanish). ANTEL also buys some equipment from Huawei and ZTE for the operation of its monopoly of fixed lines, which includes fiber optic networks for data. Finally, the Chinese company BCNOOC, through the partial ownership of AXION, operates a network of service stations in the retail market of fuel distribution.

Conclusions and Policy Suggestions

Chinese OFDI in Uruguay is of minor importance for national economic activity. There is an asymmetry between China's role as Uruguay's most significant buyer and its limited investment in the country. Uruguayan authorities claim to aspire to a greater presence of Chinese firms in the country. However, the government's intention to attract Chinese OFDI is not borne out in practice. And also, maybe the government does not want any kind of Chinese OFDI.

Probably, Chinese investment in meat processing plants will no longer be encouraged, for example. The Uruguayan state made important investments in public goods for this sector, like the traceability of livestock), so this production chain is strong and capable of exporting to high-paying diversified markets. The country does not sell more beef because of supply limitations. Greater Chinese presence in the industrial phase of the production chain may channel a more than desirable proportion of meat exports to its markets, compromising export markets diversification.

Chinese investments in manufacturing or infrastructure, both of which are limited or nonexistent, would be more welcome. The Uruguayan government has managed to sign a strategic association agreement with China and a Free Trade Agreement (FTA) like the agreements that Chile, Peru, and Costa Rica have already signed with China is frequently discussed in government and business circles.

China looks for a greater depth of linkage with LAC as a whole by means of a Strategic Cooperative Association with the Community of Latin American and Caribbean States (CELAC) but structural differences and development policies make it difficult for CELAC to reach deep agreements (Bittencourt 2016). For its part, in its bilateral relationship with the LAC countries, China has selected priority countries with which it has reached two steps of deepening: Strategic Association Agreements (SAA) and Integral Strategic Association (ISA). These agreements imply the willingness to more deeply economic and political cooperation (according to the tables presented by Malena et al. 2015:13-16). Almost all the prioritized countries have moved towards the status of ISA (Argentina, Brazil, Mexico, Peru and Venezuela), with the exception of Chile and Uruguay, which remain in SAA status.

In contrast, Peru and Brazil have received considerable Chinese OFDI. Therefore, ISA status appears as a necessary but not sufficient condition for the reception of OFDI China with certain significance (Bittencourt 2017). Only countries with ISA status received significant Chinese OFDI amounts, but some countries within the same level did not.

Why have other LAC countries with ISA status not received Chinese OFDI? Venezuela received credits in exchange for oil but presents an adverse environment for FDI (from any origin) including Chinese investors. Mexico maintains its link preferentially with the USA apart from its lack of commercial complementarity with China due to its manufacturing specialization (unlike South America). Argentina was the last to sign an ISA (2014) shortly before a change in government that resulted in Argentina shifting back towards a reintegration into the Washington financial circuit.

Could a FTA lead to an increase in Chinese investments in Uruguay? An ISA does not exclude the possibility of an FTA, as the case of Peru shows, but it does not seem the general case. In fact, China did not sign ISAs with the other countries with which it has FTAs in LAC, which are Chile and Costa Rica. In the Uruguayan case, the deepening of the relationship with China through something like an ISA is a necessary condition for a significant increase in OFDI China. If an FTA leads in that direction, it would be welcome. However, signing FTAs does not seem to have been a relevant factor for the productive integration with China through OFDI seen in Chile and Costa Rica.

Uruguay's membership in Mercosur also complicates the situation regarding a bilateral FTA with China. Argentina and Brazil are countries in which the industrial manufacturing sector still matters, so they would not choose to sign an FTA with China, which ensures that such a possibility does not exist for Mercosur (Bittencourt 2017). If any of the smaller partners in MERCOSUR sign an FTA with China, the major partners will point out this action as a potential violation of the customs union obligations of this treaty. Uruguay would face consequences in terms of regional free trade and market access in neighboring countries if it were to enter into such an agreement with China. An FTA with China would have negative consequences especially upon Uruguayan exports to its neighbors.

Increasing cooperation in scientific and technological matters may be one means of increasing Chinese OFDI. Uruguay already took some important steps in this direction. The National Institute of Agricultural Research of Uruguay (INIA) and the Chinese Agriculture Academy of Science (CAAS) are developing a project that includes R&D and the exchange of technical information and skills in soybeans for high quality human consumption (Gutierrez 2018). These activities may be followed or supplemented by other technological projects looking to improve the quality of agricultural production in such a way that may appeal to the palate of Chinese consumers. It could be an interesting way to both diversify exports with differentiated products and to attract investors to new sectors

An Integral Strategic Association may be promoted through other channels. The Uruguayan government could encourage Chinese participation in infrastructure, attract Chinese banks to finance commercial and investment activities, and promote foreign trade operations in Renminbi. The promotion of cultural exchanges between universities can also be an important tool.

Any of these alternatives may be as relevant as the signing of an FTA if they have the support of the Uruguayan state. From a commercial point of view, the advantages of an FTA are negligible, particularly in comparison with the costs that it would bring with partners in the Mercosur agreement (Torres Ledezma 2017).

It is very unlikely that Brazil would accept an FTA between Mercosur and China. If the Mercosur partners allowed a stand-alone Uruguay-China FTA and it led to an ISA, the FTA would be welcome (Bittencourt 2017). Fortunately, the Uruguayan government seems to have recently assumed a line of thought similar to this, according to Foreign Affairs Minister Nin Novoa claims.

References

Bartesaghi, Ignacio. 2018. "Las relaciones comerciales entre Uruguay y China". Informe semestral enero-junio 2018. Año 7. Nº 13. Departamento Negocios Internacionales e Integración, Universidad Católica del Uruguay.

Bittencourt, Gustavo and Reig, Nicolás. 2014. "China-Uruguay: el caso de la automotrices Chery y Lifan". In, Dussel Peters, Enrique (coord.). *La Inversión Extranjera Directa de China en América Latina: 10 estudios de caso*. México: Red Académica de América Latina y el Caribe sobre China (Red ALC-China), UDUAL y UNAM/Cechimex, pp. 227-271.

Bittencourt, Gustavo. 2016. "Estrategia de América Latina hacia la IED buscando Complementación Productiva con China". In, Bartesaghi, Ignacio (coord.). *Explorando espacios para la integración productiva entre América Latina y Asia Pacífico. Montevideo:* Observatorio América Latina-Asia Pacífico ALADI-CAF-CEPAL, pp. 63-94

Bittencourt, Gustavo. 2017. "Inversiones chinas y la firma de un TLC China-Uruguay." *Escenario* 4 (ORALC. FCS-UDELAR).

Bittencourt, Gustavo. 2018. "Notas sobre efectos de la desaceleración china en el crecimiento de la economía uruguaya". In, Arostica, Pamela and Cesarín, Sergio (eds.). *La Nueva Fase de China: Implicaciones para América Latina*. Santiago de Chile: REDCAEM and Editorial Universitaria de la Universidad de Chile. To be published.

Dussel Peters, Enrique. 2019. *Monitor of Chinese* OFDI *in Latin America and the Caribbean 2018*. Mexico: Academic Network of Latin America and the Caribbean/Red ALC-China.

Gutiérrez, N. 2018. "Cooperación Científica y Tecnológica entre Uruguay y China". Presentación en *Jornadas Académicas: 30 años de relaciones Uruguay-China*. FCS-UDELAR, Montevideo, April.

Malena, Jorge, Ramón-Berjano, Carola and Velloso, Miguel. 2015. "El Relacionamiento de China con América Latina y Argentina. Significado de la Alianza Estratégica Integral y de los Acuerdos Bilaterales". *CARI/Consejo Argentino para las Relaciones Internacionales. Documentos de Trabajo* 96, pp. 1-121.

Torres Ledezma, Sebastián. 2017. "Impactos sectoriales en Uruguay de la firma de un tratado de libre comercio entre el Mercosur y China". *Revista Estado & Comunes*, pp. 199-215.

Uruguay XXI. 2018. *Ficha País. China*. Montevideo: Uruguay XXI/ Promoción de inversiones y exportaciones.

Uruguay XXI. 2018a. *Informe Anual de Comercio Exterior 2017*. Montevideo: Uruguay XXI/Promoción de inversiones y exportaciones.

CHINESE OFDI IN BRAZIL

TRENDS AND IMPACTS, 2000-2017

Celio Hiratuka

Introduction

Economic relations between Brazil and China have shown remarkable dynamism since the beginning of the 2000s. International trade was the main vector of economic relations between the two countries, with a total trade flow that jumped from US$ 2.3 billion in 2000 to US$ 76 billion in 2017. However, since 2011, trade relations have shown less vitality and greater fluctuation, including a strong contraction in 2015 and 2016.

At the same time that trade flows slowed, Chinese outbound foreign direct investments (OFDI) in Brazil began to gain momentum. Specially as of 2010 when a change in relation to previous years became evident with respect to the more visible presence of Chinese companies investing in Brazil. This chapter seeks to analyze the growing presence of Chinese OFDI in the Brazilian economy while highlighting its main characteristics and impacts.

Although Chinese companies still have a much smaller role than companies from traditional investor countries in Brazil such as the United States and Western European countries, the speed of growth and future prospects suggest that Chinese OFDI will continue to grow and increase in importance. After an overview of the relationship, the following section briefly reviews the literature on economic relations between Brazil and China, especially the prominence of trade relations. The third section analyzes Chinese OFDI in greater depth with an emphasis on the profile of investments and their impacts on the Brazilian economy, based on information on foreign direct investments flows and stocks in Brazil from the Brazilian Central Bank (BCB) and the Monitor of Chinese OFDI in Latin America and the Caribbean database compiled by Red ALC-China. The last section presents the main conclusions and some economic policy proposals.

The Chinese Economic Relationship with Brazil (2000-2017)

Brazil established diplomatic relations with China in 1974, but it was only in the first decade of the twenty-first century that Brazilian relations with China began to gain more relevance. At first, economic relations between Brazil and China were highly concentrated in trade flows. From an average level of about US$ 1 billion in exports and imports between 1995 and 2000, bilateral trade experienced very strong growth from 2001 (Figure 1). In 2017, the total trade flow between Brazil and China reached US$ 74 billion and represented 20% of the Brazilian trade flow.

On the export side, besides Brazil's strong international competitiveness in several primary commodities, it is also important to emphasize the effect of the Chinese development model itself on the demand and prices of these products. The recent dynamism of the Chinese economy stems from an investment-led urbanization/industrialization process. At the beginning of 2000, China's rate of urbanization was only 36% and then jumped to 57% by 2016, according to National Bureau of Statistics of China (2017). Specially since the end of 1990s, this huge change was accompanied by large expenditures in infrastructure for urban expansion and interconnection between big metropolises, which meant high volumes of investments in civil construction, transportation, energy, telecommunications, and sanitation (Huang 2017, Glaeser et al. 2017). These changes resulted in demand growth and price increases in metallic, energy, and mineral commodities. In addition, the accompanying increase in *per capita* income also meant important changes in consumption patterns that consequently affected agricultural commodities and demand for processed food.

In 2000, China accounted for about 2% of Brazilian exports and was Brazil's 12th export destination. By 2005, China had already become Brazil's third largest export destination and by 2009, China had displaced the United States as the country's top export destination. Despite the slowdown observed in 2012, exports to China continued to grow until 2013, representing 19% of total Brazilian exports that year. The drop observed starting in 2014 reflected both lower growth of the Chinese economy and the reduction in commodity prices caused by that slowdown. In only two years, between 2014 and 2015, the Brazilian exports to China plummeted by about US$ 10 billion. Brazil's exports to China finally resumed growth in 2017, in part because of the recovery in commodity prices, to reach a record high of US$ 47 billion and 22% share of total exports.

Figure 1. Brazil: Bilateral Trade with China, 1995-2017

(US$ billion and % of Total Trade)

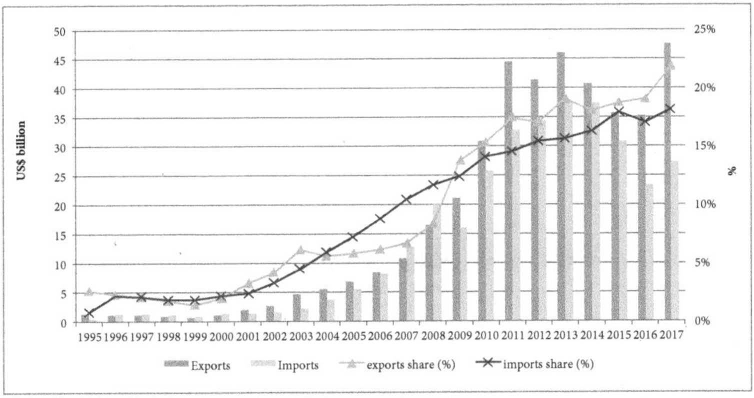

Source: author's elaboration based on UNCTAD (http://unctadstat.unctad.org/EN/Index.html).

On the import side, the robust evolution of China's competitiveness in manufactured goods coupled with a period of strong Brazilian domestic demand growth between 2004 and 2014, the appreciation of the exchange rate, and a decline in the competitiveness of several domestic manufacturing sectors resulted in growing imports to Brazil (Hiratuka and Sarti 2016). In 2000, China was the 11th largest supplier to Brazil and by 2012, surpassed the United States to become the number one source of imports. Imports continued to grow until 2014, reaching US$ 37 billion and representing 16% of Brazilian imports that year. The Brazilian crisis, however, strongly affected imports, which fell to US$ 23 billion in 2016. In 2017, imports from China resumed growth, reaching US$ 29 billion and representing 18% of all Brazilian imports.

In addition to strong growth, another important feature of the trade relation between Brazil and China is the asymmetry that exists in the profile of exported and imported products. Strong growth was accompanied by an increase in the concentration of the main exported commodities. The three main products according to the harmonized system (HS) for classifying goods at 4 digits, accounted for 60% of exports in 2001. In 2010 the share of the three main products (soybeans, iron ore. and crude oil) has

Figure 2. Brazil and China: Trade Balance by Product Group, Classified by Technological Intensity, 2000-2017 (US$ billion)

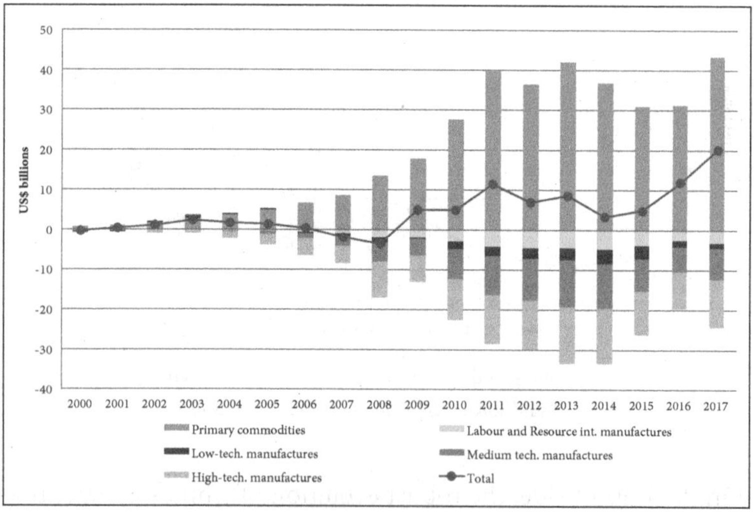

Source: author's elaboration based on UNCTAD (http://unctadstat.unctad.org/EN/Index.html).

reached 80% and fluctuated around this level until 2017. While exports were concentrated in a few primary commodities, imports have included a larger set of manufactured products from different sectors, mainly from medium and high technology segments, which has resulted in a rather asymmetrical trade pattern (Barbosa and Jenkins 2012; Jenkins et al. 2015). The difference observed in the profile of exports and imports can be seen in Figure 2.

The trade balance, which has been favorable to Brazil over time, is a result of the positive trade balances in primary commodities while in manufactured products, there is a high trade deficit. This deficit is concentrated in products classified as high technology (mainly electronics) and medium technology manufacturing products (machinery and equipment, auto parts, and chemicals, among others) and also in labor intensive products (textile, garment, and footwear). The rapid penetration of Chinese exports in the Brazilian market of manufactured products has raised concerns regarding the survival of national industrial producers, who are threatened by displacement in both the domestic market and in important third markets for Brazilian exports such as Mercosur (Jenkins et al. 2015; Hiratuka and Sarti 2016; Hiratuka 2016).

While trade flows have been the main vector of economic relations between Brazil and China, other dimensions like finance and OFDI have gained more relevance in recent years. With regard to financial flows, Gallagher and Myers (2017) show significant volumes of financing provided by Chinese state-owned banks, specially the China Development Bank (CDB) for projects in Brazil (US$ 42 billion between 2007 and 2017). In 2017, the joint Brazil-China Fund for Cooperation on Expansion of Productive Capacity was launched with an initial sum of US$ 20 billion to finance investment projects in Brazil that are of interest to both countries.

To a large extent, these changes are related to China's own post-crisis strategy. The growth pattern based on the expansion of fixed investment has been reinforced through China's policy of further stimulating investments, either through credit or fiscal stimulus, to sustain the growth rate (Paulino and Pires 2016). While global and domestic demand fell, production capacity has strongly expanded, resulting in idle capacity in several Chinese industrial sectors (Cintra and Pinto 2017; European Chamber 2016). This expanded capacity has increased trade tensions in the global market due to the combination of demand stagnation and aggressive foreign market search policies. In addition to a greater effort to reach foreign markets through exports, China has directed capital abroad to give an outlet to surplus capacity. The next section will survey how these principles are shaping the trajectory of Chinese OFDI and its impacts on the Brazilian economy.

Trends and Impacts of Chinese OFDI in Brazil (2000-2017)

This section aims to highlight the main trends, characteristics, and impacts of China's OFDI in Brazil since the beginning of 21th century. However, before addressing the specifics of Chinese investments, it is important to put foreign investments in the Brazilian economy in historical perspective.

One of the basic characteristics of the Brazilian economy is the internationalization of the productive structure, with a large number of foreign affiliates leading in a number of economic sectors. This is by no means a new phenomenon. The presence of Foreign Direct Investment (FDI) and the dominant role of transnational corporations (TNCs) in the most dynamic sectors has been a feature of Brazilian industrialization, particularly from the post-war period up through the 1970s when TNC affiliates were fundamental to the development and consolidation of a diversified productive structure.

In the 1980s, the external debt crisis interrupted the long cycle of Brazilian economic growth. The economy suffered from low and volatile growth rates and continual inflation. During this time, FDI in Brazil fell but foreign affiliates kept their position in the country as they waited for improvements in the domestic market and limited any major investments.

FDI resumed during the 1990s as part of the wave of globalization, and TNCs in Brazil pursued again more aggressive strategies. The liberalization of trade, privatization, and macroeconomic stability, followed by an increase in demand for consumer durables goods motivated TNCs to expand their presence in the Brazilian economy again, especially in the second half of the 1990s. From approximately US$ 1.5 billion annually in the 1980s and early 1990s, FDI inflows increased to an average level of US$ 24 billion yearly between 1995 and 2000.

The resumption of investments in this period was accompanied by substantial changes in the sectoral recipients of FDI. Unlike the import substitution period, when most investments were directed to manufacturing, the majority were then concentrated in the service sector, primarily in telecommunications, electrical energy, and financial services where privatization was occurring. In terms of FDI origin, countries like Spain and Portugal joined large traditional investors in the Brazil such as the United States, Japan and developed European countries.

Regarding Chinese OFDI, the inflow of investment from China remained very low until 2009, not exceeding US$ 100 million in any year between 2001 and 2009 (Figure 3). The annual average in that period was only US$ 24 million. As of 2010, a significant increase is observed, and, in spite of fluctuations, the invested values become more substantial. Between 2010 and 2013, the cumulative

Figure 3. Brazil: Foreign Direct Investment* Flows of Chinese Origin, 2001-2017

(US$ million and %)

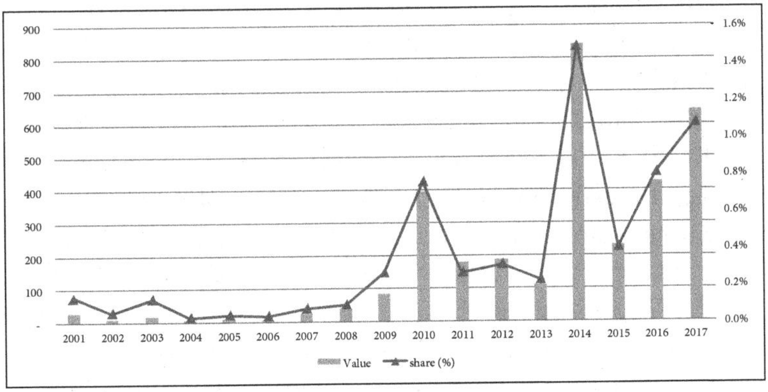

*Equity capital, excluding intra-firm loans and reinvested earning
Source: author´s elaboration based on BCB
(https://www.bcb.gov.br/rex/censoCE/port/censo.asp?idpai=cambio).

FDI inflow under equity modality reached US$ 870 million, with an annual average value about US$ 200 million. From 2014 to 2017, the cumulative Chinese investment was US$ 2.1 billion, with a yearly average of US$ 535 million. In terms of share, from a practically null value in the first period, it increased to represent about 0.4% of total between 2010 and 2013 and 0.9% between 2014 and 2017.

It's important to consider that the analysis of FDI inflows by investing countries from BCB is subject to methodological difficulties, since operations often occur through tax havens, making it difficult to identify the original investor country. Considering the Chinese sources of OFDI, it is possible to notice the same difficult due to passage through Hong Kong and other countries to attain tax advantages. According to MOFCON data, in 2016, the flow of overseas investment directed to Brazil reached US$ 124 million, much less than the US$ 425 million recorded as FDI inflow from China by BCB in the same year.

Information on FDI stock in Brazil presents more precise information about investing countries, since the Census of Foreign Capital organized by BCB seeks to identify the ultimate owner of the foreign assets. It is possible to see that in 2005, only US$ 326 million of Chinese Capital invested directly in Brazil were registered (See Table 1). This figure corresponded to only 0.2% of foreign capital in Brazil. This amount increased to US$ 7.8 billion in 2010 and reached US$ 11.9 billion in 2016. The increase was quite significant, but in 2016 it still represented 2.5% of the total, ranking China in the 13th position, far below traditional investors like the United States, Western European countries, and Japan.

By 2015, 193 registered companies (only 1.1% of the 17,534 foreign funded companies) had at least 10% of their shares held by Chinese capital, as compared to 126 companies in 2010.

Looking at the breakdown by sector, it is possible to notice some changes. In 2010, about 90% of Chinese investments were in the extractive sector. By 2016, Chinese investors had diversified their interests in other sectors, especially electricity and financial services (with 35% and 8.2% respectively of the total Chinese FDI stock in Brazil).

Table 1. Stock of Foreign Direct Investment* with Chinese Origin
(US$ million and %)

Sector	2005		2010		2016	
	Value	%	Value	%	Value	%
Agriculture	-	-	6.2	0.1	7.8	0.1
Mining and Oil Extraction	16.7	5.1	7,146.6	90.8	4,843.9	40.4
Manufacturing	281.9	86.3	209.5	2.7	401.7	3.3
Electricity and Water	-	-	-	-	4,202.1	35.0
Construction	2.7	0.8	1.4	0.0	2.9	0.0
Trade and Auto Repair	22.5	6.9	75.3	1.0	484.0	4.0
Transport and Storage	0.0	0.0	1.5	0.0	3.5	0.0
Information and Telecom.	0.5	0.2	47.0	0.6	299.5	2.5
Financial Services	-	-	372.2	4.7	981.5	8.2
Real State	1.0	0.3	0.3	0.0	128.3	1.1
Other services	2.0	0.6	14.1	0.2	638.9	5.3
Total	326.6	100.0	7,874.0	100.0	11,994.1	100.0
Share in Brazilian Total	0.2%		1.3%		2.5%	

*Equity capital, excluding intra-firm loans and reinvested earning
Source: author´s elaboration based on BCB (https://www.bcb.gov.br/rex/censoCE/port/censo.asp?idpai=cambio).

The information analyzed so far shows a significant increase in Chinese investments in Brazil, especially in the most recent period. To a large extent this process is linked to the more intense internationalization strategy carried out by the Chinese government and by the Chinese companies in the most recent period, especially after the international crisis (CBEC 2013; Barbosa 2014 and Santos and Milan 2014). Gao and Wang (2017) and (Jaguaribe 2017) also highlight the strong coordination between state-owned enterprises, development banks, government agencies and the private productive system to achieve long-term goals in terms of Chinese international insertion, including the quest to improve the profitability profile of Chinese assets abroad, still largely tied to US treasury bonds. Finally, it should be noted that since 2011 a process of devaluation of the Brazilian currency has been observed, which has made Brazilian domestic assets cheaper for foreign investors.

Furthermore, it is worth remembering China's own quest to change its pattern of development. The 13th Five Year plan stresses that China must address a number of challenges in the coming years. The main one is to move towards a new pattern of growth that is less dependent on capital-intensive investments and more efficient in the use of natural resources and at the same time reduces social and regional inequalities and expand social services to the population. Simultaneously, this transition involves changes in how China manage its economic international relations, especially with respect to the need to increase foreign direct investments and infrastructure expansion projects abroad as a way to reduce domestic idle capacity (Aglietta and Bai 2016; Koleski 2017).

Further detail on the profile of Chinese investments can be obtained from alternative sources to the data of the BCB and MOFCOM. As several studies have pointed out (Hiratuka, 2018, Kupfer et all, 2018), these alternative sources, although unofficial, can complement the official data by the greater possibility of detailing sectors of activity, the profile of investing company and the type of investment (greenfield or merger and acquisition-M&A).

In this work, the OFDI Monitor of China in Latin America, organized by the Latin American Academic Network on China (LAC-China Network) was used. The Monitor gathers information from different sources, covering information on greenfield and mergers and acquisitions investment announcements. From the information consolidated by the Monitor, a work was carried out to analyze each record and verify from the announced investments, which were actually confirmed. The exclusion of announced investments and for which no information was found to confirm the investment resulted in the data analyzed in the following pages.

It is worth remembering that the investment value captured by the database does not refer to the concept of FDI that is used by the official sources. The investment information in the database can be different, either because some of the resources can be financed by institutions in the destination country, or because, although investments flows are expected to occur over several years, the total amount can be captured in a single year.

As can be seen in Figure 4, the values estimated from the OFDI Monitor are much higher than those provided by the BCB in Figure 3. The trend is also somewhat different due to some major operations in a few years, such as Sinopec's investment in the Oil sector (US$ 7.1 billion) in 2010. However, it is possible to observe that, as of 2010, investments present a level that is higher in relation to the previous period. Between 2010 and 2014 there was a downward trend, which is reversed from 2015 onwards. When one looks to the data on the number of transactions, it's possible also see an upward trend over the period.

Figure 4. Brazil: Investment by Chinese Companies, 2003-2017
(US$ million and number of transactions)

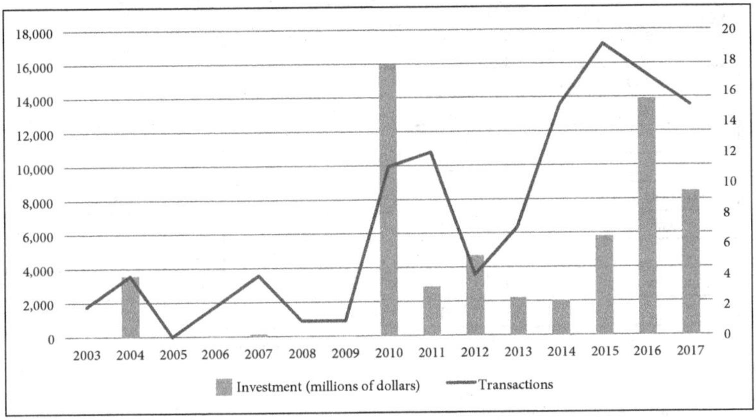

Source: author´s elaboration based on LAC-China Network (2019).

Considering the evolution of values and the sectoral distribution of Chinese OFDI in Brazil, the whole period can be subdivided in three subperiods (Tables 2 and 3). In the first one (2003-2009), when the number of transactions and the invested amount was still reduced, the mining sector is clearly the one that most concentrated investments, while the manufacturing had more importance in the number of transactions. The second one (2010-2013) is characterized by an increase mainly in the invested values but also in the number of transactions, with a beginning of diversification, with the entry of companies in the service sector as in financial services and electricity. In the third period (2014-2017), the invested values remained at relatively high levels and the number of transactions shows a significant increase. Manufacturing loses relative importance in value between 2014 and 2017 but it increases significantly in terms of number of transactions, from 17 operations in the 2010-2013 period to 29 in 2014-2017. The mining sector also loses relative importance in terms of invested amounts, while the service sectors becomes the main highlight.

Regarding the service sector, it is worth emphasizing the importance of the electric power sector, where Chinese companies

Table 2. Brazil: Investment by Chinese Companies by Sector, 2003-2017
(US$ million and number of transactions)

Sector	2003-2009		2010-2013		2014-2017	
	Value	%	Value	%	Value	%
Agriculture	-	-	59.5	0.2	1,405.7	4.7
Mining and Oil Extraction	3,560.0	92.9	18,530.0	72.2	1,694.9	5.6
Manufacturing	168.0	4.4	2,193.8	8.5	1,249.5	4.1
Services	103.7	2.7	4,895.2	19.1	25,771.4	85.6
Electricity and Water	-	-	2,737.4	10.7	22,543.0	74.8
Transport and Storage	-	-	230.0	0.9	1,473.6	4.9
Financial Services	85.0	2.2	1,804.0	7.0	842.5	2.8
Trade	-	-	120.0	0.5	218.7	0.7
Other services	18.7	0.5	3.8	0.0	693.6	2.3
Total	**3,831.7**	**100.0**	**25,678.5**	**100.0**	**30,121.5**	**100.0**

Source: author´s elaboration based on LAC-China Network (2019).

Table 3. Brazil: Investment by Chinese Companies by Sector, 2003-2016
(% of total value and number of transactions)

Sector	2003-2009		2010-2013		2014-2017	
	N.	%	N.	%	N.	%
Agriculture	0	-	1	2.9	3	4.5
Mining and Oil Extraction	3	21.4	7	20.6	3	4.5
Manufacturing	8	57.1	17	50.0	29	43.9
Services	3	21.4	9	26.5	31	47.0
Electricity and Water	0	-	3	8.8	10	15.2
Transport and Storage	0	-	1	2.9	5	7.6
Financial Services	2	14.3	2	5.9	3	4.5
Trade	0	-	1	2.9	5	7.6
Other services	1	7.1	2	5.9	8	12.1
Total	**14**	**100.0**	**34**	**100.0**	**66**	**100.0**

Source: author´s elaboration based on LAC-China Network (2019).

(State Grid and China Three Gorges) have become major players in the Brazilian market (Junqueira 2017; CEBC 2017; Hiratuka 2018). The electricity sector was the main segment in the 2014-2017 period, accounting for almost 75% of the entire invested amount. In terms of number of transactions, there was also an increase in the number of operations in the services not only in the electric power sector, but also in the area of transportation, trade, financial services and other services.

As several analysts point out, one distinctive aspect of the process of internationalization of Chinese enterprises is the strong influence of the State planning as the driver and organizer of the process, not only through state-owned enterprises of central government and provincial governments, but also by the influence over private enterprises , through a series of fiscal and financial incentives mechanisms and supervision and political control (Pearson 2015; Naughton 2015; Dussel Peters 2015; Jaguaribe 2018).

In the case of Chinese investments in Brazil this influence is very sharp (Table 4). Although the reduction in the relative share of investments made by companies with public ownership in the investment value, they accounted for 84.5% of the total in the last period. In previous periods, the participation was over 90%. To a large extent, investments values led by public companies is much higher than that of private companies but in terms of number of transactions the share of private companies is somewhat higher. In the period 2014-2017, which concentrates the largest number

Table 4. Brazil: Investment by Chinese Companies by Ownership, 2003-2017 (US$ million, number of transactions and %)

	US$ million			Transactions		
Value	2003-2009	2010-2013	2014-2017	2003-2009	2010-2013	2014-2017
Private	246.7	2,466.10	4,672.80	10	18	41
Public	3,585.00	23,212.40	25,448.60	4	16	26
Total	3,831.70	25,678.50	30,121.50	14	34	66
%	2003-2009	2010-2013	2014-2017	2003-2009	2010-2013	2014-2017
Private	6.4	9.6	15.5	71.4	52.9	62.1
Public	93.6	90.4	84.5	28.6	47.1	39.4
Total	100	100	100	100	100	100

Source: author´s elaboration based on LAC-China Network (2019).

of operations, private companies accounted for 62.1% of total transactions, but for 15.5% of the invested amount. The average transaction value of the two groups of companies in this period was US$ 115 million and US$ 978 million respectively.

Investments of public and private companies had a very different sectoral distribution. In sectors considered strategic (Pearson 2015), such as in the mining, oil extraction and electricity, public enterprises predominated (e.g. State Grid, China Three Gorges, Sinopec, CNOOC and CNPC). Private companies, in turn, concentrated mainly in manufacturing activities, especially in automotive, electronics and telecommunications products and machinery and equipment.

Another relevant information is the distinction between investment involving on one hand new or expansion investments (greenfield), and on the other M&A. As can be seen from figure 5, over the periods, investments made through M&A become predominant, accounting for 95% of the invested value between 2014 and 2017. In addition, new investments fall in absolute terms between 2010-2013 and 2014-2017. This is a worrying aspect, since new investments result in greater impacts on the capital formation process and on the generation of value added and new jobs. In general, operations involving M&A have much higher average values,

Figure 5. Brazil: Chinese Investments by Type of Operation (US$ million)

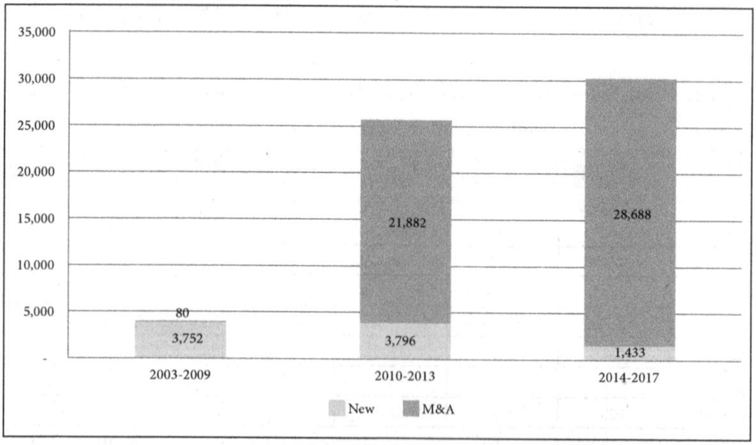

Source: author´s elaboration based on LAC-China Network (2019).

since new investments represented the major part of transactions (86% of the total in the first period, 62% in the second and 60% on the third).

Still regarding the distinction between greenfield investments and M&A, it seems to be a very distinctive feature of Chinese investments. Considering the total data for Brazil compiled by UNCTAD, in the period 2014-2017, the value of M&A with Brazilian companies as target represented 47% of the sum of M&A and greenfield investments (against 95% in Chinese investments). This increase can be largely associated with the preference of public companies for this modality, since they accounted for 98% of all M&A in the period 2010-2013 and 87% 2014-2017.

Finally, one last aspect to be highlighted is the estimated employment generated by the investments. Figure 6 shows that the employment affected by Chinese investments in Brazil has been increasing. However, the estimation of effectively new jobs is relatively small. Throughout the period, new investments have had an impact of just over 25,000 jobs. On the other hand, a much larger volume was affected by M&A processes. In this case, these are jobs which already existed before and start to be controlled or to have some equity involvement from Chinese companies. As seen

Figure 6. Brazil: Effect of Chinese Investments on Employment by Type of Investment

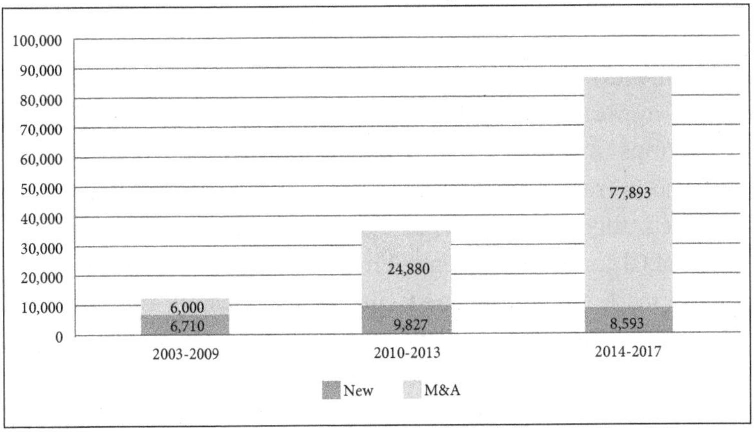

Source: author's elaboration based on LAC-China Network (2019).

in M&A transactions, the M&A affected jobs were quite significant and increasing. But the effects of these operations are difficult to analyze since they would depend on a more detailed follow-up of post-acquisition changes in terms of generated or eliminated jobs, wages and working conditions.

Conclusions and Policy Suggestions

The information analyzed throughout this chapter showed that while trade flows between Brazil and China have grown fast since the early 2000s, Chinese FDI in Brazil has become more important only as of 2010, reflecting the intensification of the internationalization of Chinese companies and the devaluation of asset prices in Brazil.

The increase in Chinese investments inflows was accompanied by important changes. While investments in the extractive sector prevailed up to 2009, sectoral diversification has been observed since 2010. Between 2010 and 2013, although the extractive sector still concentrated most of the investments, manufacturing gained importance, as do the electric energy and financial sectors. In the period 2014-2017, the electric energy sector becomes the main destination of Chinese OFDI in Brazil, with the Chinese companies buying some of most important domestic companies. Information on the number of transactions for the period 2014-2017 points more clearly to a sectoral diversification of Chinese investments in Brazil, with the manufacturing industry accounting for an important part of total and an increase in the number of operations in the service sectors, not only in the electric energy, but also in transportation, trade, finance and other services.

The information analyzed also showed some distinctive features of Chinese investments. First, the importance of the investments made by state-owned enterprises. Despite the reduction of relative importance in the periods analyzed, investments by public owned companies accounted for 84.5% of the total invested amount and 39.4% of operations between 2014 and 2017. These data are related with the central role of state planning in the China's internationalization process and its articulation with the national development strategy, whether directly through public enterprises investment abroad or through of several mechanisms of support and financing to public companies. Second, the predominance of M&A, which represented 95% of the total invested between 204 and 2017. The high concentration on M&A is one of the major sources of concern regarding the profile of Chinese OFDI in Brazil, since can result in relatively small impacts on macroeconomic investments and generation of new value added and jobs.

Considering the analysis carried out in this chapter, the following policy proposals can be highlighted.

- The strategic character of Chinese investments makes it more evident that Brazilian policymakers must also take a strategic approach, seeking to maximize potential positive results and mitigate risks. It is not a question of adopting a restrictive or discriminatory policy, but of the ability to prioritize actions and coordinate instruments so as to take full advantage of the potential opportunities that Chinese investments may represent. The fact that a large part of OFDI is carried out by state-owned enterprises is a major challenge, since purely economic motivations are not at the forefront of these enterprises investment decisions. A greater understanding of the more general Chinese development strategy and the role that the internationalization of Public and Private Companies fulfill in this process is fundamental, so that actions can be taken to maximize the benefits to the Brazilian economy and society.
- Regarding the type of investments, it would be important to seek to increase the relative importance of greenfield projects in relation to M&A. In terms of impacts on host economies, greenfield are much more effective in terms of impacts on expanding productive capacity and generating new value added and jobs. The need to raise the rate of Gross Capital Formation in the Brazilian economy makes this aspect even more central.

- Regarding sectoral distribution, an area where potential impacts are very large are investments in infrastructure sectors. In the electric power sector the Chinese companies have already a relevant position, but invested basically through M&A. Infrastructure is an area where Brazil has chronic deficiencies, and one of the main areas of expansion of Chinese investments in the world. In addition, the involvement of the Chinese public banks and the Brazil China Cooperation Fund for Capacity Building may play an important role in the funding projects in transportation, energy (including clean energy) and construction. However, it is important to have a strategy that maximizes the benefits of these projects, which means maintaining and perfecting mechanisms to monitor, regulate and generate positive effects on the country in terms of quality of services, employment generation, good environmental and labor conditions, linkages with domestic productive chains and technological spillovers.
- Still regarding sectoral distribution, the recent diversification can mean interesting prospects, but greater investments in industrial and service sectors that are more technology- and knowledge-intensive should be targeted. The dynamism and rapid transition of the Chinese economy towards more knowledge-intensive sectors requires an effort of monitoring and analysis by the government, academia and productive sector. That could help in the exploration of new opportunities for investment and bilateral cooperation, as well as the establishment of closer relations which could guarantee wider benefits from the point of view of generating more spillovers on the Brazilian economy.
- Finally, a more effective strategy in all the above items would require an effort to strengthen the coordination among the several public sector institutions responsible for general or sectoral attraction, promotion, incentives, financing, regulation and supervision of investments (e.g. Ministry of Foreign Affairs, Secretariat for International Affairs of the Ministry of Planning, Brazilian Export Promotion Agency-APEX, Ministry of Industry, Development and Trade,

Ministry of Transportation, Brazilian Bank of Development-BNDES, Brazilian Institute of the Environment and Natural Resources-IBAMA and Regulatory Agencies as National Agency of Electric Energy-ANEEL and National Agency of Petroleum- ANP).

References

Aglietta, Michel, Bai, Guo. 2016. "China's 13th Five-Year Plan. In Pursuit of a "Moderately Prosperous" Society". *CEPII Policy Brief* 12, pp. 1-16.

Barbosa, Alexandre de Freitas. 2014. *"Las relaciones económicas entre Brasil y China a partir del desempeño de las empresas State Grid y Lenovo"*. In, Dussel Peters, Enrique (coord.). *La inversión extranjera directa de China en América Latina: 10 estudios de caso.* Mexico: Red ALC-China and UDUAL, pp. 61-132.

CEBC (Conselho Empresarial Brasil China). 2013. *Uma análise dos investimentos chineses no Brasil: 2007-2012. São Paulo:* CEBC.

Cintra, Marcos Antonio, Pinto, Eduardo Costa. 2017. "China em transformação: transição e estratégias de desenvolvimento". *Revista de Economia Política* 37(2), p. 381-400.

Dussel Peters, Enrique. 2015. "The omnipresent role of China's public sector in its relationship with Latin America and the Caribbean". In, Dussel Peters, Enrique and Armony, Ariel (coords.). Beyond raw materials. Who are the actors in the Latin America and Caribbean-China relationship? Mexico: Nueva Sociedad, Friedrich-Ebert-Stiftung and Red ALC-China, pp. 50-72.

European Chamber of Commerce in China. 2016. Overcapacity in China: an impediment to the Party's reform agenda. Beijing: European Union Chamber of Commerce in China.

Gallagher, Kevin and Myers Margaret. 2017. *China-Latin America Finance Database.* Washington, D.C.: Inter-American Dialogue.

Glaeser, Edward, Huang, Wei. Ma, Yueran and Shleifer, Andrei. 2017. "A real estate boom with Chinese characteristics". *Journal of Economic Perspectives* 31(1), p. 93-116.

Hiratuka, Celio, Castilho, Marta, Dussel Peters, Enrique, Bianco, Carlos and Carracelas, Gastón. 2012. "Avaliação da competição comercial chinesa em terceiros mercados". In: Bittencourt, Gustavo (Org.) *El impacto de China en AL: comercio e inversiones*. Serie Red Mercosur 20.

Hiratuka, Celio and Fernando Sarti. 2016. "Relações econômicas entre Brasil e China: análise dos fluxos de comércio e investimento direto estrangeiro". *Revista Tempo do Mundo* (IPEA) 2(1), pp. 83-98.

Hiratuka, Celio. 2018. "Chinese Infrastructure Projects in Brazil: two cases studies". In, Dussel Peters, Enrique, Armony, Ariel and Shoujun, Cui. *Building development for a new era: China's infrastructure projects in Latin America and the Caribbean*. Mexico: University of Pittsburgh and Red Académica de América Latina y el Caribe sobre China, pp. 122-143.

Hiratuka. Celio. 2016. "Impactos de China sobre el proceso de integración regional de Mercosur". In, Dussel Peters, Enrique. *La Nueva relación Comercial de América Latina y el Caribe con China. ¿Integración o desitegración regional?* Mexico: Red ALC-China and Unión de Universidades de América Latina y el Caribe, pp. 195-244.

Jaguaribe, Anna. 2018. "Characteristics and Direction of China's Global Investment Drive". In, Jaguaribe, Anna. (org). *Direction of Chinese global investments : implications for Brazil*. Brasilia: FUNAG, pp 17-50.

Jenkins, Rhys. 2015. "Is Chinese Competition Causing Deindustrialization in Brazil?" *Latin American Perspectives* (6), pp. 42-63.

Junqueira, Leandro Leone. 2017. *A Estratégia das Empresas e a Consolidação do Segmento de Distribuição de Energia Elétrica*. Master Dissertation Thesis. Faculade de Enegenharia Mecânica. Unicamp.

Koleski, Kathrin. 2017. *The 13th Five Year Plan*. Staff Research Report. US-China Economic and Security Review Commission. Washington, D.C.: USCESR.

Kupfer, David, Rocha, Felipe Freitas. 2018. "Direções do investimento chinês no Brasil 2010-2016: estratégia nacional ou busca de oportunidades". In, Jaguaribe, Anna. (org). *Direction of Chinese global investments: implications for Brazil.* Brasilia: FUNAG, pp 215-266.

MOFCOM (Ministry of Commerce People's Republic of China). 2017 *Statistical Bulletin of China's Outward Foreign Direct Investment 2016.* Beijing: MOFCOM.

Monitor de la OFDI de China en ALC. 2019. *Monitor de la OFDI de China en ALC 2019.* Mexico: Red ALC-China.

Naughton, Barry. 2015. "The Transformation of the State Sector: SASAC, the Market Economy, and the New National Champions". In, Naughton, Barry, Tsai, Kellee S. *State capitalism, institutional adaptation, and the Chinese miracle.* Cambridge: Cambridge University Press, pp. 46-74.

Ortiz Velásquez, Samuel. 2016. Monitor de La OFDI de China en América Latina y El Caribe. Aspectos metodológicos. Mexico: Red ALC-China.

Paulino, Luis Antonio, Pires, Marcos Cordeiro. 2015. "As relações entre China e AL frente ao novo normal da economia chinesa". *Revista Economia e Políticas Públicas* 4(1), pp. 9-28..

Pearson, Margaret. 2015. "State-Owned Business and Party-State Regulation in China's Modern Political Economy". In, Naughton, Barry and Tsai, Kellee S. *State capitalism, institutional adaptation, and the Chinese miracle.* Cambridge: Cambridge University Press, pp. 27-45.

Santos, Leandro and Milan, Marcelo. 2014. "Determinantes dos investimentos diretos externos chineses: aspectos econômicos e geopolíticos". *Revista Contexto Internacional* 36(2), pp. 457-486.

Secretaria de Assuntos Internacionais MPOG. 2018. *Boletim Bimestral sobre Investimentos Chineses.* http://www.planejamento.gov.br/assuntos/internacionais/arquivos/boletimfdichina2edicaojaneiro2018.pdf.

CHINA'S FOREIGN DIRECT INVESTMENT IN COLOMBIA

Benjamin Creutzfeldt

Introduction

Among the principal economies of Latin America, Colombia has long been the least open to investment or immigration from Asia and has benefited only marginally from the economic transformation of the Far East since the 1960s and the explosive economic growth of China since the 1990s. The country's internal conflict, which has repeatedly flared into violent civil war since the 1960s, has done little to attract foreign investors. Some progress has been made in expanding state control and security since the beginning of the 21st century, but foreign direct investment (FDI) in Colombia has not risen more than in other Latin American economies, and attention from the fastest-growing capital-exporting economy –the People's Republic of China– has been negligible.

The present chapter sheds light on the reasons for Colombia's tardiness to the phenomenon of Chinese-driven growth in Latin America, provides a panorama of the handful of Chinese firms that have successfully established themselves in the country, and summarizes the significant changes that have occurred in the bilateral relationship since 2016. This chapter opens with an overview of Sino-Colombian relations since the late 20th century and the diplomacy on either side that underpins the relationship. This is followed by a synopsis of significant Chinese investment by sector, and includes analysis of the challenges companies have faced and the progress made in recent years. The chapter closes by reviewing the opportunities and risks implicit in the growing Chinese presence in Colombia, and offers policy recommendations that point to the importance of learning from neighbouring countries in the region –in particular those of the Pacific Alliance– and to the value that North American and European experiences can bring to bear on this transpacific relationship.

An Overview of Chinese-Colombian Relations

Historically, the presence of China in Colombia has been minimal and its impact almost imperceptible, in contrast to Cuba, Peru, Mexico, Brazil, and other countries in the region, which saw waves of immigration from China throughout the 19th and 20th centuries. This situation has not changed significantly in the last few decades, despite China's rise since the 1978 reforms and its position today as one of the leading players in the global economy. Several researchers have attempted to track and better understand the presence of Chinese citizens, companies, and their respective activities in Colombia, but none have succeeded in profiling this diverse group. One of the earliest attempts was made by the anthropologist Friederike Fleischer (2005), now a professor at Los Andes University in Bogotá, who identified the shortcomings of preceding efforts to identify and differentiate Chinese immigrants. Natalia Marriaga (2012) applied a similar anthropological approach and a compelling journalistic style, but her reports are centred on individual shop owners and do not attempt to present the overall demographics of these immigrants. Gómez and Díaz (2016) describe migration and bilateral institutions since the 1970s, but fail to qualify either methodically. Studies that attempt to engage with the Chinese business community often fall short, illustrating the linguistic and cultural barriers that persist –barriers that scholars like Rudas and Cabrera (2015) do not overcome when seeking to engage with Chinese visitors or permanent residents.

Even today, it is the minimal presence of Asian corporations in Colombia that is striking, both in comparison to the number of investors from other parts of the world, and in contrast with the experiences of its Pacific Alliance partners Chile, Mexico, and Peru. Although the country has been an indirect beneficiary of the rise in commodities prices in the first decade of the 21st century due to the strength of global demand driven primarily by China, Colombia has long lacked significant engagement in terms of foreign trade (Reina & Oviedo 2014). This has been exacerbated by latent xenophobia towards Asia in particular, and very low levels of migration from Asia compared to most neighbours, resulting in a profound lack of familiarity with those cultures (Creutzfeldt 2018). This tendency can be traced back in time to the Colombian government's restrictions on migration from Asia in the 1920s (Sanmiguel 2006), its decision to support the United States in the War against North Korea in the 1950s –and by extension, against the Soviet Union and the People's Republic of China– and its persecution of domestic communists in the 1980s (Marín Rivas 2017).

It is only with this background that we can begin to understand and evaluate the relatively low level of Chinese investment in Colombia today, given that purely economic analyses of the fourth-largest economy in Latin America and the performance of its stock market would suggest otherwise. UNCTAD data shows that Colombia's inward FDI has broadly increased since the early 2000s (see Figure 1), but it received only 14% of the FDI inflow for the region in 2017. Chinese FDI does not even register on the charts.

Figure 1. Colombia's total inward FDI 2000-2017

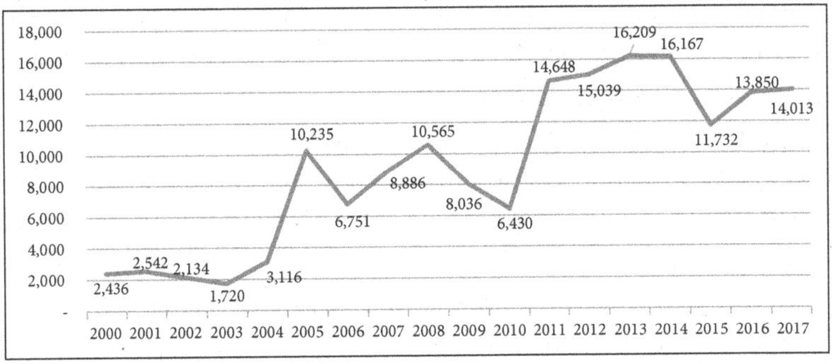

Source: author's elaboration based on UNCTAD (2018, July).

Today, estimates of the Chinese population in Colombia, including emigrants from Taiwan and descendants of first-generation immigrants, range from fifteen to twenty thousand individuals, a third of whom are based in the coastal city of Barranquilla (where China's only consulate in Colombia was located until it closed in mid-2017). The presence of Chinese in Colombia has played a negligible role in bilateral relations. This stands in stark contrast to tiny neighbour Panama, a province of Colombia until 1904, where an estimated populace of around 300,000 ethnic Chinese constitutes almost six percent of the national population (Torrijos Legazpi 2014).

An important factor in the recent past has been Colombia's closeness with, and strong support from, the United States (cf. Creutzfeldt 2012). This was especially significant during the government of Álvaro Uribe, the president from 2002 to 2010, who was at times described as "Washington's faithful vassal in South America" (Wieland 2007:1). In the year 2004, the United States Institute of Peace reported that "with more than 2,000 personnel from 32 U.S. agencies, the embassy in Bogotá surpassed that in Cairo as the largest U.S. embassy in the world" (USIP 2004:114). At that time, Colombia was also the fourth-largest recipient of US foreign aid and played a key role in Washington's "War on Drugs." At the very time that China's government and its more adventurous business executives and traders were eyeing Latin America, Bogotá was making every effort to reaffirm its early twentieth century 'Respice Polum' foreign policy, which focused almost exclusively on the relationship with the United States (Bermúdez Torres 2010). Washington spent heavily on its principal ally in the region and maintained it as a hub for regional anti-narcotics and intelligence-gathering operations.

It is not surprising that at least until 2016, the rapprochement between China and Colombia was cautious, and the tenor of this relationship is not easily transformed. Although Colombia now has three Confucius Institutes and a considerable number of private teaching initiatives for Mandarin, broader skills for professional engagement are lacking due to the weaknesses of primary and secondary education in the country (Oviedo, Fizbein and

Sucre 2015). The lack of coordination between establishments of higher education and competition between private universities impedes the advancement of knowledge production in any field, including the study of China and East Asia, though some efforts by academics in Colombia to build knowledge on China are noteworthy (García Tobón 2009; Creutzfeldt 2012; Vieira 2013; Pastrana and Gehring 2017).

Bilateral leadership visits between China and Colombia have been few and far between. Premier Zhao Ziyang was the first Chinese head of state to visit Colombia in 1985, at the invitation of President Belisario Betancur (Beijing Review 1985:6). The first return visit was by President Ernesto Samper to Beijing in October 1996, followed by that of Andrés Pastrana in 1999. Álvaro Uribe made a trip to China in 2005, as did his successor, Juan Manuel Santos, in 2012. Xi Jinping, visited Colombia in 2009 as vice president, making a point of coaxing Colombia into last-minute participation in the Shanghai World Exposition 2010 (Latin American Herald Tribune 2009). Premier Li Keqiang made a short stopover in Bogotá in May 2015. This contrasts with neighbouring countries: Hugo Chávez and his successor Nicolás Maduro in Venezuela paid as many as fifteen visits to China in as many years, and Luiz Inácio Lula da Silva of Brazil and his counterpart Hu Jintao met a dozen times in the first decade of the century.

Beijing's diplomatic strategy towards Colombia is embedded within a well-coordinated broader regional plan, involving multiple government and party agencies: the Ministries of Foreign Affairs and Commerce, the Development and Reform Commission, and organizations within the Chinese Communist Party such as the International Department, the Organization Department, and the United Front Work Department. Staff rotates not only between embassies, but also in and out of the aforementioned agencies and the vast majority of senior embassy personnel have a strong command of the Spanish language.

In addition to visits by heads of state, diplomatic profiles are another indicator of the strength of bilateral relations. The backgrounds of the ambassadors on either side of the relationship offer significant insights into the nature and level of binational relations.

Ambassador 居一杰 Ju Yijie, ambassador to Colombia from February 2000 to May 2003, was previously the representative of the Panama Trade Development Office, and after leaving Bogotá, became ambassador in Caracas. His successor in Bogotá, 吴长胜 Wu Changsheng, headed embassies in Bolivia and the Bahamas prior to taking office in Bogotá from August 2003 to February 2007. 李长华 Li Changhua, the ambassador from March 2007 to July 2009, had risen through the diplomatic ranks for over two decades, with experience in in Mexico, Venezuela and Uruguay, came from Chile where he had overseen the negotiations and signing of China's first Free Trade Agreement (FTA). 高正月 Gao Zhengyue had been ambassador to Peru before assuming the Colombian position between August 2009 and June 2011. 汪晓源 Wang Xiaoyuan, ambassador in Bogotá between 2011 and 2016, was a senior diplomat who had headed his country's embassies in Equatorial Guinea and Uruguay, and holds the distinction of having been the first PRC head of mission in Costa Rica. His seniority and experience were important factors in ensuring the smooth implementation of the first visit by a Chinese Prime Minister to Colombia since Premier Zhao Ziyang's Latin America tour in 1985. Since 2016, 李念平 Li Nianping has raised the visibility of his position and his country by traveling to 20 of Colombia's 32 departments, and engaging in other public relations efforts exhaustively documented in an October 2018 Special Edition of *Semana* Magazine.

Colombia's ambassadors to Beijing during the same period have been political and business-focused nominees with limited formal diplomatic experience. None spoke Chinese and some had only a limited command of English. Alfonso Campo Soto, a conservative senator of Cesar Province, was followed by the longest-serving ambassador to Beijing, Guillermo Ricardo Vélez, formerly representative in London for Colombia's export promotion entity Proexport (later renamed Procolombia). His tenure, from 2004-2011, coincided with President Álvaro Uribe's visit to China in 2005 and oversaw rapid trade growth between the two countries, followed by personal efforts by the former ambassador after his retirement to negotiate bilateral business deals.

His successor Carlos Urrea lasted only eleven months on the job, citing obligations in his family business for his hurried departure. He resigned during President Juan Manuel Santos' visit to Beijing in 2012, making follow-through of the nine agreements signed in Beijing unfeasible. He was succeeded by Carmenza Jaramillo, also a former Proexport country director, who had limited political influence either in China or in Colombia to effectively change the dominant tendencies. Óscar Rueda García, ambassador since 2016, is a tourism professional for whom Beijing is his first diplomatic mission, a posting seen by many as political reward for his work as treasurer for the political party founded by Álvaro Uribe.

In short, bilateral relations have been marked by a lack of focus and specialized engagement on the Colombian side, making it harder for Chinese corporations to engage constructively. Lack of information and the persistence of prejudice against Chinese businesses and their products have derailed what could have become innovative collaborations (see for instance Bermúdez Liévano 2018). China-Colombia relations have been further hampered by societal tension and mistrust. Neoliberal development under presidents Uribe, Santos, and now Duque has emphasized large-scale, export-capable industries, free trade agreements, and capital markets. These policies have benefited large corporations but generated employment (compare Sanborn 2018), and affected low-income Colombian labourers by inhibiting their ability to organize and pressure for wages and working conditions. The resulting inequalities and tensions have left many Colombians disenchanted with foreigners and their economic influence, which in turn has translated into negative perceptions of both the U.S. and China. In a recent survey by the Pew Research Center, 48% of Latin America viewed China favourably, but in Colombia this number fell to 28%. More than 45% of Colombians thought China's expansion in Latin America was bad for their country, one of the highest negative perceptions in the region (Koop 2015).

However, the Trump administration in the United States has also led to disenchantment in many parts of Latin America, including Colombia. This trend coincides with a concerted effort by China under Xi Jinping to grow trade, investment and infrastructure development (MoFA 2015), spearheaded in Colombia by the aforementioned charm offensive under Beijing's ambassador Li Nianping. Going forward, a key area of bilateral activity will be infrastructure. As a new frontier in Sino-Colombian cooperation, infrastructure is at the core of President Xi Jinping's Belt and Road Initiative, an important interest of Chinese corporations, and a vital element for Colombia's development and its regional and global integration.

Up until 2015, Capital Airport Holdings represented the only significant Chinese activity in this sector, winning bids to manage and expand six airports across the north of the country (China-CEA 2015). In contrast, Hydrochina has made headlines regularly since 2009 for financing a feasibility study for the development of the Magdalena River for shipping and energy generation, but this has not led to concrete participation in projects as of the time of writing (China en América Latina 2016). Other projects have been discussed and dropped, such as a "dry canal" rail and pipeline link in the northeast of the country to connect Caribbean and Pacific ports in 2011 (Semana 2011), a deep-water port on the Pacific coast north of Buenaventura, and the ill-fated Ituango hydroelectric dam. Since 2016, a growing number of Chinese corporations have entered into cooperation agreements and joint ventures with Colombian companies and bid with growing frequency –and occasional success– on public tenders for projects in highway construction and electricity generation. These lie outside the scope of the present discussion, as they do not typically represent investments unless they include concessions for revenue generation over several decades. Chinese companies have also been impeded by the same labyrinth of obstacles that their Colombian and foreign competitors face, including demanding procurement processes and local interests seeking a portion of any project taking place in their territory (Ellis 2017).

China's Foreign Direct Investment in Colombia since 2000

There are approximately 70 Chinese companies operating in Colombia as of October 2018, though the number stands at over 100 if we include commercial traders of Chinese nationality who entered the market since late 2015.[1] The cumulative investment in Colombia of Chinese origin, or the total capital interests in the country, is estimated at a little over US$3 billion. This figure is a conservative approximation reached in coordination with UNAM's *Red ALC-China*, through publically obtainable records in Colombia, press and specialist industry reports, and interviews with several of the relevant companies, conducted with the support of the principal binational chamber of commerce *(Cámara Colombo-China de Inversión y Comercio, CCCIC)* and the Association of Chinese Companies in Colombia *(Asociación Empresarial Colombo-China, AECC)*. It is a figure that has grown since 2015, when it was around US$ 2.3 billion and the Trade Attaché at the Chinese Embassy in Bogotá confirmed that that figure was "pretty close to our own data" (Communication from the Trade Counselor's office of the Chinese Embassy in Bogotá, June 2015). The number of Chinese companies that have established representative offices has also risen. The AECC, founded at the behest of the Chinese ambassador in October 2016, has a membership of 34 companies. The CCCIC has also put together a list of 63 Chinese companies with offices in Colombia, though less than a dozen of these are among the Chamber's 130 registered members (the vast majority being Colombian trading companies and law firms).

1 After many years of complaints by Chinese business persons and the Chinese embassy in Bogotá, lamenting the difficulties faced by Chinese citizens when soliciting visas for entry to Colombia, the Colombian Foreign Office initiated significant changes: in February 2015 it allowed Chinese nationals holding Schengen or U.S. visas to enter freely. This led to a sudden influx: several dozen traders, many of them previously importing and wholesaling clothing and apparel in Europe or other Latin American countries, availed themselves of this opportunity and set up shop in the commercial district of San Victorino in central Bogotá. Moreover, in 2017, the Pacific Alliance countries decided to recognize each other's visas issues to citizens of third countries.

Even in the midst of an exploration of foreign direct investment, it is worth remembering that there are multiple definitions of what comprises FDI, as has been discussed elsewhere (Ortiz Velásquez 2017; Umaña 2016). In essence, it is a form of cross-border investment with the objective of establishing a lasting interest that an enterprise based in one country might have in an enterprise operating in another country. Lasting interest implies a significant degree of influence on the management of the enterprise along with building a long-term rapport between the direct investor and the direct investment enterprise. According to the OECD (2008), ownership of 10% of the voting power by the foreign investor is evidence of such a relationship. FDI can be achieved by either setting up new factories and plants from the ground up (greenfield investment), or through cross-border mergers and acquisitions that involve acquiring an existing foreign enterprise in the country of interest (brownfield investment). More broadly, FDI includes mergers and acquisitions, building new facilities, reinvesting profits earned from overseas operations and intra-company loans, but not infrastructure projects commissioned by the government or companies in the host country. Be that as it may, we have not here considered separately the reinvestment of profits, although in the cases of foreign companies whose principal income is from sales within Colombia, such as Lenovo, Huawei, ZTE, Kerui and Foton, it is important to note that many of these are likely to be significant.

The figures listed in Table 1, above, diverge considerably from the official figures published by Colombia's Central Bank (Banco de la República 2018), as this institution limits its records to direct binational transactions, when in fact the majority of Chinese investments have not been direct but through acquisitions in third countries. For instance, Sinochem's acquisition of Emerald Petroleum in 2009 took place in London, where Emerald was listed at the time (Reuters 2009). It has developed operations in 14 fields across Colombia. Similarly, CNOOC's acquisition of assets in Colombia in 2012 was part and parcel of the company's takeover of Canadian oil giant Nexen (Cattaneo 2012).

Table 1. List of Chinese companies with quantifiable investment in Colombia, 2000-2017

Date	Investing Company	Target company	Destination sector	Employment (number of workers)	Investment (millions US dollars)
2016/11	Hytera Communications	Hytera Communications	Communications	25	4
2015/02	Foton Motor	Foton AKT (Funza)	Automotive OEM	70	12
2014/12	Huawei Technologies	Huawei Technologies Services	Communications	800	31
2013/03	Sinopec Int'l Petroleum	Mansarovar Energy Colombia Ltd	Oil	500	750
2012/07	CNOOC	Nexen Petroleum Colombia Ltd.	Oil & Gas	n/a	185
2011/09	ZTE	ZTE Colombia SAS	Communications	647	2
2010/10	Huawei	Javeriana laboratory	Communications	n/a	4
2010/08	Sinopec	Hupecol	Oil & Gas	84	280
2009/10	Sinochem	Emerald Energia	Oil & Gas	130	188
2009/05	Shandong Kerui	Kerui Colombia	Oil & Gas	167	878
2006/08	Mansarovar Energy	Mansarovar Energy Columbia Ltd	Oil & Gas	550	48
2004/05	Huawei Technologies	Huawei Technologies Colombia SAS	Communications	355	425
2004/02	ZTE Corporation	ZTE Corporation Sucursal Colombia	Communications	31	58
2000/09	Huawei Technologies	Huawei Technologies Sucursal Colombia	Communications	1	240

Source: author's compilation, incorporating material from Red ALC-China (2019).

In a case of direct involvement, Sinopec entered the oil sector when it joined forces with Indian ONGC Videsh to acquire equal parts in Omimex, renamed Mansarovar Energy Colombia and operating jointly with Ecopetrol of Colombia (Hindu Business Line 2006). This group has expanded in important ways since it was first founded, investing as much as US$ 1.5 billion within the first five years of operations, and has announced further investments to expand production (Siddiqui & Saikia 2016). In doing so, it has encountered the challenge of local resistance. In late 2018, several referendums were held by communities to vote on extractive industry activities, resulting in the rejection of these projects. However, the country's constitutional court ruled in favour of the multinational, citing the country's ownership of the subsoil (Reuters 2018). Sinochem's Emerald Industries had faced a similar situation in 2016 when local communities in the Department of

Caquetá objected to the environmental study presented by the company and argued that the environmental impact of future activities on water resources had not been properly assessed and that the license should therefore not be granted (Bermúdez 2016). Such conflicts are gaining greater visibility across Latin America, leading to a United Nations initiative to monitor Chinese companies with regards to their protection of indigenous communities and their environments (InfoAmazonia 2018).

A number of smaller firms operate as suppliers to the oil industry, such as the Colombian subsidiary of Shandong Province's Kerui Petroleum Equipment. As a result of these and other activities, the petroleum sector is the largest in terms of Chinese investments in Colombia. Chinese-owned firms are responsible for an estimated seven percent of the country's annual oil exports. Explorations have occasionally exposed engineers to risks in remote parts of Colombia controlled by armed groups rather than the government. In 2011, three employees of Emerald Energy were kidnapped together with their translator (El Tiempo 2011). Negotiations led by the company and interventions by the Colombian vice president and the Chinese embassy made their release possible a year later (see also Ma 2016).

Another prominent sector in which Chinese multinationals have made significant investments is telecommunications. Huawei has been active in Colombia since 1999 and has made several new investments since that time (see Table 1, above). Its initial efforts were geared at business-to-business marketing and it was able to gain a foothold in national telephone networks. The company broke in to smartphone production worldwide in 2009 and has since established itself as a major brand in the cell phone market globally, including Colombia. Building on strong sales, reported at US$ 678 million for 2013, Huawei opened multiple stores across the country in 2014. It expanded its visibility by becoming a leading sponsor of the Colombian national football team and signing star footballer James Rodríguez as its 'brand ambassador' for two years (EFE 2015). State-owned Zhongxing, or ZTE, has also made inroads since it was first established there in 2005 but has achieved only limited visibility. Both Huawei and ZTE have become important suppliers of data management and security surveillance systems, most notably in Ecuador, Bolivia and Venezuela. This is an area that has recently come under scrutiny from the United States –ostensibly for reasons of national security, though principally for motives of business competition and corporate self-preservation[2].

Chinese investment in the automotive sector remains nascent. Much like telecommunications, Colombia is recognized as a significant market and investments are oriented towards sales, with limited assembly taking place in the country. Only two Chinese brands, Jincheng and Jialing, have operated assembly plants in Barranquilla and Cali, respectively (Ellis 2017). While most car brands have only pursued exploratory sales in the market, Medellín-based conglomerate AKT Corbeta joined forces in 2015 with Foton of Changping near Beijing to produce mid-size pickup trucks adapted for the Colombian market (El Tiempo 2015). Six Chinese companies led by BYD failed to qualify for a public tender for electric buses to modernize Bogotá's Transmilenio bus fleet (Bermúdez 2018). The growing attention to opportunities in the Colombian market promises further Chinese involvement in the future.

In extractive sectors outside of oil, there has been only limited interest from Chinese corporations with respect to mining. This presents a significant contrast with Peru, where Chinese firms have been active since the 1990s and today are important players in the field (Creutzfeldt 2016). Chinese firms have made initial explorations and have become involved in informal (i.e. non-licensed, small-scale) mining activities with an emphasis on gold and coltan. These are highly problematic ventures often involving criminal groups and in conflict with vulnerable communities (cf. CICDHA).

Intentions to invest or otherwise engage in the Colombian market are nonetheless difficult to predict. Comments by Colombian trade representatives quoted in leaked US diplomatic cables reveal declarations of interest by Chinese companies but only a few have acted upon those statements. A senior executive for Chinese

2 Cf. comments made by the unofficial Trump advisor Steve Bannon, cited by Jun Mai in "Steve Bannon says killing Huawei more important than trade deal with China," in the *South China Morning Post*, May 22, 2019.

home appliances manufacturer Haier, for instance, accompanied vice president Xi Jinping on his 2009 visit to Bogotá and made favourable comparisons on the potential of Colombia's market and stability compared to Venezuela, but there is no evidence of subsequent investment. Colombia "is not viewed as prime FDI material by the Chinese [due to its] endemic competitiveness issues, from onerous taxes to high labour costs to poor infrastructure" (Wikileaks 2008). This status quo persists, despite the bilateral investment treaty signed between the two countries in 2008, which went into effect in 2013 (UNCTAD 2013).

Inversely, Colombian traders have been actively increasing imports of manufactured goods from China, which has helped bring down costs for consumers, benefitting the economically challenged bottom half of the country's population but also drastically inflating the trade imbalance. Chinese goods have displaced considerable segments of Colombia's own clothing, ceramic, toy, and shoe sectors. Domestic manufacturers have persuaded their government to implement safeguards to prevent dumping of Chinese consumer products on several occasions through quota restrictions on competing Chinese imports. Larger corporations, meanwhile, have instead begun entering the Chinese manufacturing sector directly by establishing offices in China and seeking cost reductions on supplies.

Conclusions and Policy Suggestions

In sum, China's interest in Colombia as an investment destination is modest in regional comparison but growing and has found new impetus since 2016. This can be explained in part by the improved security situation overall and the historic signing of the peace agreement that year. It is also important to underscore the role a charismatic ambassador has played in raising the profile of China in the country and in creating a framework to help newcomers harness the experience of established Chinese companies, helping them as they contend with the risks implicit in a highly unequal society with an extremely violent past, fiercely independent regions, and largely unchecked corruption.[3]

In Colombia, China has followed a pattern evident in other cases of investing most heavily in the extractive sector, which generates the fewest jobs and leaves Colombia poorly positioned in global value chains. An analysis of *per capita* foreign trade figures shows that although the Colombian economy is the fourth in size in the Latin American region, it occupies a modest tenth position in exports *per capita*. Despite almost twenty years of concerted efforts by the Colombian government to attract strategic investment from abroad, their economy is far from fully inserted into global markets (Reina et al. 2016:51). It remains to be seen whether Beijing's efforts to position its companies overseas can improve this situation for Colombia and help it overcome the challenges presented by the recent U.S. –led drift towards protectionism.

The responsible ministries within the Colombian government must develop the ability to better define and publicize the priorities in attracting Chinese investment, while learning from the experiences of Peru, Chile, Argentina, and Ecuador how to best tailor national goals and demands to Chinese interests. The Pacific Alliance should encourage more proactive engagement with East Asian economies, and this is an area where Colombia can learn much from the success especially Peru and Chile have had in expanding product and brand presence in the Chinese market.

Colombia would also do well to build on Memorandums signed during the Santos presidency and recognize the value of the Chinese companies with hands-on experience in the country, by fomenting consortiums and helping build trust between actors from both sides. Beijing has made clear its intentions to increase rather than reduce its footprint in Colombia –the size and location of the projected new embassy is as clear a statement of intent as any (Taylor 2018). The possibilities of enhanced bilateral engagement have been researched and outlined by the Chinese (Chai

3 Even in the aftermath of the *Lava Jato* scandal that saw political leaders from Brazil, Peru and other countries removed from power and placed behind bars, Colombia has not seen a comparable process despite the evidence, thanks to the firm grip on power held by a deeply corrupt elite unafraid of violent suppression of witnesses.

et al. 2012), but Colombia has been unable to properly set forth a vision. It is likely that President Ivan Duque, the country's leader since August 2018, will undertake a mission to China within his first year in office, but it is unclear if his cabinet has the capacity to improve on the limp record of the last presidential visit (cf. Puyana 2012).

Finally, it is essential for Colombian civil society to prepare adequately for the likely growth of Chinese activities in the extractive sector. The People's Republic of China, though rich in guidelines, has a poor track record in terms of the protection of the environment and the rights of ethnic minorities. National interests declared by the Colombian government are typically defined by the political elite and frequently run counter to local interests and priorities, as evidenced by the growing number of community protests. While Chinese companies lean on the Communist Party apparatus to quash dissent, companies in Colombia habitually resort to criminal organizations and hired assassins. It is not in the interest of the people of Colombia to sacrifice their land and their well-being to the over-hyped phantom of economic growth.

References

Banco de la República de Colombia. 2018. *Flujos de inversión directa – balanza de pagos.* BRC: Bogotá. www.banrep.gov.co/es/inversion-directa.

Beijing Review. 1985. "Zhao in Latin America: Seeing Is Believing." Vol 28, no. 47 (November), pp. 6-7.

Bermúdez Liévano, Andrés. 2016. "Sinochem Stuck without 'Social Licence' to Extract Oil in Colombia." *Diálogo Chino,* 21st November.

_____ 2018. "Bogotá Rejects Chinese Electric Buses." *Diálogo Chino,* 8th November.

Bermúdez Torres, César Augusto. 2010. "La Doctrina Respice Polum ('Mirar hacia el Norte') en la práctica de las relaciones internacionales de Colombia durante el siglo XX." *Memorias* 7, no. 12: 189-222.

Cattaneo, Claudia. 2012. "China's CNOOC to buy Nexen for $15.1-billion." *Financial Post,* 23 July.

Chai Yu et al. 2012. "中国-哥伦比亚自由贸易协定研究 [Study on the China-Colombia Free Trade Agreement]." 拉丁美洲研究 *[Latin American Research]* 34(4), pp. 3-13.

ChinaCEA. 2015. "Capital Airport Holding Company CAH – Colombia Project." 25 March. www.chinacea.com/en/content/details_53_1044.html.

China en América Latina. 2016. "Plan Maestro del Río Magdalena." 8 August. www.chinaenamericalatina.info/es/2016/08/08/plan-maestro-del-rio-magdalena-2/.

Colombia, Ministerio de Relaciones Exteriores. 2010. *Colombia y China: Treinta años de amistad y cooperación*. Bogotá: Ministerio de Relaciones Exteriores.

Colombia, Ministerio de Comercio, Industria y Turismo. 2018. *Investigaciones con Derechos Antidumping Vigentes,* July.

Colombia Reports. 2018 (July). "Foreign Direct Investment (FDI)." https://data.colombiareports.com/colombia-fdi-statistics/.

Creutzfeldt, Benjamin. 2012. *China en América Latina: Reflexiones sobre las Relaciones Transpacíficas*. Bogotá: Universidad Externado de Colombia.

____ 2016. "Not All Plain Sailing: Opportunities and Pitfalls for Chinese Investment in Peru." *Asian Perspective* 40, no. 4: 603-26.

____ 2018. "Diplomacia cultural china en Colombia, alcances y resistencias." *La política cultural de China en América Latina*. In, Cornejo, Romer (edit.). *La política cultural de China en América Latina*. Mexico: Colegio de Mexico, pp. 199-228.

Creutzfeldt, Benjamin and Tatiana Gélvez. 2011. "Un dragón en Colombia: Realidad o cuento chino?" *Revista Zero* 25, pp. 110-115.

EFE. 2015. "James Rodríguez será la imagen de Huawei en Colombia por dos años." 8th May, www.efe.com/efe/america/gente/james-rodriguez-sera-la-imagen-de-huawei-en-colombia-por-dos-anos/20000014-2606972.

Ellis, R. Evan. 2017. "Chinese Advances and Setbacks in Colombia." *IndraStra* 3(5).

El Tiempo. 2011. "Secuestran a tres chinos en Caquetá." 9 June, www.eltiempo.com/archivo/documento/CMS-9573466.

El Tiempo. 2015. "Foton inauguró su planta de ensamblaje en Colombia." 25 August.

Fleischer, Friederike. 2005. "La diáspora china en Colombia" *(Manuscript)*. Universidad Nacional de Colombia.

García Tobón, Carlos. 2009. *China: Su Larga Marcha hasta la Globalización*. Bogotá: Universidad Javeriana.

Gómez Díaz, Diana Andrea and Luz M. Díaz. 2016. "Las organizaciones chinas en Colombia." *Migración y Desarrollo* 14(26), pp. 75-110.

Gómez Peña, Natalia and Karla Díaz. 2017. *Inversiones Chinas en Colombia: ¿Cómo van los Proyectos con Participación China en el País?* Bogotá: Asociación Ambiente y Sociedad.

Hindu Business Line. 2006. "ONGC-Sinopec acquires Columbian oil firm." 22nd September, www.thehindubusinessline.com/todays-paper/tp-corporate/ONGC-Sinopec-acquires-Columbian-oil-firm/article20222164.ece?ref=archive.

InfoAmazonia. 2018. "Inversiones chinas en la Cuenca Amazónica, bajo la lupa de Naciones Unidas." *El Espectador,* 8th November.

Koop, Fermin. 2015. "China enfrenta problemas de imagen en Colombia." *Diálogo Chino,* 20 August.

Latin American Herald Tribune. 2009. "China Vice President Xi Jinping Meets With Colombia's Uribe About Investments." 17th February.

Ma, Tianjie. 2016. "Oil, Monkeys and Guerrillas: Chinese Companies Face Problems in the Amazon." *Diálogo Chino,* 22nd November.

Marín Rivas, María del Pilar. 2017. "Las violaciones de Derechos Humanos en Colombia durante los años 80 del siglo XX: Acercamiento a su comprensión histórica desde la degradación y el fortalecimiento de la defensa." *Anuario de Historia Regional y de las Fronteras* 22(1), pp. 113-35.

Marriaga, Natalia. 2012. "Crónicas de China en Colombia: Esperando al Señor Chang." *China Files.* 21 November.

Ministry of Foreign Affairs, People's Republic of China (MoFa). 2015. "中国与拉美和加勒比国家合作规划 [Cooperation Plan between China and the Countries of Latin America and Caribbean]." Beijing.

____ 2018 (August). "中国同哥伦比亚的关系 [China's Relations with Colombia]." Beijing.

OECD. 2008. *Benchmark Definition of Foreign Direct Investment (4th Edition)*. Paris: OECD Publishing.

Ortiz Velásquez, Samuel. 2017. "Inversión Extranjera Directa de China en América Latina y el Caribe, aspectos metodológicos y tendencias durante 2001-2016." *Economía Informa*, no. 406: 4-17.

Pastrana Buelvas, Eduardo, and Hubert Gehring (eds.). 2017. *La Proyección de China en América Latina y el Caribe*. Bogotá: Editorial Javeriana.

Puyana, Guillermo. 2012. "Fuegos Fatuos (Santos en China)." *Portafolio*, 15th May.

Reina, Mauricio and Sandra Oviedo. 2014. "Colombia and Asia: Trying to Make up for Lost Time." In, Arnson, Cynthia, Jorge Heine and Christine Zaino (edits.). *Reaching across the Pacific: Latin America and Asia in the New Century*. Washington, DC: Woodrow Wilson Center, pp. 253-291.

Reina, Mauricio (et al.). 2016. *Impacto Económico de la Inversión Extranjera Directa en Colombia*. Bogotá, DC: Fedesarrollo, Centro de Investigación Económica y Social.

Reuters. 2009. "Sinochem agrees $878 million buy of Emerald Energy." Thomson Reuters, 12th August, www.reuters.com/article/us-sinochem-emerald-idUSTRE57B1SF20090812.

Reuters. 2009. "UPDATE 1-Court says Colombia votes cannot block mining, oil projects." CNBC, 11th October, www.cnbc.com/2018/10/11/reuters-america-update-1-court-says-colombia-votes-cannot-block-mining-oil-projects.html.

Revista Semana. 2018. "China: Poder, Tradición, Comercio, Innovación (Edición Especial). October.

Rudas Lleras, Guillermo and Mauricio Cabrera Leal. 2015. "Colombia and China: Social and Environmental Impact of Trade and Foreign Direct Investment." In, Ray, Rebecca, Kevin P. Gallagher, Andrés López and Cynthia Sanborn (edits.). *China in Latin America.* Boston: Global Economic Governance Initiative.

Sanborn, Cynthia. 2018. "From Extraction to Construction." *ReVista: Harvard Review of Latin America,* Fall.

Sanmiguel, Inés. 2006. "Japoneses en Colombia: Historia de inmigración, sus descendientes en Japón." *Revista de Estudios Sociales,* no. 23 (April): 81-96.

Seligman, Lara. 2018. "U.S. Military Targets Growing Russian and Chinese Influence in Latin America." *Foreign Policy,* 19 November.

Semana. 2011. "Chinos realizan estudio preliminar de 'canal seco' en Colombia." 18 February, www.semana.com/economia/articulo/chinos-realizan-estudio-preliminar-canal-seco-colombia/235705-3.

Siddiqui, Huma and Siddhartha P. Saikia. 2016. "ONCG Videsh plans to invest $500 million to up output from Colombia." *Financial Express,* 9th March.

Taylor, Luke. 2018. "A Dead Drug Lord's Mansion and China's New Colombian Connections." *South China Morning Post,* 9th September.

Torrijos Legazpi, José María. 2014. "Chinos en Panamá: Una Mayoría Desconocida." *La Estrella de Panamá,* 30th March.

UNCTAD. 2018. "Foreign Direct Investment: Inward and Outward Flows and Stock, Annual." http://unctadstat.unctad.org/wds/ReportFolders/reportFolders.aspx.

Vieira Posada, Edgar, ed. 2013. *La Transformación de China y su impacto para Colombia.* Bogotá: CESA.

Wieland, Carsten. 2007. "Uribes Kampf an Doppelter Front." *KAS-Länderberichte.* Bonn: Konrad-Adenauer-Stiftung.

Wikileaks. 2008. *Taming the Dragon: Colombia's Economic Relationship with China.* Bogotá: U.S. Embassy.

Other links

AECC. Asociación de Empresas Chinas en Colombia, www.aecc.com.co

CCCIC. Cámara Colombo-China de Inversión y Comercio, www.camaracolombochina.com

CICDHA. Colectivo sobre Financiamiento e Inversiones Chinas, Derechos Humanos y Ambiente, http://chinaambienteyderechos.lat/

CHINESE OFDI IN VENEZUELA (2000-2017)

CONDITIONS, CHALLENGES AND POLICY PROPOSALS

Carlos Eduardo Piña

Introduction

The relationship between the People's Republic of China and Venezuela has been one of the most dynamic alliances that the Asian nation has had with a Latin American country since it began implementing its global opening strategy in the year 2000. The confluence of foreign policy views, both countries' need to diversify energy markets, and the possibility of increasing large-scale commercial exchanges set in motion the establishment of a unique cooperation model in Latin America.

The Chinese-Venezuelan alliance has fostered numerous studies exploring the scope of the loans which the Asian nation has made to Venezuela. But studies of outbound foreign direct investment (OFDI) from China to this South American country have not been as abundant, suggesting an academic void on the topic.

The purpose of this article is to analyze the impact of the outflows of foreign direct investment from China to Venezuela between 2000-2017, as well as collaborate with the efforts made by the Chinese-ALC Academic Network regarding the collection of data on transactions made between 2000 and 2017.

This chapter first aims to describe the most important aspects of the relationship between China and Venezuela since Hugo Chávez came to power in 1999. The impact of China's outbound foreign direct investment on Venezuelan economy is then analyzed, using figures provided by the OFDI Monitor and other official sources. Finally, the third chapter provides a series of conclusions and policy suggestions with the aim of suggesting improvements in the decision-making process for public policies.

China's Relationship with Venezuela (2000-2017)

Venezuela and China established diplomatic relations in June 1974 during the presidency of Carlos Andrés Pérez. By then, the South American country was diversifying its political and economic ties, based on its role as an oil exporter, founder of OPEC, and driving force for North-South dialogue (Elsa Cardozo 1992). By 1999, they had signed 36 cooperation agreements in scientific and technical areas, commercial, agricultural, livestock and fishing, and even in the hydrocarbon sector, generating an exchange between 1974-1999 of close to US$ 100 million (White Book, MPPRE 2013).

Hugo Chávez made four official visits to China, starting when he came to power in 1999, 2001, 2004 and in 2006. The first meetings' objective was to design the "China-Venezuela Energy Strategic Plan 2001-2011" and define the "High Level Mixed Commission". This vision of foreign policy as a strategic exchange, which became evident in the following six years of Chávez/s government, was guided by 1) the Economic and Social Development Plan of the Nation 2001-2007; and 2) the National Project Simon Bolivar 2007-2013 : the First Socialist Economic and Social Development Plan of the Nation 2007-2013 (Brandt 2016).

In the beginning, there was a degree of continuity in Venezuela's traditional foreign policy. However, the changes implemented by Chávez progressively became more evident, especially the promotion of Latin American cooperation and integration, with an emphasis on the Caribbean and South America, and the diversification of political, economic and commercial relations with non-traditional nations, particularly with China. These relationships were based upon principles of interdependence, mutual respect, cooperation and self-determination, with an eye on promoting multi-polarity.

These transformations in Venezuela's foreign policy were influenced by ideological and geopolitical determinants and financed with their oil export revenues. The 2002 failed coup d'état and a 63-day oil strike led to the deterioration of relations with the United States and increased the confluence of the interests between Caracas and Beijing. While the former sought to reduce its dependence on the power of the north using its energy resources, mainly hydrocarbons, the latter, advancing an "internationalization process" strategically positioned itself in the Orinoco Oil Belt and the Mining Arc (Brandt 2016).

The result of these events was an increase in the trade balance between both countries. In 2001, the trade balance was around US$ 437 million; by 2017 this figure had reached US$ 8.95 billion, a twentyfold increase. Moreover, it should be noted that by 2017 China had become Venezuela´s second most important trading partner behind the United States, surpassing the European Union and India (World Trade Map; European Commission 2018). The trade balance between both countries has been favorable to Venezuela since 2005, due to the income generated by oil exports and a fall in imports from China to the South American country.

Meanwhile, outbound foreign direct investment (OFDI) from China to Venezuela has been approximately US$ 3.1 billion in the last 17 years (Monitor of China's OFDI and MOFCOM 2018). This OFDI can be divided in three different stages: the first one between 2000 and 2006, which there were investments close to US$ 38 million. In the second one, during 2007 and 2011 period, Chinese OFDI grew by US$ 674 million, which constitutes a leap equivalent to 17 times the previous amount, and was aimed at the automotive, oil, telecommunications, electronic equipment and mining sectors. Finally, during the 2012-2016 period, investments showed a 335% growth, standing at US$ 2.2 billion, with construction (housing) being the highest expenditure followed by developments in the Orinoco Oil Belt, automotive industry, and equipment for the construction sector. It should be noted that at the time of writing this document, it was not possible to verify new investments in

2017. Per sector, 55% of Chinese OFDI in Venezuela has been invested in the service sector, with disbursements of US$ 1.6 billion, US$ 696 million or 23.4% in raw materials, and finally US$ 627 million or its equivalent of 21.08% in the industrial sector.

This disaggregated review highlights infrastructure works such as Ciudad Tiuna (housing) in Gran Misión Vivienda Venezuela, the developments of Barrio Nuevo Barrio Tricolor, the construction of the section of the Santa Lucía-Kempis highway in Miranda state, construction in the oil sector, and other projects which for many reasons did not materialize, such as the national railway system.

Venezuelan-Chinese Joint Financing Fund (FFCCV)

In order to better understand Chinese OFDI in Venezuela it is necessary to analyze the financing that the Asian country has granted it through short and long-term revolving funds. Public investment projects are executed under cooperation schemes in which Venezuela diversifies its oil placements and China exports the goods and services required in agreed projects. These arrangements position both public and private companies to benefit and promote investments in Latin America and the Caribbean.

Venezuela has received resources from China for US$ 62.2 billion, with which 790 projects have been financed, both public investments and FDI in fusion with Chinese state companies. Out of these, 495 have been completed, 205 are in progress, and 90 are in the start-up phase (Reuters News, July 2018)

Sino-Venezuelan funds sometimes use technological transfers in key economic sectors to increase productivity in Venezuela. They are created via Chinese contributions through the China Development Bank (CDB) and Venezuelan contributions through the National Development Fund. Resources received through the Venezuelan Chinese Joint Financing Fund are payable within a maximum term of up to three years and those received by the Long Term Volume Fund (LTVF) up to ten, with both applying a quarterly LIBOR rate (short term) and half yearly (long term). Also, LTVF loan included SHIBOR rate- in the case of the part established in Yuan Ren Min Bi –plus a margin that ranges between 50 and 300 basis points approximately (Díaz 2017).

Once each of the tranches has been canceled, they are reimbursable and renewable up to two times. So, between 2007 and 2017, Venezuela received US$ 50 billion through the FFCCV and the LTVF. Likewise, the South American country has made contributions for US$ 12 billion, for a total of resources from the FFCCV of US$ 62 billion. Out of the contributions made by China, US$ 16 billion have been fully paid for tranches A and B and their first renewals (See Table 1).

Table 1. China-Venezuela Joint Fund Structure (in $US million)

Total Amounts (MM USD)		Contributions from China	Contributions from Venezuela
Date		Short Term Funds	
Nov-07	Tranche A	4,000	2,000
Apr-09	Tranche B	4,000	2,000
Jun-11	Tranche A-II	4,000	2,000
Aug-12	Tranche B-II	4,000	2,000
Nov-13	Tranche C	5,000	1,000
Jul-14	Tranche A-III	4,000	2,000
Apr-15	Tranche B-III	5,000	1,000
SUB - TOTAL		**30,000**	**12,000**
Date		Long Term Funds	
Aug-10	Tranche I (USD)	10,000	0
Aug-10	Tranche II (RMB)*	10,000	0
SUB - TOTAL		20,000	0
TOTAL		**50,000**	**12,000**

Source: author's elaboration based on PDVSA (2017).

In accounting and methodological terms, for purposes of classification in national accounts, the financing received through China represents a liability for Venezuela and is paid with oil barrels equivalent to the depreciation, capital, and interest payments. Payments are calculated based on the interest rate, payment terms, and the maturity of the loan received. Public investments executed with resources from the Chinese-Venezuelan Funds are not therefore Chinese OFDI in Venezuela. However, some investments realized by Chinese enterprises were channeled through FFCCV, especially those in which joint ventures have been established and a participation in share capital, under previous agreement, has been set aside for Chinese companies.

Notable examples would include the following joint ventures: Venezolana de Industrias Tecnológicas (VIT), Empresa Venezolana de Telecomunicaciones (VTELCA), Orinoquia telephone company, HAIER Venezuela, and YUTONG Venezuela. Venezuela has also seen the creation of some joint ventures servicing the oil sector such as ITC and CV Shipping.

The bilateral relationship between Venezuela and China, viewed from the broad perspective of OFDI from the Asian country by sectors and amounts, the activities of the Venezuelan Chinese Joint Financing Fund, and trade balance statistics, now appears to fit the characterization made by Sun Hungbo (2013): "Cooperation between China and Venezuela is a fairly mature model, being of plural cooperation with energy as its main axis."

Figure 1. Venezuela's Foreign Direct Investment Inflows and Outflows (2000-2017) (in $US million)

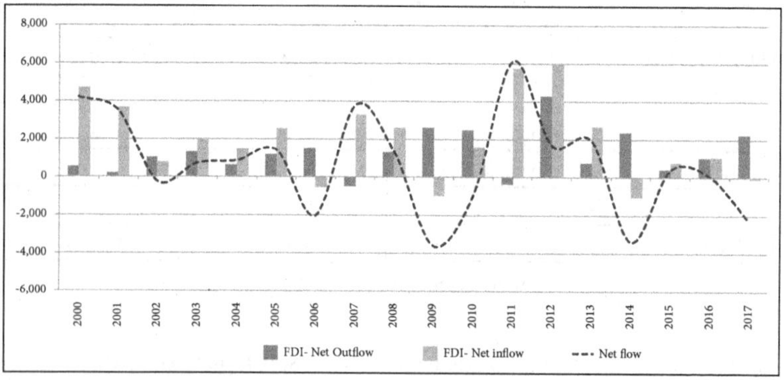

Source: author's elaboration based on BCV of Payments Quarterly Brief and UNCTAD (2018)

Foreign Direct Investment (FDI) in Venezuela has demonstrated variable behavior both in inflows and outflows to the economy between 2000-2017. In most years, investment inflow has been higher than the outflow but from 2002, in addition to increasing the outflows, the investment inflows fell abruptly. From then on both flows became more volatile.

Some events that explain the behavior of FDI inflows and outflows in Venezuela between 2000 and 2017 are the following:

1) In 1996, an adjustment program supported by the International Monetary Fund (IMF) called "Agenda Venezuela" was applied in Venezuela to attract FDI in the oil sector through operational agreements, strategic partnerships, and shared profits
2) 2002-2003 were years of political instability, producing an economic contraction, which in turn triggered the process of restructuring national public debt and the application of an exchange control regime
3) During 2004-2008, there was a recovery in oil prices, which allowed for economic growth, the accumulation of international reserves, and the creation of parafiscal structures that enhanced public investment
4) 2007-2008 saw the beginning of nationalization and the expropriation of private companies, the revocation of concessions and the activation of a secondary capital market, which, in tandem with other factors, caused capital flight
5) Also in 2007, financing from China as a complement to the National Development Fund began to flow into Venezuela, bolstering public investment
6) In 2008, the global financial crisis broke out and oil prices collapsed, causing the contraction of imports between 2009-2010 and slowing economic growth
7) The Presidential elections of 2012 required securing new investments to maintain public spending to complete public works in execution. In 2013 with the death of President Hugo Chávez, the economy entered a phase of slowdown with rising inflation, resulting from the exhaustion of foreign currency liquidity. Imports fell, and the overall situation was aggravated by the fall in international oil prices during the second half of 2014.

Chinese OFDI in Venezuela (2000-2017)

Chinese OFDI in Venezuela between 2000 and 2017 was US$ 3.1 billion (Monitor of China's OFDI and others, 2018). This figure represents approximately 8.1% of the total FDI inflows into the country during this period (BCV, Report 18K and others).

Chinese OFDI in Venezuela can be divided into different stages between 2000 and 2017. There was a period of low dynamism between 2000-2006, a moderate stage of dynamism with average investments around US$ 100 and US$ 200 million between 2007 and 2011, another period of high investments but with some volatility between 2012 and 2016, and finally, a marked fall in 2017, a year in which there were no investment inflows from the Asian country (see Figure 2).

Figure 2. Chinese ODFI in Venezuela (2000-2017)

(in $US million)

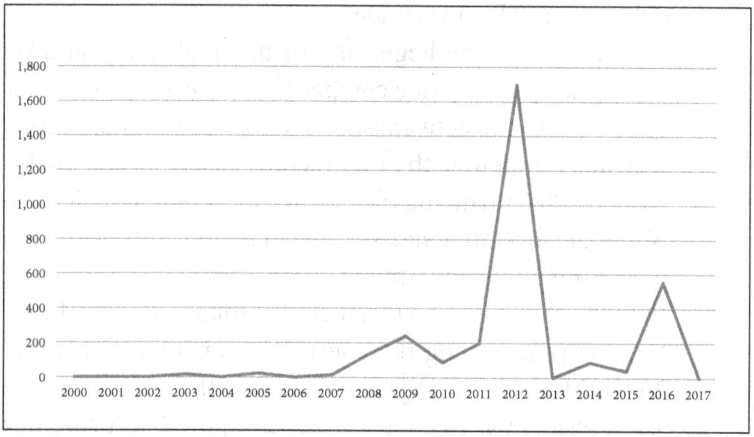

Source: author's elaboration based on Red ALC-China (2018) and MOFCOM.

In comparison with the rest of Latin America, Venezuela accounts for 2.8% of the total Chinese FDI inflows in the region, which stood at US$ 109.1 billion (Monitor of China's OFDI and MOFCOM, several years). Venezuela ranks sixth in Latin American countries among recipients of Chinese OFDI in the 21st century, surpassed by Brazil, Peru, Argentina, Chile, and Mexico.

The number of transactions carried out by Chinese companies in Venezuela during 2000 and 2017 was 19, which represents 5.8% of the total transactions made in Latin America during that period (Dussel Peters 2018). This number of disbursements contrasts with the number of projects transacted via the FFCCV, which reached 790 in the same period. The preference for debt mechanisms as a primary means of channeling investments and trade exchanges reflects a difference between the Chinese-Venezuelan cooperation model applied to Venezuela and the schemes that the Asian nation has applied to the rest of Latin America.[1]

It is possible to identify patterns of transactions within Venezuelan economy (Ortiz Velázquez 2017). For example, Chinese investments made in the automotive industry through Chery, Yutong, and Great Wall Motors, in telecommunications by Huawei and ZTE, and in electronic components by Haier have been made through a business model in which the Venezuelan state ensured the purchase of all the production of these companies. This arrangement was made possible by the state-partner nature of these joint ventures.

Similar patterns emerged in the construction sector, especially with the Ciudad Tiuna housing complex built by CITIC, which aimed to benefit social sectors with few economic resources (CITIC Annual Report 2014). Again, the Venezuelan state ended up acquiring ownership of the houses built (Ellis 2014). Meanwhile, the participation of Chinese OFDI in the oil sector was intended to pay the commitments acquired by Venezuela through the agreement of the FFCCV (Hongbo 2014; Gerdel 2016).

With regard to type of investment, approximately 70% of Chinese OFDI in Venezuela has been directed to greenfield projects and the remaining 30% in mergers and acquisitions. This is different from the patterns observed in the rest of Latin America, where mergers and acquisitions have represented the largest share of Chinese OFDI in the region (Dussel Peters 2018).

1 Data regarding Outbound Foreign Direct Investment (OFDI) from China to Venezuela, especially information related to transactions, amounts and employment, was extracted from the Monitor of Chinese OFDI in Latin America and the Caribbean.

Most of the greenfield projects took place between 2011 and 2016 and were related to the opening of commercial offices, factories, and expansion of capital in businesses that were already positioned in the country, such as Huawei, the China Development Bank, and Chery Automobile (Monitor of China's OFDI 2018).

Mergers and acquisitions between 2005 and 2010 were largely joint-ventures in which the Venezuelan state was guaranteed the majority of the shareholding. A series of companies were formed between Chinese companies and their Venezuelan counterparts in telecommunications, electronic equipment, hydrocarbons, and automotive industries.

With the exception of the oil sector, most initial investments on the part of Venezuelan came from the FFCCV and Chinese contributions were granted in exchange for the transfer of technology in sectors with high added value products. The following companies demonstrate the trend:

- Venezolana de Industrias Tecnológicas (VIT) (2005): between the Ministry of Basic Industries of Venezuela and Langchao, with a participation of 51% and 49%, respectively
- Compañía Venezolana de Telecomunicaciones (VTELCA) (2007): between the state business, Corpivensa, and ZTE, with a shareholding of 84.3% and 15.7%, respectively (Prensa Vtelca, Official Gazette 38.784, 2007)
- Compañía de Teléfonos Orinoquia (2009): between the Venezuelan company Telecom Venezuela and Huawei, with a share percentage of 65/35%, respectively (Prensa CONAPRI; Huawei Annual Report 2009; Official Gazette 39.150)
- Haier Venezuela Assembly Plant (2010): between Corpivensa and Haier Group Company, with a shareholding of 85/15%, respectively (Venezuelas News Agency; Haier Venezuela 2012)
- Yutong Venezuela Bus Assembly Plant (2015): between the Ministries of Transport and Commerce of Venezuela and Yutong Hong Kong Limited, with a participation of 85/15%, respectively (Official Gazette 40.763 2015)

- In the oil sector, an alliance between CNPC and PDVSA stands out through Petrourica, Petrozumano, Petrolera Sinovensa, and Petrolera Sinovenezolana (PDVSA 2017).

Chinese OFDI and its Impact on Employment Generation

Chinese OFDI in Venezuela has generated approximately 14,601 jobs distributed in the main sectors of Venezuelan economy. For each position generated there has been an investment of US$ 211,697, a figure that is below the trend registered in Latin America, which was US$ 370,348 (Dussel Peters 2018).

Job positions per sector are distributed as follows: 1) Manufacturing with 11,794 jobs (80.8%); 2) services with 2,169 jobs (14.8%); and 3) raw materials with 633 jobs (4.3%). Most of the positions created by Chinese OFDI in Venezuela have been related to the installation of factories for Haier, ZTE, Huawei, and Yutong, as well as the Chery assembly plants.

Trends are mixed with respect to the quality of employment. In the raw materials sector, the use of unskilled labor has been privileged. Meanwhile, in the industrial and services sectors, specifically in those factories with higher added value products, Venezuela has made sure to have a portion of native staff trained at the headquarters of Chinese companies (VTELCA 2005; Ministry of University Education 2012; VIT 2011).

Debates and Discussions about Chinese OFDI in Venezuela 2000-2017

The negotiation, approval, and implementation of the tranches of the Chinese-Venezuelan Joint Financing Fund have captured most of the attention of analysts inside and outside Venezuela, in no small part because of the amount of money that has entered the country through this route. The debate on transactions carried out from FDI has been relegated to second place in terms of importance. Other discussions have revolved around the incentive structure offered by the Venezuelan government in order to guarantee the lowest risk to Chinese investments. These incentives guaranteed the purchase of Chinese products by state companies, the allocation of foreign currency, and the creation of a legal framework in accordance with the Asian country's business interests.[2] As a result, Chinese investments in Venezuela increased exponentially between 2007 and 2015 at the same time that Venezuela lost OFDI from other countries.

In addition, it is important to remark that between 2016 and 2017 Venezuela faced an economic crisis due to a collapse of international oil prices, causing a drop in the country's gross domestic product and a slowdown in goods and services consumption. In consequence, a great amount of Chinese direct investments in Venezuela have stalled or even been abandoned. Some analysts and opposition politicians considered this stagnation as a failure in China's economic strategy in Venezuela, which has resulted in a debate aimed at understanding whether the Chinese strategy has been successful or not.

Conclusions

1) China's foreign direct investment in Venezuela between 2000 and 2017 reached US$3,1 billon, which represents 8.1% of the total FDI the country has received during that period. Within Latin America, Venezuela represents 2.8% of the total invested
2) Chinese investors preferred to use OFDI mechanisms to carry out construction and manufacturing projects with high added value, while the FFCCV has channeled most of inflows to oil and mining sectors

2 One of the most notable cases of Venezuelan state cooperation with Chinese enterprises has been in the automotive sector, where since 2001 a public-private company named "Corporación ZGT" sold some car assembly factories to produce cars under the Chery brand. The Great Wall Motors plant was expropriated in Carabobo State in 2013 and acquired a few days later for Corporation ZGT to produce Chery cars in Venezuela

3) The cooperation model established by both countries between 2000 and 2017 has been characterized by strong dynamism in all of its areas, having the structure of the Chinese-Venezuelan Joint Financing Fund as its main axis
4) Disbursements by concept of OFDI look relatively small compared to the resources delivered through debt
5) Commercial exchange has been handled exclusively by the Venezuelan State, which reduces the risks inherent to the investment and made it easier for the Asian country to position some of its companies and brands in areas such as telecommunications, mobile communications, and the automotive industry
6) It is necessary to consider the strategic approach of the presence of China in the country with the largest proven oil reserves and one of the largest reserves of gold, coltan and minerals and rare earths in the world. This is perhaps a significant reason for the Asian country to continue its investments in this nation, despite criticisms made in academic circles both in China and the world, which question such decision.
7) Caracas has forged a privileged relationship with Beijing in spite of the economic difficulties faced in Venezuela in recent years. Even in 2014, the year in which international oil prices collapsed, Presidents Xi Jinping and Nicolás Maduro elevated the bilateral relationship to the level of an "Integral Strategic Alliance"
8) However, Venezuela shows institutional and operational vulnerability which has prevented it from negotiating its relationship with China on better terms that would strengthen the areas that could truly result in development

Policy Suggestions

1. Venezuela should review its relationship with China to obtain advantageous treatment in the medium and long term. It should promote improvements in its technical and technological capabilities so that it can become more than a supplier of raw materials in exchange for economic resources from loans and credit lines
2. Venezuela should improve its economic and social indicators to ensure greater stability and attract Chinese OFDI in areas besides oil and mining
3. Greater transparency in terms of access to information regarding Chinese OFDI as well as other types of financing granted by that China is needed
4. Venezuela should increase compliance with the comptroller and surveillance mechanisms established in its legal system

References

Agencia Venezolana de Noticias. 2012. "Planta de electrodomésticos Haier en Yare: un complejo industrial que producirá 815.000 electrodomésticos al año". November 16; available at: https://www.aporrea.org/actualidad/n218268.html

Agencia Venezolana de Noticias. 2016. "Balance: 30 mil millones de dólares en inversión petrolera reflejan confianza en Venezuela". December 31; available at: https://www.aporrea.org/energia/n302185.html

América Economía. 2013. "Venezuela expropia firma Great Wall para aumentar producción de Chery" August 07; available at: https://www.americaeconomia.com/negocios-industrias/venezuela-expropia-firma-great-wall-para-aumentar-produccion-de-chery

BBC Mundo. 2017. "De 170.000 a 2.768 vehículos por año: las cifras de la debacle de la producción de autos en Venezuela"; available at: https://www.bbc.com/mundo/noticias-america-latina-38646110

Brandt, Carlos. 2016. *Hacia la construcción de la seguridad energética Suramericana. La propuesta petrolera de Venezuela (2002-2012)*. Doctoral Thesis, Universidad Central de Venezuela: Caracas.

Cardozo, Elsa. 1992. *Continuidad y consistencia en quince años de la política exterior venezolana 1969-1984*. Venezuela: UCV.

CEPAL (Economic Commission for Latin America and the Caribbean). 2015. "Latin American Economic Outlook 2016: Toward a New Partnership with China"; available at: http://www.cepal.org/en/node/35347

ChinaCarTimes.com. 2011. "Chery to invest 200 million in Venezuela with new Factory"; available at: https://autowise.com/chery-to-invest-200-million-in-venezuela-with-new-factory

CITIC (China International Trust and Investment Corporation). 2014. *Annual Report 2014*; available at: https://www.citic.com/uploadfile/2017/0425/20170425013556270.pdf

Computerworld.com. 2012. "Huawei inaugura en Caracas su primera tienda comercial fuera de China". May 25; available at: http://www.cwv.com.ve/huawei-inaugura-en-caracas-su-primera-tienda-comercial-fuera-de-china/

CONAPRI. 2009. "Estiman iniciar en diciembre operaciones de Industria Electrónica Orinoquia". November 26; available at: http://bpi.conapri.org/ArticleDetailIV.asp?articleid=348092&CategoryId2=15143

Culshaw, Fabiana. 2014. "El Fondo Chino auxilia al gobierno venezolano en la crisis económica" *Debates IESA*, pp.64-66

Dussel Peters, Enrique. 2018. Monitor of Chinese OFDI in Latin America and the Caribbean 2018. Red ALC-China: México; available at: http://www.redalc2china.org/monitor/images/pdfs/menuprincipal/DusselPeters_MonitorOFDI_201 8_Eng.pdf

Ellis, Evan. 2014. *China on the Groud in Latin America: challenges for the Chinese and impacts on the Region*. London: Palgrave McMillan.

Escuela Venezolana de Planificación (EVP). 2012. *Lecturas de China. Cuadernos Notas Docentes*. Caracas: Ediciones EVP.

Finanzas Digital. 2014. "Mi Casa Bien Equipada ha colocado más de 3 millones de electrodomésticos chinos en 4 años". May 14; available at: http://www.finanzasdigital.com/2014/05/mi-casa-bien-equipada-ha-vendido-mas-de-3-millones-de-electrodomesticos-chinos-en-4-anos/

Gerdel, Aymara. 2018. *China en la política de diversificación de mercados del sector petrolero venezolano durante el siglo XXI*. Universidad Central de Venezuela.

Huawei. 2009. *Huawei Annual Report 2009*; available at: https://www.huawei.com/ucmf/groups/public/documents/webasset/hw_092117.pdf

ICBC. 2011. "China's Chery Auto to Build Plant in Venezuela"; available at: http://www.icbc.com.cn/icbc/market%20review/chinas%20chery%20auto%20to%20build%20plant%20in%20venezuela.htm

Informe 21. 2016. "Venezuela firma acuerdos con CNPC de China por $2.200 millones". November 17; available at: https://informe21.com/economia/venezuela-firma-acuerdos-con-cnpc-de-china-por-2200-millones

Inter-American Dialogue. 2018. "Chinese Finance to Latin America and the Caribbean in 2017". March 8; available at: https://www.thedialogue.org/analysis/chinese-finance-to-latin-america-and-the-caribbean-in-2017/

"La mina Sosa Méndez". 2015. Correo del Caroní, May 18; available at: http://correodelcaroni.com/index.php/opinion/item/31761-la-mina-sosa-mendez

La Radio del Sur. 2016. "Eulogio Del Pino: Firma de acuerdos con CNPC incrementará producción en Faja del Orinoco". November 18; available at: https://laradiodelsur.com.ve/eulogio-del-pino-firma-de-acuerdos-con-cnpc-incrementara-produccion-en-faja-del-orinoco/

MEDIUM. 2017. "Financiamientos desde el Fondo Conjunto Chino-Venezolano". August 31. In: https://medium.com/@bienvo89/financiamientos-desde-el-fondo-conjunto-chino-venezolano-b6cf132ab932

MINCI (Ministerio del Poder Popular para la Comunicación e Información). 2017. "Un total de 472 acuerdos han sido suscritos entre China y Venezuela en los últimos años". December 22; available at: www.minci.gov.ve

Ministerio del Poder Popular para las Relaciones Exteriores, 2012. Acuerdos suscritos entre la República Bolivariana de Venezuela y la República Popular China. Material mimeografiado.

Ministerio del Poder Popular para las Relaciones Exteriores, 2013. White Paper. Caracas: Venezuela.

Ministerio del Poder Popular para las Relaciones Exteriores. Embajada de Venezuela en China. 2014. "Inaugurada oficina de representación del Banco de Desarrollo de China en Caracas". July 20. available at: http://china.embajada.gob.ve

Ortiz Velazquez, Samuel. 2016. *Performance of China's* OFDI *(2005-2014) According to Two Methodological Approaches: Asset/Liability and Directional.* Red ALC-China: Mexico.

PDVSA (Petróleos de Venezuela S.A). 2017. *Informe de gestión anual de 2016*; available at: http://www.pdvsa.com/index.php?option=com_content&view=article&id=6538&Itemid=1186&lang=es

Portafolio.com. 2007. "ZTE producirá un millón de celulares en Venezuela". June 21; available at: http://www.portafolio.co/economia/finanzas/zte-producira-millon-celulares-venezuela-170092

Rendón, Moises and Sarah Baumunk. 2018. "When Investment Hurts: Chinese Influence in Venezuela". *Center for Strategic and International Studies*; available at: https://www.csis.org/analysis/when-investment-hurts-chinese-influence-venezuela

Reporte confidencial. 2013. "Expropian firma Great Wall para aumentar producción de Chery" August 07; available at: http://www.reporteconfidencial.info/noticia/3199855/expropian-firma-great-wall-para-aumentar-produccion-de-chery/

Reuters. 2015. "A FONDO-Industrias chinas en Venezuela no arrancan, pero el gigante asiático hace un negocio redondo". June 23; available at: https://lta.reuters.com/article/businessNews/idLTAKBN0P31P420150623

Reuters. 2015. "Chinese firms do brisk business in Venezuela despite idle factories"; disponible en: https://www.reuters.com/article/us-venezuela-china-insight/chinese-firms-do-brisk-business-in-venezuela-despite-idle-factories-idUSKBN-0P31BD20150623

Reuters. 2016. "IFR-Venezuela podría tener que reestructurar deuda con China por caída del petróleo: Barclays". February 26; available at: https://lta.reuters.com/article/companyNews/idLTAL2N15H1LA

SEC (Securities and Exchange Commission) 2018. *Reporte anual de Gobierno y Sub-Divisiones Política: Reporte Anual (Forma 18K) de Venezuela*; available at: https://www.sec.gov/Archives/edgar/data/103198/000119312517376486/d505622dex99d.htm

Sun Hungbo, 2014. "Modelo de cooperación energética entre China y América Latina. Revista Problemas del Desarrollo available at: https://www.sciencedirect.com/science/article/pii/S030170361470848X

TELESUR. 2015. "Venezuela tiene la fábrica de autobuses más grande de A. Latina"; available at: https://www.telesurtv.net/news/Venezuela-inaugura-fabrica-de-autobuses-mas-grande-de-Latinoamerica-20151202-0020.html

Vasquez, Patricia. 2018. *China, Oil, and Latin America: Myth vs Reality*. Atlantic Council; available at: http://www.atlanticcouncil.org/images/publications/china-oil-latam-final.pdf

Venezuela Official Gazette 38.784 (Gaceta oficial no. 38.784). Published November 5 2007; available at: http://historico.tsj.gob.ve/gaceta/octubre/051007/051007-38784-02.html

Venezuela Official Gazette 39.150 (Gaceta oficial no. 39.150. Published March 31 2009; available at: http://historico.tsj.gob.ve/gaceta/marzo/310309/310309-39150-22.html

Venezuela Official Gazette 40.763 (Gaceta oficial no. 40.763). Published October 08 2015; available at: http://historico.tsj.gob.ve/gaceta/octubre/081015/081015-40763-03.html

Xinhua. 2015. "Chinese company to build new residential zones in Venezuela". April 30. http://www.xinhuanet.com/english/2015-05/06/c_134212814.htm

Yutong.com. 2018. "Yutong Venezuelan Factory is put into operation"; available at: https://en.yutong.com/plus/ourmarket/latinamerica/MarketsFocus/2016/2016CPK2LcMBtI.html

CHINA'S FOREIGN DIRECT INVESTMENT IN PANAMA

Nehemías José Jaén Celada

Introduction

The study of the political economy of Panama has always been tied to its relationship with the United States, its service-driven economy, and its geographic position. Panama, in large part because of the canal, has served as a natural convergence point not only for the region but for the entire world. The last decade of the past century was marked by a post-U.S. invasion period in which Panamanian society sought to recover from a profound deterioration of the country's institutions after a 21-year military dictatorship (1968-1989) was terminated by the controversial intervention of Washington. The post-invasion recovery path was guided by International Monetary Fund (IMF) and the World Bank (WB) policies pushing for a deeper liberalization of the Panamanian economy. These neoliberal policies resulted in improvements in Panama's key economic indicators but these same policies did little to improve agriculture, education, or health and social welfare in ways that may have benefited the Panamanian society overall.

Between 1989 and 1999, the two successively elected civilian governments made substantial progress reestablishing a democratic environment, conveying a sense of rule of law that attracted diversified foreign direct investment (FDI) into the country. Between the return to democracy and the twilight of the twentieth century, Panama achieved an average growth rate of 5.76% and its gross domestic product went from US$6.4 billion in 1990 to US$12.1 billion in 1999.

The outset of the twenty-first century is considered a turning point in the history of Panama. The United States handed the ownership and control of the Panama Canal to the Panamanian State and withdrew the last troops stationed in Panamanian territory on December 31, 1999, as required by the clauses of the Torrijos-Carter Treaty on the Panama Canal signed in 1977. These events signified the beginning of a decline in U.S. influence on Panama and the rest of the Latin American and Caribbean region. As of 2000, the country began to experience a steady increase of FDI inflow that –coupled with a higher rate of government spending, GDP growth rate and external debt as a percentage of gross national income– suggests that the change in ownership and control of the Panama Canal has been significant in determining FDI into Panama (Lloyd 2018).

The period between 2000 and 2009 was characterized by the implementation of policies aimed at improving the attractiveness of the country as well as the capacity and capability of its services platform. These policies were jointly promoted and advocated by interest groups and the central government. In 2007, a referendum led to an estimated US$5 billion expansion project of the Panama Canal, which was inaugurated on June 26, 2016. This milestone created the conditions for the transformation of Panama's long-term maritime development, with implications for the region as well.

Panama's remarkably economic performance *vis-à-vis* the rest of the region coincided with the reengagement of China in Latin America and the Caribbean. From a hemispheric perspective, China's recent involvement in Latin America is surprising in its suddenness and scale that in turn has led to a proliferation of commentary, debate and policy analysis, particularly in the realms of strategic thinking, political economy and bilateral relations (Armony and Strauss 2012:1). From a Panamanian perspective, strong cultural links with the Chinese have existed since the second half of the nineteenth century during the last Chinese imperial dynasty of the Qing that ruled from 1644 to 1912 and the arrival of the first Chinese coolies in the isthmus.

In its reengagement, China's sought to employ its distinctive approach in the region, which uses economic power to mask the political interests of its global soft-power strategy, at the same time that Latin America's political spectrum was shifting. These sociopolitical transformations allowed Beijing to pursue its national interests within certain countries, primarily in South America, that then became major suppliers of war materials feeding China's overwhelming appetite. In the case of Panama, despite the lack of diplomatic relations with the People's Republic of China for almost seventy years, Beijing's increasing economic leverage played a significant role in strengthening the presence of Chinese actors in the isthmus in the realm of bilateral trade and investment; presence that further consolidated when Panama ditched its longstanding diplomatic ties with the Republic of China (Taiwan) and adhered the country to the 'One China Principle.'

This chapter on China's foreign direct investment in Panama summarizes the historical trajectory of Sino-Panamanian ties and introduces the patterns of investment of this Asian power in the most strategic country in the Western Hemisphere and Washington's longstanding traditional ally.

The Trajectory of the Relationship between Panama and China

Historical records indicate that the first encounters between Panamanians and Chinese occurred more than 150 years ago. At the time, Chinas was still ruled by an imperial dynasty and Panama was part of Colombia, to which it had adhered right after gaining independence from Spain in late 1821. In determining the trajectory of this relationship, the historical analysis can be segmented in three main timeframes. The first period, running from the mid-nineteenth century up through the first half of the twentieth century, saw the first waves of Chinese migrants reaching Latin American ports, including Panama, the consolidation of an independent country, the decay of imperial China, the inauguration of the Panama Canal, World War I, the Chinese Civil War and World War II. The second period starts at the end of World War II followed by the defeat of the Chinese nationalists, the relocation of the Republic of China to Taiwan, and the foundation of the People's Republic of China by the Chinese Communists in 1949. The long decades of the Cold War, which shaped U.S. influence over Latin America and the Isthmus of Panama, followed. The experience with the United States undoubtedly shaped Panama's foreign policy towards Beijing and Taipei. The third period runs through the 1980s and 1990s, and includes the Tiananmen Square uprising, the fall of the Berlin Wall, the U.S. invasion of Panama and the fall of the Soviet Union, concluding with the 1999 transfer of the Canal from U.S. control to Panamanian.

Scholarship about the relation between Panama and China is relatively scarce and consists of predominantly historical and anthropological research that narrates contact in the nineteenth and twentieth century. However, the dramatic expansion of Chinese interests in Latin America and the Caribbean, with China using Panama as its operation hub, demands greater engagement on the relationship and greater expertise on China and its activities in the region.

Contacts between China and Latin America can be traced back to the 1570s when trade across the Pacific began to flourish. China exported silk, porcelain, and cotton yarn to Mexico and Peru in exchange for silver coins and other items. The geographical distance between China and Latin America determined that "no wars or disputes over territory, cultures or values of their very different peoples, have constituted the basis of the relationship between them" (Villafañe 2011:20). Nonetheless, it was more than three hundred years before significant numbers of Chinese migrants, mostly peasants from southern Mainland China, the so-colled "coolies," arrived in the region hired as contract laborers to work in mines, plantations, railway construction, and other industries in the late nineteenth century. Historians estimate that approximately 1,600 Chinese laborers arrived in the isthmus of Panama between 1852 and 1854 to work in the construction of the trans-isthmian railroad of Panama (Chen 2018). A few years later, Chinese migrants also took part in the courageous excavation of a ditch that would shape the course of world history, as members of the workforce of the Panama Canal. This first wave of Chinese migration to Panama would become one of the strongest ethnographic influences shaping race and diversity in Panama since the colonial era. Towards the end of the nineteenth century, more than 10,000 Chinese could have arrived in Panama to work in the construction of the Panama Canal; as they began to root in the isthmus, this fostered anti-Chinese immigration sentiments that were later on incorporated into the domestic political discourse of the professional Panamanian middle-class.

The French failure to complete the construction of the canal marked the consolidation of the U.S. presence in the most strategic point of the Americas, as Washington not only overtook the project but also supported the Panamanian independence movement that resulted in the foundation of the Republic of Panama. The U.S. took this opportunity to station military forces alongside the canal stripe; stark presence and controversial influence that would last for the next one hundred years.

In Mainland China, the first three decades of the past century were characterized by several internal political upheavals that evolved into a longstanding bloody civil war. The first part of the so-called Chinese Civil War spanned from 1927 to 1937 when Japanese forces invaded Mainland China; confronted with this menace, communists and nationalists conformed a united front to fight Japanese: this was the prelude of World War II, the most remarkable turning point in modern history. With the surrender of Japan in 1945, communists and nationalists failed at conforming a coalition government thus, both parties plunged –again– in a civil war that resulted in the defeat of the nationalists governing the Republic of China, and the establishment of the People's Republic of China by CPC's leader Mao Zedong. This prompted the nationalists to relocate the government of the Republic of China to the island of Taiwan –whose status in the international arena is still a matter of controversy and ambiguity– with which Panama maintained diplomatic relations for over one hundred years until

June 2017 when the Central American country decided to adhere itself to the so-called 'One China Principle.' Thus, recognizing the government of the People's Republic of China as the sole and legitimate government of China –including Hong Kong, Macao, Taiwan and several disputed islands.

The second half of the twentieth century was a period of constant sociopolitical and economic transformations in Panama. The occupation of a vast territory alongside the Panama Canal by the US Army was considered a humiliating violation of Panama's national sovereignty. It exacerbated nationalist feelings among Panamanians and others in Latin American and Caribbean.

Undoubtedly, the Cold War marked the political history of Latin America and the Caribbean. This period was not unnoticed to Panama and most countries south of Rio Grande, as containing the advancement of communism became the main policy goal of Washington in the region *vis-à-vis* the Soviet Union in first instance and, then, Communist China. This translated into unrestrictive U.S. support to right-wing and populist military governments all across the region, including Panama's revolutionary leader, Omar Torrijos (1968-81). Unsurprisingly, despite several rapprochements between Panama and the People's Republic of China, Torrijos' government not only abstained in 1971 from endorsing the replacement of the Republic of China with the Chinese communists governing the Mainland, but also never took concrete steps towards the normalization of relations with Beijing not to jeopardize the cause of the reversion of the Canal to Panamanian hands. Despite such global dynamics, the relationship between Panama and Mainland China began to focus on the commercial realm as Beijing's policy of 'reform and opening up' –so-called socialism with Chinese characteristics– from 1978, radically transformed the global industrial production environment with China becoming the 'world's factory.'

With the return to democracy, after 21 years of dictatorship, the government of President Guillermo Endara Galimany prioritized economic recovery and the strengthening of the rule of law. No steps were taken to normalize diplomatic and political relations with Mainland China despite the global tendency of recognizing the Chinese government in Beijing and also the continuous inflow of Chinese illegal migrants in Panama. In 1994, the Democratic Revolutionary Party, the political group that supported Torrijos and Noriega, won the general elections, prompting to resume contacts with Beijing. No long after been sworn in office, President Ernesto Perez Balladares negotiated with the government of Mainland China the establishment of "non-governmental" representative liaison offices in both capitals, directly subordinated to each country's ministry of foreign affairs and labeled as trade development representative offices. Notwithstanding the absence of diplomatic ties, both offices operated at the highest level in spite of the non-governmental mask.

During his term, President Balladares challenged the traditional U.S. and European corporate establishment when two key container ports were granted in concession for 25-years to a Hong Kong-based conglomerate, perhaps the first significant investment of a Chinese company in Panama. Under the terms of the deal, which covers the twin ports of Cristobal and Balboa, Hutchinson Port Holding agreed to pay US$22.2 million in annual rent and a one-time lump sum payment of US$10 million for the purchase of existing equipment at the ports (South China Morning Post, 4 March 1997). The deal coincided with Britain's reversion of the colony of Hong Kong to Beijing and occurred two years before the U.S. army total withdrawal from Panama and the transfer of control and ownership of the canal to the Panamanian people.

By the end of the century, bilateral trade between Panama and China consolidated. The development of Panama's logistic platform played to the advantage of China. The Colon Free Zone, founded in 1948, became the hub for the re-exportation of Chinese manufactured goods across the region of Latin America and the Caribbean. Contrary to Panama's experience with China, Beijing's re-engagement with countries in the Southern Cone occurred when the region experienced a political wave that shifted several countries to the left.

The government of President Mireya Moscoso (1999-2004) did not alter the course of Panama's relationship with Taiwan. This, perhaps unintentionally, weakened and constrained the advancement of Beijing into the region of Central America and the Caribbean Zone (CACZ) for the years to come. Moreover, the lack of high talks between President Moscoso administration and the Chinese government in Beijing, prompted certain Panamanian interest groups and political parties to independently maintain contacts with the Chinese Communist Party.

In spite of the new political conditions in South America in early 2000s, countries in CACZ did not change their foreign policy of recognizing the government of Taiwan, mainly due their reliance on economic and financial help from and geographical proximity to Washington, and the assistance and investments Taiwan has executed in the sub-region for decades. In the case of Panama, none of the democratically elected governments after 1990 have shown much assertiveness in either domestic or international policies. Beyond the general consensus that Panama's relationship with the United States is strategic, successive Panamanian governments have repeatedly failed at setting consistent foreign policy priorities in the last three decades. The country, for example, has not taken advantage of its prime relationship with Japan and the so-called 'Four Asian Tigers' (Hong Kong, Singapore, Korea and Taiwan) to attract greater investment in the isthmus.

While Beijing saw in Panama a long-term goal, Taipei considered the Central American nation to be its most significant diplomatic ally, regionally and globally. Taipei rightly assumed that any alteration of its relationship with Panama might transform the diplomatic chessboard of Latin America and the Caribbean. Taiwanese interests in Panama have been driven by a mix of political objectives and business-oriented decisions subjected to Panama's political oscillation from one political party to another every presidential term.

The Torrijos administration (2004-2009) resumed secret talks with Beijing aimed at establishing diplomatic relations. However, domestic issues overshadowed President Torrijos's interests on China. The administration embarked on two key economic and political subjects directly linked to U.S. interests in Panama: a free trade agreement (FTA) between Panama and the U.S., and the expansion project of the Panama Canal. Moreover, from 2008 in Taiwan, the return to power of the Nationalist Party of China (KMT) dismissed any attempt of Panama to establish diplomatic relations with Beijing as both governments across the Taiwan Strait sought to advance a joint economic and political agenda considered as a truce constraining each other's diplomatic strategy. This so-called "diplomatic truce" would last until 2016.

The Administration of President Ricardo Martinelli (2009-2014) misread the magnitude of the issues between the People's Republic of China and Taiwan, and the increasing tensions over territorial disputes in the East and South China Sea. Instead of taking advantage of the diplomatic ties with Taiwan, commercial ones with the PRC, and traditional longstanding connections with Japan by fostering the attraction of direct investment into the Isthmus, President Martinelli committed several faux pas to the detriment of Panama's relations with all three actors (La Prensa, 23 October 2012). Panama was only able to attract a few Chinese companies willing to invest in the country. These companies shared a few common characteristics: they were private, and therefore less restricted by regulations governing outbound capital; they were restructuring their operations primarily in Mexico and South America; and, they were developing a strategy to engage with Central American and Caribbean nations. It goes without saying that early Chinese investment in Panama have failed in their attempt to replicate their past and current experiences in Africa, Southeast Asia and South America, where they mistakenly underestimated market regulations and the rule of law.

In 2016, the return to power of the Democratic Progressive Party (DPP), with Dr. Tsai Ying-wen as president, precipitated a communication rupture between Beijing and Taipei –despite her well-known political moderation. This prompted China to relaunch its no-longer-subtle diplomatic long-term strategy of gaining diplomatic recognition from the remaining countries with which Taipei still maintained formal ties, principally Panama in Central America and the Dominican Republic in the Caribbean. China took this opportunity to reshape its new role in the region in a period in which China and Lain America and the Caribbean began transitioning from complementarity to cooperation, prompting new economic commitments and policy priorities between both actors, and Panama has emerged as China's key instrument for its long-term strategic interests in the region.

Beijing's soft-landing in Latin America and the Caribbean has been considered an instance of hegemonic challenge to Washington's dominant position in the Western Hemisphere. However, is still not clear "if China's growing economic size and power (in trade, investment, and finance), coupled with growing military might may prevent or increase the possibilities of hegemonic challenge, as well as whether recovery or decline in the United States may forecast any outcome" (Paz 2012:34). This new reality has prompted Latin American political actor to foretell the end of the 'Washington Consensus' and the emergence of the 'Beijing Consensus' –also called "China Model."

Chinese Patterns of Investment in Panama

Panama's strategic relevance in the realms of global economics, finance and trade has made of it a unique case in the study of China's direct investment into Latin America and the Caribbean. Undoubtedly, China's bilateral approach to selected South American countries is not a model fits-all in the region at large. In turn, in recent years, Beijing began to bet for multilateralism, through the China-CELAC Forum (Community of Latin American and Caribbean States), aiming to tackle regional sociopolitical and economic issues not prioritized before. For Beijing, this was a unique opportunity, a way of dealing with a region barely known through a single multilateral platform; for Latin America, policy coordination was the imperative goal to better take advantage of China's Latin American policy redefinition (Doria and Jaen Celada 2017:125). However, due to its perceived politicization and lack of contribution from Latin American counterparts, China-CELAC Forum has gradually lost preponderance in Sino-Latin American relations.

In 2014, Beijing announced the China-LAC Cooperation Plan (2015-2019), which sought to achieve inclusive growth and sustainable development through 3 main engines: trade, investment, and financial cooperation. The plan focused on 6 areas: boosting China-LAC industry connections with energy and resources, infrastructure construction, agriculture, manufacturing, scientific and technological innovation, and information technologies and cooperation priorities. In 2018, China announced the continuation of this cooperation plan (2019-2021) and added a new element: the Belt and Road Initiative (BRI). Both the China-CELAC Cooperation Plan and the Belt and Road Initiative coupled with the antagonistic relationship between the top leaders across the Taiwan Strait since 2016, precipitated a rapprochement between Panama and China that resulted in the establishment of diplomatic relations in June 2017. The third section of the chapter summarizes this turning point in the relationship between both countries, and the implications with respect to Chinese direct investment in Panama in recent years.

How and when the governments of Panama and China began formal negotiations on the establishment of diplomatic relations will remain the best-kept secret of the remarkable announcement made on June 12, 2017, by President Varela. The president itself communicated the rupture of Panama's longstanding ties with the Republic of China (Taiwan) and the normalization of formal diplomatic and political relations with the People's Republic of China, which brought Panama into alignment with Beijing's "One China Principle." Panama had been keen to attract Chinese direct investment into the country and become a beneficiary of China's global and Latin American policies. From China's perspective, luring Panama into its sphere of influence was the missing piece in its Western Hemisphere strategy. Panama's decision to normalize relations with China was at first applauded by different interest groups in Panamanian society, but later resulted in a wide range of speculation and anxieties about the impact of Chinese businesses on Panamanian SMEs, the agricultural sector, and even security.

As predicted, the establishment of diplomatic ties between Panama and China provoked a domino effect. On April 30, 2018, the Dominican Republic severed diplomatic ties with Taiwan and established diplomatic relations with the People's Republic of

China; four months later, El Salvador followed suit. If Panama's and the Dominican Republic's China decision was a bucket of cold water for Washington, El Salvador's was the drop that spilled the glass. The White House, stated that this was "a decision that affects not just El Salvador, but also the economic health and security of the entire Americas region" (White House 2018). Moreover, the U.S. government also noted that "countries seeking to establish or expand relations with China in order to attract state-directed investment that will stimulate short-term economic growth and infrastructure development may be disappointed over the long run" (ibid.). But if there is a great difference between Panama and these two countries, is that Panama at seems to have a short-term roadmap on developing its relationship with China, as it shows more experience dealing with Chinese investments prior the establishment of diplomatic relations.

On the heels of diplomatic recognition, the presence of Chinese companies in Panama steadily became a remarkable fact; thus, for Panama, the lack of formal ties with Beijing was clearly a matter affecting China's participation in different sectors of its economy. Throughout the last four decades, three patterns of Chinese investment can be observed in Panama: portraying the advancement of China's interest in the Central American country and the region.

In the 1980s and 1990s, several private Chinese SMEs established operations in Colon Free Trade Zone, using this strategic commercial area as a trampoline to the CACZ and the Andean region, which is considered as the first and most traditional pattern of Chinese investment in the country targeting an economic/commercial pillar.

The second pattern emerged in the early 2000s when private Chinese engineering companies arrived in Panama as partners or contractors in medium-size concessions projects, mainly in the hydroelectric sector. During the same period, Panama consolidated the privatization of its state-owned port infrastructure –a process that had begun in last years of the previous century and attracted Chinese port operators in key shipping terminals on both sides of the Panama Canal. These investments almost went unnoticed, but became the spearhead for more Chinese companies to explore potential opportunities in the isthmus.

Between 2004 and 2019, Panama's general investment program has had a total budget of approximately US$40 billion primarily allocated in six action lines and several key sectors. Such an aggressive and unprecedented investment in public infrastructure, called the attention of Chinese state-owned, public and private construction enterprises –most of which were already operating in the region– to participate in public tenders and mid-and-long-term concessions. These Chinese SOEs created the perception that China was increasing its investments in the country. However, it has slowly become clear that such companies were not cataloged as Chinese foreign direct investment as they only bid for projects directly financed by the Panamanian central government.

Aside from the notable presence of Chinese SOEs in public tenders in the country, the main challenge Panama faced *vis-à-vis* China's expansion in the Americas was how to attract Chinese direct investment into key sectors of the Panamanian economy to fill the vacuum left by North American and European investors. Prior to the establishment of diplomatic relations between the two countries, major Chinese state-owned banks like the China Development Bank (CDB) and the Export-Import Bank of China (Exim Bank of China) had imposed restrictions on financing Chinese projects overseas in countries with which China did not maintain diplomatic ties. Chinese public and private enterprises were limited in terms of capital for their business opportunities in the isthmus and as a result, only few companies managed to enter Panama during this period, such as the Chinese ITC giant Huawei.

However, this tendency changed immediately after June 2017 with the normalization of diplomatic relations. Soon after, Chinese enterprises began to target key projects in Panama's logistics and port sectors, along with the energy sector, especially natural gas. The steady advancement of relations between Panama and China has also accelerated the settling of Chinese flagship banks in Panama to support Chinese foreign direct investment in Panama and the region. This new active role of Chinese capital in strategic economic sectors in Panama constituted the third wave of Chinese investment in the Central American country.

Panama's mid-and-long-term development depends upon the successful implementation of several national economic strategies created with the assistance and funding of regional development banks such as the Inter-American Development Bank (IDB) and CAF Development Bank of Latin America, in collaboration with government entities and interest groups. In recent years, these national strategies have been focused on two main strategic sectors that are Panama's key economic pillars: the logistics and maritime sector, and energy sector.

Well before the establishment of diplomatic ties between Panama and China, Chinese interests were focused on potential projects proposed as part of Panama's logistics development roadmap: the national maritime strategy, and the national energy strategy. Between 2014 and 2018, Chinese direct investment into Panama totaled approximately US$3.5 billion. The establishment of diplomatic relations in 2017 brought about an immediate impact: in the majority of the total amount of Chinese FDI inflow has been felt in the last twenty months.

In 2016, China Landbridge Group Co., Ltd. (Landbridge Group), a privately owned company based in the northern Chinese port of Rizhao, Shandong province, acquired the concession rights to develop Panama's largest seaport: Margarita Island Port. Located at the Panama Canal's entrance to the Atlantic Ocean and opposite to the Hong Kong-owned Cristobal Port, Margarita Island Port is an important stop en-route to the Panama Canal. It is part of the Colon Free Trade Zone, the largest in the Western Hemisphere and one of the world's few cargo distribution centers with sea-land-air-rail multimodal transport. This strategic expansion decision came after the company's successful experience securing Australia's Darwin Port and it is part of the company's master plan to build a highly modernized and efficient deep-water container port to meet the present and future operational demand of the Panama Canal (ChinaGoAbroad 2016). At the June 7, 2017 "first stone ceremony," less than a week before the unexpected establishment of diplomatic ties between Panama and China, Panamanian president Juan Carlos Varela commented that "the port was the most important Chinese investment in Panama so far" (Global Construction Review 2017).

The US$1 billion megaport built to serve the "One Belt, One Road Initiative" (OBOR), will be carried out in three stages. The first will increase the port's handling capacity to 2.5 million TEU and add a liquefied natural gas terminal. According to the master plan, "when the first stage is complete in the second quarter of 2019, PCCP will have four berths with a total quay length of 1.2 km and a depth of 18m; the second and third stages will add a logistics park and more cranes to the port" (ChinaGoAbroad 2016). According to some analysts and people involved in this investment, "the steady progress of the project is attributed to the development of China-Panama relations" (China Daily 2018). The developer of this project has contracted China's biggest construction company, China Communications and Construction Company (CCCC), to lead the construction of this port.

As part of the strategic investment in key economic sectors, Landbridge Group jointly with its Chinese partner in Panama, Shanghai Gorgeous Investment Development Co. Ltd., are also investing in the natural gas energy sector in Colon province. These two companies bought Martano, a Panamanian power generation company established in 2007, for approximately $200 million. In 2015, Martano was awarded a 15-years concession to build and operate a 400MW combined-cycle natural gas plant in Isla Margarita. Martano beat out fourteen companies competing to supply power to the electricity distribution companies Ensa, Edemet and Edechi during the period from 2019 to 2033 (Central America Data 2015). It has been reported that Martano offered 8.5 cents per kilowatt-hour for generation based on natural gas, 30% lower than a previous bid, which was won by Gas Natural del Atlántico, part of AES group. This project is being developed on a plot of ten hectares located completely in the terrestrial sector of Rio Alejandro Energy Park located in the township of Puerto Limón. The main subcontractor of this project is the well-known Shanghai Electric Group one of the largest engineering companies in this sector worldwide.

The total investment on this project is estimated at approximately at US$900 million. At the end of 2018, it was announced that Royal Dutch Shell Plc won a long-term contract to provide liquefied natural gas to this project. The deal with the Shell-trading unit comes as a trade dispute between the United States and China has put global LNG exports in the spotlight. Terms of the 15-year deal, which will meet all the fuel needs of the LNG-fueled plant, were not disclosed. The facility will require roughly 400,000 tons per year of LNG (Reuters 2018).

In the second decade of this century, Panama also positioned itself as a hub for ITC companies with very competitive and aggressive regional strategies. In this sense, China's conglomerate Huawei identified Panama as the best platform for its regional headquarter. The well-known mobile phones manufacturer sought to concentrate in Panama its top human resource, operations and logistics/distribution in Panama. This corporate decision has meant a direct investment of more than US$50 million in almost 9 years of presence in Panama. Huawei's direct investment includes but is not limited to the establishment of its regional training center for US$7 million and the construction of its sixth global distribution/logistic center of 10,000 square meters for approximately US$42 million. The latter encompasses 15 different production lines designed for the Latin America and Caribbean market. Huawei's presence in Panama has generated more than 300 jobs in the last few years (Global Times 2015).

In the early 2000s, the first Chinese attempts to directly invest in the country were mainly in the solar energy sector and also fisheries. However, most, if not all, of those attempts failed. According to several actors formerly involved in these cases, the lack of an energy strategy or roadmap, not to mention a regulatory structure, played out in detriment to these Chinese initiatives. In the case of fisheries, Panama has not taken concrete steps to reform the laws, regulations and protocols involving several state institutions directly governing this sector. Chinese investors turned to countries with a clearer, and perhaps more convenient, fisheries platforms.

With the establishment of diplomatic relations between Panama and China, the Asian giant has deepened and accelerated its geo-economic expansion plan in the Western Hemisphere. However, *vis-à-vis* China's geopolitical role, Panama lacks a concise evaluation of the long-term effects on its economic development and shows signs of overreliance on Chinese interests, alienating its most important, longstanding and traditional partners.

Policy Recommendations

The establishment of diplomatic relations between Panama and the People's Republic of China has led to an ambitious bilateral agenda. China has inserted itself into the heart of Latin America and the Caribbean by strategically positioning its massive capital in Panama's key economic pillars. Beyond the cliché of Panama and China having a relationship of more than 150 years and of China being the second most important user of the Panama Canal, it is important for both nations to deepen their common knowledge of each other aiming at avoiding potential misunderstandings as well the emergence of misperceptions that could play in detriment of the positive development of this relationship. This section of the chapter proposes a number of policies that can be implemented by Panama.

Since the early twentieth century, Panama's geographical position and the construction of the Panama Canal have determined the fate of the country. These two factors have also shaped the economic grid of Panama, with 80% of its GPD deriving from a service-driven platform mainly composed of financial and legal services, the Panama Canal and all related ancillary industries, along with tourism in recent years. In light of profound changes in the dynamic of globalization, including tributary governance, Panama is being compelled to transform its economy by strengthening its competitive advantages that forcibly requires: upgrade (modernization) and expansion of its special economic zones; development of existing logistics nodes beyond port facilities; development of strategic industrial parks; and, most importantly, the integration of all these components. This transformation could be achieved if the country succeeds at increasing the attraction of FDI especially from Northeast Asian countries.

The Ministry of Foreign Affairs, the Ministry of Commerce and Industry, and the Ministry of Economy and Finance of Panama shall jointly establish a task force on Asia Pacific in general, China in particular within the structure of the first. This task force shall be made up of Panamanian experts on Asia/China to clearly define, design, develop, and execute a mid-and-long-term policy towards the Asia Pacific region with a focus on East Asian economies. With the alignment of policy priorities among these three key ministries, Panama can effectively promote its unique characteristics to meet the goal of increasing diversified foreign direct investment. Moreover, the existing agency called Proinvex, entitled to promote investments attraction and exports, shall be rebranded into 'Pro Panama' and relocated to the Ministry of Foreign Affairs; therefore, the task force on Asia Pacific/China could serve as the technical support of Pro Panama on matters regarding the world's most dynamic region.

Panama's economic pillars and its role in the international community, suggests the need the country has to improve its capability to study and research global issues affecting or influencing its own development. Thus, it is necessary the creation of a think tank on global political and economic studies by Panama's main academic institutions, sponsored by the central government and regional developments banks. In partnership with renowned foreign academic institutions, this initiative will allocate human capital and resource on the study of crucial issues in global affairs. In the long run, this institution should be the main resource of policy advice to the Panamanian state, the private sector, and society. This think tank should also coordinate relevant training programs for public servants and also the private sector.

Conclusions

Since the late 90s, Chinese companies in Panama created the mistaken perception that China was investing heavily in the country. In reality, most of these companies were merely competing to provide services to the Panamanian government. It was not until the last decade that Panama began to receive Chinese direct investment in key economic sectors like ITC, ports & logistics, and energy. The establishment of diplomatic relations between Panama and China has not only accelerated and consolidated the presence of this extra-regional actor in the isthmus of Central America but has also increased the economic and political leverage of China at large in the Western Hemisphere.

Panama's shift of diplomatic allegiance from Taipei to Beijing provoked a domino effect in the CACZ, with the Dominican Republic and El Salvador following Panama's precedent. China's presence in LAC has been boosted with the normalization of diplomatic and political relations with Panama. Since June 2017, more than 40 documents have been signed between Panama and China in different matters. Panamanian President Juan Carlos Varela also visited President Xi Jinping less than 6 months after the establishment of diplomatic relations and the latter paid a visit to Panama in December 2018. With the incorporation of Panama in the Belt and Road Initiative, signed during the visit of Panamanian President Juan Carlos Varela to China in November 2017, and the advancement of Chinese strategic investments in Panama's key economic pillars, U.S. dominant interests in the region in general, and Panama in particular, are being challenged and eroded.

China's active role in Panama has coincided with the need to transform the country's economy, which has been negatively affected by the "Panama Papers" scandal, and the imposition of global fiscal rules emanating from a group of developed nations incapable of enforcing internal regimes. Furthermore, Washington's apparent disinterest on and ambiguous policy toward Panama have created the perception, among Panamanian society, of an imperative need for aligning certain national interests with China's agenda. This, in turn, has fostered an exaggerated and unmeasured overreliance on matters related to China. Thirty years after the return to democracy, Panama is still considered to have immeasurable levels of corruption undermining its nature as the point of convergence for global services, capital flow, human mobility and political diversity.

China's remarkable presence in Panama and the Central American isthmus have collided with the U.S. traditional core interests. The recent visits of high-ranking U.S. officials to Panama, including State Secretary Pompeo, the Special Assistant to the President and Senior Director for Western Hemisphere Affairs of the US National Security Council Mauricio Claver-Carone, among others, suggest that Washington is unwilling to surrender its core interests in Panama and the region to China and has made clear its concerns to the recent elected government of Panama. The United States perceives the advancement of China in the region as a challenge to its sphere of influence; thus, Panama shall avoid getting trapped between both powers. It is unlikely that the United States will remain oblivious to Chinese attempts to raise its profile in Panama. If Washington appeared to be indifferent to the establishment of diplomatic relations between Panama and China, it has now launched a campaign to reaffirm itself in Panama. However, Washington's ability to reassert itself in Panama may be limited by the economic strength shown by China and its ability to channel massive investments and trade levels to one of its newest partners in the region, not to mention its soft-power strategy spreading its own culture and values among economic, political and social elites.

References

Chen, Berta Alicia. 2018. *Panamá y China: una relación de tres siglos*. Panama: Management Development Corporation.

"Chinese firm starts work on $1bn Panamanian megaport." 2017. *Global Construction Review*, June 12. http://www.globalconstructionreview.com/news/chinese-firm-starts-w7rk-1bn-panama7nian-meg7aport/

Doria, Gaio and Jaen Celada, Nehemias José. 2016. "CELAC and China in Perspective: Regional Integration and Engagement Redefinition". In, Cui, Shoujun and Manuel Perez Garcia (eds.). *China and Latin America in Transition: Policy Dynamics, Economic Commitments and Social Impacts*. New York: Palgrave Macmillan, pp. 113-128.

González, José. 2012. "Califican de desacertadas las declaraciones de Martinelli en Japón." *La Prensa*, October 23. https://www.prensa.com/jose_gonzalez_pinilla/Califican-desacertadas-declaraciones-Martinelli-Japon_0_3508899129.html

Hampton, Liz. 2018. "Exclusive: Shell wins LNG deal to supply Chinese firm's power plant in Panama." *Reuters*, September 20. https://www.reuters.com/article/us-shell-lng-panama-exclusive/exclusive-shell-wins-lng-deal-to-supply-chinese-firms-power-plant-in-panama-idUSKCN1M02IS

"Huawei opens Latin American Distribution center in Panama." 2015. *Global Times*, October 20. http://www.globaltimes.cn/content/945380.shtml

"Landbridge Group connects three ports with acquisition of Margarita Island Port." 2016. *ChinaGoAbroad*, May 25. http://www.chinagoabroad.com/en/recent_transaction/20530

Li, Xiaoxiao and Chen, Xiaowei. 2018. "Chinese-invested Panamanian port expansion project in smooth progress." *China Daily*, November 30. http://www.chinadaily.com.cn/a/201811/30/WS5c0097ada310eff30328bfc5.html

Lloyd, Robert A. 2018. "The Panama Canal as a Determinant of FDI in Panama". *Review of Integrative Business and Economics Research*, pp. 87-102.

"Panama: Agreement for 350 MW of Thermal Energy." 2015. *Central America Data*, December 11. https://www.centralamericadata.com/en/article/home/Panama_Agreement_for_350_MW_of_Thermal_Energy

Paz, Gonzalo. 2012. "China, the United States and Hegemonic Challenge in Latin America: An Overview and Some Lessons from Previous Instances of Hegemonic Challenge in the Region." In, Julia C. Strauss and Ariel C. Armony (eds.). *From the Great Wall to the New World: China and Latin America in the 21st Century*. Cambridge: Cambridge University Press, pp. 18-34.

Renteria, Nelson. 2019. "Salvadoran president-elect to assess relationship with China: aide." *Reuters*, February 3. https://www.reuters.com/article/us-el-salvador-politics/salvadoran-president-elect-to-assess-relationship-with-china-aide-idUSKCN1PX06J

"Siemens to provide tech for Panama's LNG-fuled power plant."2018. LNG *World News*, May 15. https://www.lngworldnews.com/siemens-to-provide-tech-for-panamas-lng-fueled-power-plant/

Strauss, Julia and Armony, Ariel C. 2012. "From Going Out (zou chuqu) to Arriving In (desembarco): Constructing a New Field of Enquiry in China-Latin America Interactions". In, Strauss, Julia and, Armony, Ariel C. *From the Great World to the New World: China and Latin America in the 21st Century*. Cambridge: Cambridge University Press, pp. 1.17.

Tam, Juan. 2006. "Huellas Chinas en Panamá: 150 años de presencia". Panama: Único Impresores.

Wallis, Keith. 1997. "Hutchison completes Panama Canal deal." *South China Morning Post*, March 4. https://www.scmp.com/article/186992/hutchison-completes-panama-canal-deal

López Villafañe, Víctor. 2011. "Chinese Policy toward Latin America: Implications for Japan and the US." *Korean Review of International Studies* 14(1), pp. 19-32.

CHINESE FDI IN COSTA RICA

Rafael Arias R. and Luis Vargas M.

Introduction

Costa Rica is a small and very open economy. These tendencies were strengthened by structural reforms implemented during the second half of the 1980s. Macroeconomic stabilization policies were complemented by a development strategy that focused on the attraction of foreign direct investment (FDI) and the promotion of non-traditional exports to non-traditional markets. This process allowed the Costa Rican economy to position itself as one of the Latin American countries with the best indicators of FDI attraction in recent decades and a very dynamic export sector (Arias and Muñoz 2007).

Costa Rica's competitive advantages, especially its geographical location, political and social stability, legal system, and human capital, contributed to the consolidation of its attractiveness as a destination for FDI. Intel's investments in 1997, generated a very positive impact on the economy and marked a turning point in the growth of investments in the technological and services sectors. Nevertheless, at the beginning of the new century, the country faces the exhaustion of the easy stage of the export promotion strategy that presented important challenges in terms of attracting investments with a greater impact on added value. Likewise, structural lags in the infrastructure, logistics, and transport sectors have limited possibilities of further growth and become obstacles to the country's competitiveness.

In view of the need to boost the country's rate of economic growth and attract investment in key sectors, former President Oscar Arias Sánchez (2006-2010) decided to establish diplomatic relations with China. This diplomatic outreach was followed by the signing of a free trade agreement in 2010, which consolidated political and economic relations between the two countries. Among the objectives of the free trade agreement, the following stand out:

a) Achieve new and greater trade opportunities between the Parties, both for the current exportable offer, and for the potential supply of goods and services.
b) Create a stable legal framework to promote and develop investments and strategic alliances in the territories of the Parties.
c) Promote cooperation and economic complementarity among the State Parties, through the implementation of specific projects on priority issues for each of the countries.

China immediately became the second biggest commerce partner of Costa Rica, behind the United States of America. Arias' administration expected that China's growing importance in the world economy would make China a strategic partner for the prospective growth and the productive transformation of the Costa Rican economy, based on investments in strategic sectors (Arias and Vargas 2017). The following pages seek to address economic relations between China and Costa Rica since the establishment of diplomatic relations and the evolution of Chinese investments in Costa Rica in recent years.

Chinese Relations with Costa Rica 2000-2017

Two historical milestones, the establishment of diplomatic relations and the signing of the 2010 Free Trade Agreement (FTA) with China, signaled the growing importance of the Chinese market for Costa Rica. In 2007, Costa Rica became the first Central American nation to establish diplomatic relations with China (Chen, 2016). The political realism of this decision was based on recognition of China's importance in the global restructuring of capital and its great potential in terms of economic growth and opportunities for development (Burgués 2009).

In 2010, after six rounds of negotiations, Costa Rica and the People's Republic of China (PRC) signed a FTA, the second such agreement between Costa Rica and an Asian country, intended to achieve greater insertion of Costa Rican goods and services in the Asian giant's market (COMEX 2010). Exports from Costa Rica to China grew ten times between 1994 and 2012 (Dussel Peters 2014). Between 2000 and 2007, exports to the Asian country grew at an annual rate of 42%, with most of those exports concentrated in integrated circuits and microstructures (Matarrita 2008).

China's importance as a trade partner for Costa Rica is even more significant when viewed from its impact on the import sector. Costa Rica has increased its participation in global value chains thanks to its commercial exchange with China (Rodil 2017). China is an important supplier of inputs to produce intermediate and finished goods and this trend has become more evident in new global trade dynamics, specifically with the consolidation of global value chains (Arias and Vargas 2017). From 2000 to 2017, it was a net importer of goods from China (Figure 1), except in 2006, 2007 and 2009, when its exports to China slightly exceeded their imported value.

As shown in Figure 1, the formalization of diplomatic relations in 2007 coincides with higher levels of trade between the two countries. However, this growth was barely sustained until 2009. By 2010, when both economies signed the FTA, Costa Rican exports to China fluctuated downward, while their imports maintained a clear tendency in the opposite direction. Costa Rican exports to China in 2014 and 2015 suffered a significant drop which coincided with the partial closure of the Intel's operations in Costa Rica (Arias and Vargas 2017).

Exports from Costa Rica to China in the last two decades have been highly concentrated in seven sub-sectors. The electrical and

Figure 1. Costa Rica. Exports, imports, and trade balance with China in billion of US dollars (2000-2017)

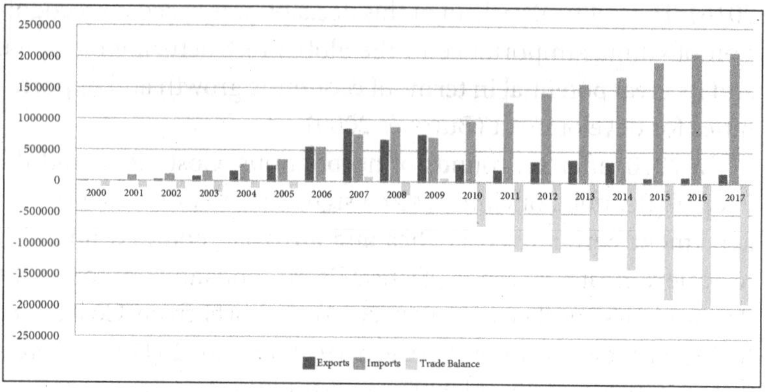

Source: author´s elaboration with data from Matarrita (2008) and PROCOMER (2018).

electronic subsector represents 89% of the value exported from Costa Rica to China, a concentration that, although it fell to 38% in 2017, is still relatively high. The additional six sub-sectors listed in Table 1 have shown significant growth in their exports' participation in the last eighteen years, ranging from 20% in the case of Food industry to 6% for Metalworking and Medical and precision equipment in 2017. According to data from PROCOMER (2018), seven hundred and twenty-one companies –Chinese, transnational, and national– operating in Costa Rica exported to China in this same period.

In terms of imports as well exports, the Electrical and electronics, Metalworking and, Textiles, leather and footwear are positioned as three of the main subsectors in bilateral trade (PROCOMER 2018). Chemistry, Transport materials, Other industrial and Plastic complete the list of the seven main subsectors that import Chinese products to Costa Rica. These subsectors account for 85% of Costa Rican imports from China, which, although still a high concentration, is not as significant as exports from Costa Rica to China.

In general, trade exchanges between the two countries are associated with low levels or no intra-industry trade (Yong and

Table 1. Costa Rica. Exports to China by subsector in thousands of US dollars. (2000-2017)

Year / Subsector	Electrical & electronics sector	Metalworking	Food industry	Textiles, leather & footwear	Meat industry	Logging sector	Medical and precision equipment
2000	6.209,01	234,69	n.d.	56,49	87,45	n.d.	190,00
2001	8.985,01	262,16	0,04	39,61	14,44	n.d.	908,53
2002	28.793,52	317,58	n.d.	3,60	4,11	136,87	1.997,40
2003	83.672,08	634,74	6,74	29,00	n.d.	440,55	239,63
2004	155.874,06	1.487,18	34,48	2.128,02	n.d.	542,46	3,78
2005	233.300,44	3.654,24	54,31	795,02	12,31	751,21	685,07
2006	543.420,59	8.376,95	761,66	784,47	45,82	273,43	623,41
2007	827.201,14	9.965,24	1.841,83	456,27	22,75	1.032,81	992,45
2008	655.257,64	10.309,53	2.531,89	3.569,72	n.d.	883,49	3.112,27
2009	743.495,94	7.846,76	3.781,21	6.779,10	n.d.	422,33	518,59
2010	247.793,75	13.300,68	4.160,83	8.279,57	178,86	1.326,79	161,16
2011	159.699,77	8.661,40	6.749,99	5.380,15	98,45	4.860,67	464,35
2012	284.563,05	14.081,43	14.902,17	4.468,46	15,00	3.886,51	1.358,40
2013	316.527,62	10.331,78	16.572,22	11.008,05	1.205,57	3.341,82	3.062,78
2014	267.184,75	6.912,49	7.591,50	10.998,90	10.806,41	8.784,66	3.635,44
2015	23.447,14	7.100,05	1.838,27	10.962,04	10.679,49	5.242,38	8.659,61
2016	60.205,16	7.187,13	817,66	4.507,95	9.763,68	7.527,62	4.403,39
2017	67.018,92	10.526,58	35.498,76	5.765,36	16.947,88	12.195,09	10.856,75
Total	4,712,649.60	121,190.64	97,143.56	76,011.79	49,882.24	51,648.71	41,873.00
Average	261.813,87	6.732,81	6.071,47	4.222,88	3.563,02	3.228,04	2.326,28

Source: authors elaboration with data from PROCOMER (2018).

Villalobos 2009; CLACDS 2014), which may be the result of the lack of complementarity between the productive structures of both economies, which hinders the integration of companies located in Costa Rica with Chinese value chains (CLACDS 2014). That lack of integration has been one of the reasons why trade between both countries has not shown greater intensity and depth over the years.

In recent years China has positioned itself as one of the main providers of international cooperation resources and infrastructure projects for Costa Rica. However, China's development cooperation in Costa Rica is characterized by low levels of investment in infrastructure projects, instability, and lack of interest in the strategic sectors for productive transformation based on technological change, innovation, and a greater articulation between productive sectors and global value chains (Arias and Vargas 2017).

As indicated by Armony, Dussel Peters and Cui (2018), infrastructure projects are the last and most ambitious phase in the complex relations between China and Latin America and the Caribbean (LAC). These authors add that the region represents a learning opportunity for Chinese companies and that, in turn, LAC could find an opportunity in the infrastructure projects of the Asian giant to close its structural lags in terms of infrastructure for development. According to the authors' estimates, the region should be investing 5% of its Gross Domestic Product (GDP) in infrastructure, instead of just 3%.

Chinese infrastructure projects in Costa Rica include the construction of the National Stadium, an oil refinery, the expansion of a national highway, the construction of a police academy and proposals for Special Economic Zones (SEZ) and distribution centers for global service providers (DeHart 2018). Of these projects, the only one that is still underway is the expansion of Route 32, the road that connects the Costa Rican Great Metropolitan Area (GAM) with its Caribbean coast (Government of the Republic of Costa Rica 2018). In this coast is located Moin Port, the main Costa Rica's point of access to the global economy. New investments for the construction of the Moin Container Terminal (TCM) in March 2019, a concession given to the Dutch company APM Terminals, will boost port development and significantly improve the country's levels of competitiveness. The improvement of Route 32 complements port development and transport and stocking logistics on a national and global scale.

Another important proposal is the Chinese Special Economic Zone (SEZ) in Costa Rica. This project initially counted with support from both governments, but it has not been realized to date. The last advance on the SEZ project in Costa Rica was in January 2015 when both countries signed a memorandum of understanding to carry out a feasibility study that would allow the project to continue (Government of the Republic of Costa Rica 2015). There has been no progress since on either negotiations or concrete measures for implementation.

A final land and port transportation project in which China is a strategic partner is led by the Inter-American Development Bank (IADB) (Mueller and Li 2018). This project consists of the expansion of Route 1 in the Barranca-Limonal stretch of the Inter-American Highway and the preparation of a master plan for maritime port activity, both on Costa Rica's pacific coast. Conversations with representatives of the Ministry of Public Works and Transportation (MOPT) and the Costa Rican Institute of Ports of the Pacific (INCOP) suggest that these plans are advancing according to the pre-established schedule. The IADB's coordination is positive in terms of generating confidence in the development of the project by both projects and could provide a solution for the development of other investment projects.

In short, the economic relations between Costa Rica and China at the level of trade, investment, cooperation, and infrastructure projects have not been as dynamic as expected after the formalization of diplomatic relations and the signing of the FTA. However, it is premature to issue a strong opinion on the future of projects between both countries as success will depend upon both countries' actions, especially those taken by Costa Rica to strengthen its relationship with China.

Impact of Chinese FDI in Costa Rica 2000-2017

The magnitude and impact of Chinese investment in LAC have been widely studied by academics and international organizations. In recent decades, China has become not only one of the largest trading partners of LAC but also one of the leading investors in the region (OECD 2007). Although Chinese investment in LAC has been focused on extraction-oriented activities like mineral resources, raw materials, and energy (Dussel Peters 2014), in recent years China has diversified its interests and the overall share of raw materials and energy has significantly decreased (Dussel Peters 2018).

Despite the growth of investments in LAC, China is not the main sources of investment in the countries of the region and only represents 1.1% of foreign direct investment (FDI) (ECLAC 2017). The only exception to this is Ecuador, where between the years 2007 and 2016, China ranked fourth as a country of origin of FDI. In general, investments in the region continue to be dominated by the United States, by countries of the European Union, and by countries of the LAC region. Specifically, the United States, the Netherlands, and Spain are situated in the first three positions (ECLAC 2017).

Beginning in the 1980s, Costa Rica's economic adjustment policies prioritized macroeconomic stabilization and economic growth through export-oriented policies and the attraction of FDI (Trejos 2008). The strategy followed by Costa Rica contributed to the creation of emerging clusters in business services, medical devices and advanced manufacturing as reflected in their relative importance in the trade with the rest of the world (OECD 2012).

As Figure 2 shows, investments in Costa Rica have been mainly in sectors of the economy with higher added value and more sophisticated exports, which positions the country in proximity to

Figure 2. Costa Rica. Foreign direct investment according to the main sectors of destination in millions of US dollars (2000-2017)

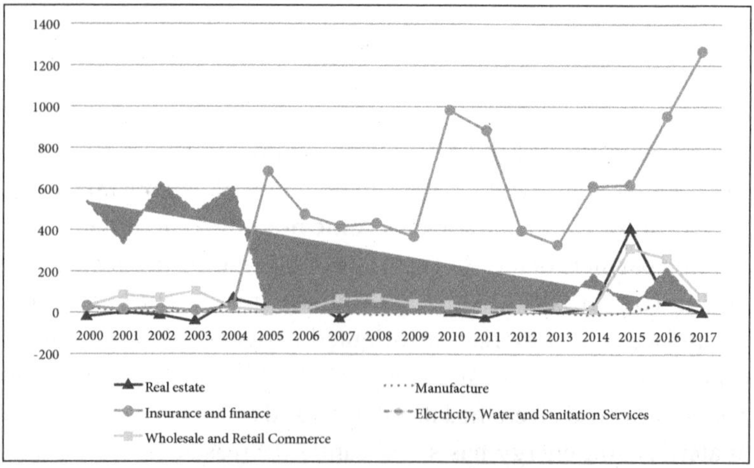

Source: author´s elaboration with data from BCCR (2018).

economies like those of Croatia and Norway but below similarly oriented economies like those of Malaysia and Ireland. This tendency coincides with the outlook of the Costa Rican external sector towards knowledge-intensive activities, in which the country has managed to position itself worldwide. As can be seen in Table 2, most of these investments are located in the regimes Companies Definitive Regime and Free Trade Zone, which, have attractive incentives for foreign investors.

Table 2. Costa Rica. Foreign direct investment according to regime of investment in million of US dollars (2000-2017)

Year/ Regime	Companies Definitive Regime	Free Trade Zone	Real Estate	Tourism Sector	Financial Sector	Inward Processing
2000	134,6	453,9	15,0	51,3	27,1	-15,0
2001	184,2	241,0	9,0	111,5	43,1	19,9
2002	427,8	294,0	21,0	76,0	17,2	-11,5
2003	218,8	359,8	31,0	88,0	2,2	-7,7
2004	174,5	555,5	178,4	41,0	22,6	4,0
2005	474,0	514,9	234,6	53,2	53,3	34,1
2006	448,9	415,1	364,0	124,0	343,4	7,2
2007	603,5	457,8	631,3	321,3	73,9	0,7
2008	987,7	503,2	472,2	291,5	28,9	36,4
2009	530,2	335,0	241,7	253,5	86,9	-3,8
2010	411,8	957,7	147,0	81,0	70,0	15,9
2011	1.158,2	828,4	228,1	113,5	107,4	25,9
2012	1.019,9	568,1	431,8	143,0	72,6	22,7
2013	808,5	536,5	1.160,7	139,7	91,9	3,8
2014	957,5	1.055,3	762,1	34,0	157,3	-39,7
2015	1.516,7	666,4	320,0	41,1	195,5	12,1
2016	1.041,8	646,2	270,0	102,6	112,6	30,7
2017	593,6	1.307,3	250,0	443,3	130,6	17,6
Average	649,6	594,2	320,4	139,4	90,9	8,5

Source: author´s elaboration with data from the BCCR (2018).

Costa Rica's strategy for attracting FDI also becomes apparent when FDI flows by country of origin are analyzed (Figure 3). The United States remains the main investor in the Costa Rican economy, surpassing the volume of investment by the Netherlands, the second country of origin, by about six times in the period between the year 2000 and 2017. Mexico, Spain, and Colombia complete the list of the five countries with the highest investments in Costa Rica in the last eighteen years. This result is consistent with what has happened in the rest of LAC, where the main FDI flows come from North America, Europe, and countries within the same region.

Figure 3. Costa Rica. Foreign Direct Investment according to the main countries of origin in million of US dollars (2000-2017)

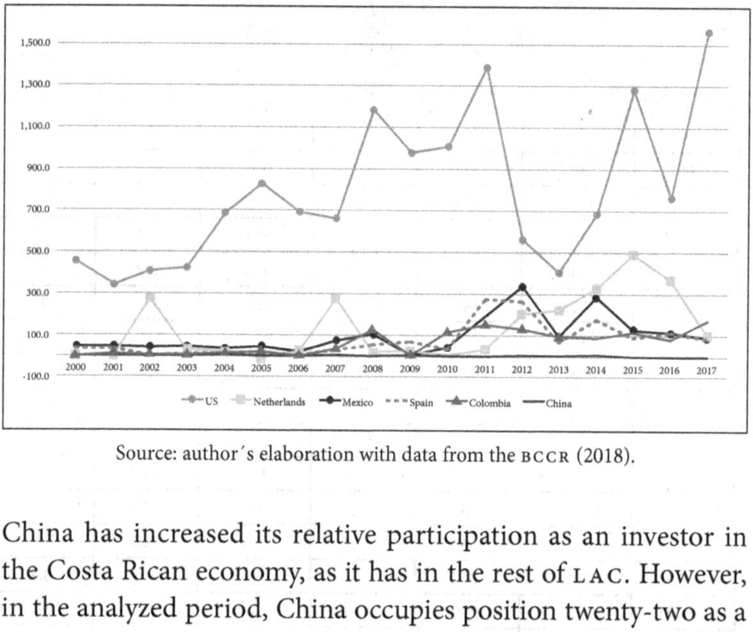

Source: author's elaboration with data from the BCCR (2018).

China has increased its relative participation as an investor in the Costa Rican economy, as it has in the rest of LAC. However, in the analyzed period, China occupies position twenty-two as a country of origin of investments in the Costa Rica. Chinese investment in Costa Rica peaked in 2014, at a rate six times higher than the average investment between 2000 and 2017. Chinese companies Huawei and ZTE entered the Costa Rican telecommunications market that year (Ellis, 2014).[1]

1 It should be noted that at the time, the Costa Rican telecommunications market represented a turning point, since there was fierce competition among telecom operators due to the recent opening of the market in 2009, effective until 2012.

Contrary to what happens with other business partners in Costa Rica, the case of China is interesting because although it is its second most important trading partner, its direct investments are not that significant (Arias and Vargas 2017).

Costa Rica has not been a major recipient of investment flows from China because of the lack of compatibility between the investments attracted by the Central American nation and the industries in which the Asian country has focused its investments abroad. As noted earlier, Costa Rica has concentrated on attracting companies with knowledge-intensive activities. This approach has been most successful in attracting companies from the United States because of Costa Rica's geographical proximity (OECD, 2012). China, in contrast, has designated most of its FDI in the region to the natural resources and energy required to sustain its high rates of industrialization in recent decades (López and Ramos 2014; de Freitas, Tepassê and Neves 2014).

In addition to the misalignment between the needs and expectations of foreign investment of both economies, cultural and legal institutional frameworks differences, generated by different political and social realities, have also been a factor. A decision-making process so mediated by different political forces has discouraged Chinese capital investments, causing stagnation and even a decline in the number of Chinese state companies operating in Costa Rican territory. According to figures from the Embassy of the People's Republic of China in Costa Rica, there are currently only ten companies with Chinese state capital in operation.[2] Legal institutional differences have become a barrier to realizing infrastructure projects financed by Chinese companies.

Another factor is the lack of interest the Costa Rican government has demonstrated in capturing investments from Chinese companies. According to interviews conducted with experts from

2 Although it was not possible to access official data from the CCPIT and the Economic Council Office of the Chinese Embassy in Costa Rica, a Chinese specialist and representatives of the Embassy itself points out that there has been an erosion in the Chinese companies that operate in Costa Rica. These same people point out that five years ago there were more than fifteen Chinese state-owned companies operating in the country.

the Coalition of Investment Initiatives (CINDE), this agency does not prioritize the monitoring of Chinese capital investments.

Chinese investment data in Costa Rica, as in other countries, is underestimated. This underestimation is explained by the bias generated by the Chinese investment flows to companies located in the Cayman Islands and the British Virgin Islands, through which Chinese companies invest in Central America and the non-obligation of Chinese private equity companies to declare their investments (CLACDS 2014). In the case of Costa Rica, even when there is no data on the private companies located in the country, observations and interviews with national and Chinese experts suggest that there is a significant amount of capital from China that is not identified and registered in the Costa Rican FDI statistics.

Academics and international organizations indicate that Costa Rica's recent strategy to attract investment must change if the country wants to continue taking advantage of capital flows to drive its economic and social development (Trejos 2008; OECD 2012). The scaling of Chinese capital towards investments in more knowledge intensive industries and infrastructure could allow Costa Rica to capitalize on a series of competitive advantages in the region to attract these investments.

Costa Rica could leverage two characteristics that initially attracted the attention of the Chinese government: 1) its geographical location in the middle of the continent as a possible hub of investment with a "market seeking" orientation to the rest of the continent, emphasizing knowledge-intensive industries and; 2) its extensive experience managing natural resources. As a laboratory of agribusiness, the generation of clean energy, and the conservation of natural resources, Costa Rica's results could then be applied and scaled in China (Chen 2016).

Costa Rica has seen significant growth in recent years in its business services market. Costa Rica has the potential to become a financial and business center for Chinese companies in the region, especially in light of the potential for expansion of Chinese companies like Alibaba. Attracting China's interest in industries of this nature could boost investment in physical and digital infrastructure (ports, airports, roads, canals, railways, telecommunications infrastructure, among others), all of which are strategic sectors for the development of the LAC countries (Niu 2018).

Conclusions and Policy Suggestions

The beginning of diplomatic relations in 2007 and the signing of the FTA in 2010 constitute the institutional arrangements that the government of Costa Rica has implemented to promote a closer relationship with China. A decade later, economic results and Chinese capital investments in the country have not produced the expected results. Although commercial relations have grown, they do not present the pace or intensity required to transform investment patterns and cooperation in sectors in which both countries have interests (Arias and Vargas 2017).

Investment volumes have been considerably low in the period analyzed, unlike the experiences of other commercial partners and in spite of the relevance of China as a partner in Costa Rica's commerce. The little data available, combined with interviews with experts, indicates that the volume of FDI has not reached the levels of investment necessary to boost the growth of strategic sectors for the Costa Rican economy.

This situation may have a pragmatic explanation, given that Chinese direct investments in LAC have been concentrated in sectors related to natural resources and raw materials. In recent years there has been growth in investments in the service and manufacturing sectors. China also provides financing in the form of loans to boost large infrastructure projects but this must not be confused with direct investment.

In the case of Costa Rica, the information available indicates that Chinese investment is still incipient. At first, it was thought that Costa Rica would be strategic for Chinese investments, not because of the size of the Costa Rican economy or because of its wealth in mineral resources, but rather because of its geographical location and legal security, which offered China competitive advantages to expand operations in the region. Costa Rican relations with China offered the possibility of investments in physical infrastructure, telecommunications, transport logistics, and stocking and energy. To date, no infrastructure project of significant scale has been executed with Chinese direct investment.

Failed attempts on behalf of both governments are found in the infrastructure and transport sector (roads), as well as in energy (oil refining). Perhaps the most promising project in terms of direct investment was the development of a Special Economic Zone in the Central Pacific of Costa Rica, which was promoted as the central project of the Development Bank of China for Costa Rica. It has remained stagnant for almost five years.

Within the context of this "cooling" in economic relations between the two countries, particularly in terms of China's interest in increasing direct investment in Costa Rica, the following policy suggestions may be useful:

1. The most important challenge for Costa Rica is to improve its legal institutional framework for doing business. Costa Rica's political process means that making decisions and finalizing contracts and investment projects with third countries can take more time than usual. It is necessary to establish clear rules of the game and a more efficient decision-making process.
2. The Government of Costa Rica should create a high-level technical secretariat to follow up on its economic relations with China and define a policy of attracting Chinese direct investment in sectors and economic activities of interest to both countries. This technical secretariat should have representation from the Ministry of Foreign Trade of Costa Rica (COMEX), private investment promotion agencies like the Foreign Trade Promoter (PROCOMER) and the Coalition of Investment Initiatives (CINDE), along with input from the Chinese Association of Costa Rica and the commerce representatives of the Chinese Embassy in Costa Rica.
3. The Costa Rican FDI authorities should identify productive sectors in which Costa Rica is a world leader that also have potential for attracting Chinese investment, such as clean energy, bioprospecting for the pharmaceutical

industry, research tourism in biodiversity, health tourism, clean transportation, and infrastructure for sustainable development.

4. Costa Rica should strengthen its commerce office in China by increasing the human resources present in China and focusing on Chinese companies with compatible interests to invest in Costa Rica, especially in knowledge-intensive activities. Greater inter-institutional coordination integrating the work of the Costa Rican "foreign trade triad" (COMEX, PROCOMER and CINDE) might achieve the kind of results that have been attained in markets such as the United States and some European countries.

References

Arias, Rafael and Juan Muñoz. 2007. "Reforma económica y modelo de promoción de exportaciones: logros y vacíos de la política de desarrollo de las últimas dos décadas". *Revista de Ciencias Económicas de la Universidad de Costa Rica 25-No. 1*, pp. 15-39.

Arias, Rafael and Luis Vargas. 2017. "Relaciones Económicas Costa Rica y China. In, Dussel Peters, Enrique (edit.). *América Latina y el Caribe y China: Economía, Comercio e Inversión 2017*. Red ALC-China, UDUAL, UNAM/Cechimex: México, pp. 215-234.

Armony, Ariel, Enrique Dussel and Shoujun Cui. 2018. "Introduction" In, Dussel Peters, Enrique, Ariel Armony and Shoujun Cui (Ed.). *Building Development for a New Era: China's Infrastructure Projects in Latin America and the Caribbean*. Mexico: Asian Studies Centre, UCIS, Red ALC-China, pp. ix-xi.

BCCR. 2018. *Inversión directa, economía declarante, anual (por actividad)* [data]. Retrieved from https://gee.bccr.fi.cr/indicadoreseconomicos/Cuadros/frmVerCatCuadro.aspx?idioma=1&CodCuadro=%202184.

BCCR. 2018. *Inversión directa, economía declarante, anual (por país de origen)* [data]. Retrieved from https://gee.bccr.fi.cr/indicadoreseconomicos/Cuadros/frmVerCatCuadro.aspx?idioma=1&CodCuadro=%202185.

BCCR. 2018. *Inversión directa, economía declarante, anual (por régimen)* [data]. Retrieved from https://gee.bccr.fi.cr/indicadores-economicos/Cuadros/frmVerCatCuadro.aspx?idioma=1&CodCuadro=%202183.

Burgués, Antonio. "Introducción". In, Trejos Montero, Marta (edit.). *Relaciones China-Costa Rica: Una referencia para Centroamérica*. CIDH: Costa Rica, pp. 7-12.

Chen Sui, Susan. 2016. "The Impact of Costa Rica's Relationship with China". *Revista Estudios* 33, pp. 1-32.

CLACDS (2014). *Comercio e Inversión entre América Central y China*. Costa Rica: CLACDS.

COMEX. 2010. *Tratado de Libre Comercio Costa Rica-China: Documento Explicativo*. Costa Rica: COMEX.

De Freitas, Alexandre, Ângela Tepassê and Marina Neves. 2018. "Las relaciones económicas entre Brasil y China a partir del desempeño de las empresas State Grid y Lenovo". In, Dussel Peters, Enrique (coord.). *La Inversión Extranjera Directa de China en América Latina: 10 casos de estudio*. Mexico: Red ALC-China, UDUAL, UNAM/CECHIMEX, pp. 61-132.

DeHart, Mónica. 2018. "1. China-Costa Rica Infrastructure Projects: Laying the Groundwork for Development?" In, Dussel Peters, Enrique, Ariel Armony and Shoujun Cui (Ed.). *Building Development for a New Era: China's Infrastructure Projects in Latin America and the Caribbean*. Mexico: Asian Studies Centre, UCIS, Red ALC-China, pp. 3-23.

Dussel Peters, Enrique. 2014. *Política económica –comercio e inversiones– de Guatemala hacia la República Popular de China: Hacia una estrategia en el corto, mediano y largo plazo*. Mexico: United Nations.

Dussel Peters, Enrique. 2018. "Introducción". In, Dussel Peters, Enrique (Coord.). *La Inversión Extranjera Directa de China en América Latina: 10 casos de estudio*. Mexico: Red ALC-China, UDUAL, UNAM/Cechimex, pp. 7-12.

Dussel Peters, Enrique. 2019. *Monitor de la OFDI de China en América Latina y el Caribe 2018*. Mexico: Red ALC-China.

ECLAC. 2017. *La Inversión Extranjera Directa en América Latina*. Santiago de Chile: ECLAC.

Ellis, R. Evan. 2014. *China on the Ground in Latin America-2014: Challenges for the Chinese and Impacts on the Region*. London: Palgrave Macmillan.

López, Andrés and Andrea Ramos. 2018. "Argentina y China: nuevos encadenamientos mercantiles globales con empresas chinas. Los casos de Huawei, CNOOC y Sinopec". In Dussel Peters, Enrique (Coord.). *La Inversión Extranjera Directa de China en América Latina: 10 casos de estudio*. Mexico: Red ALC-China, UDUAL, UNAM/Cechimex, pp. 13-60.

Matarrita, Ricardo. 2008. "Relaciones comerciales de Costa Rica con China". In, Estado de La Nación (coord.). *Decimocuarto Informe Estado de la Nación en Desarrollo Humano Sostenible*. Programa Estado de La Nación: Costa Rica.

Muller, Sven-Uwe and Fan Li. 2018. "Chinese Infrastructure Projects in Latin America and the Caribbean: The Experience of the Inter-American Development Bank". In, Dussel Peters, Enrique, Ariel Armony and Shoujun Cui (edits.). *Building Development for a New Era: China's Infrastructure Projects in Latin America and the Caribbean*. Asian Studies Centre, UCIS, Red ALC-China. Mexico, pp. 164-179.

Niu, Haibin. 2018. "A Strategic Analysis of Chinese Infrastructure Projects in Latin America and the Caribbean" In, Dussel Peters, Enrique, Ariel Armony and Shoujun Cui (Ed.). *Building Development for a New Era: China's Infrastructure Projects in Latin America and the Caribbean*. Asian Studies Centre, UCIS, Red ALC-China. Mexico, pp. 180-194.

OCDE. 2012. *Attracting Knowledge-intensive Foreign Direct Investment to Costa Rica: Challenges and Policy Options*. OECD: France.

Ortiz, Samuel. 2016. *Performance of China's* OFDI *(2005-2014), according to two methodological approaches: asset/liability and directional*. Mexico: UNAM/Cechimex.

PROCOMER. 2018. *Portal Estadístico de Comercio Exterior* [data]. Retrieved from http://sistemas.procomer.go.cr/estadisticas/inicio.aspx.

Rodil Marzábal, Óscar. 2017. "Relaciones Económicas Costa Rica y China. In, Dussel Peters, Enrique (Ed.). *América Latina y el Caribe y China: Economía, Comercio e Inversión 2017*. Red ALC-China, UDUAL, UNAM/Cechimex: Mexico, pp. 337-358.

Santiso, Javier. 2007. "Introduction". In, Santiso, Javier (edit.). *The Visible Hand of China in Latin America*. Paris: OECD, pp. 9-14.

Televisora de Costa Rica. 2018. *Terminal de Contenedores de Moín recibió segundo embarque de grúas pórticas y de patio*. Retrieved from https://teletica.com/194618 terminal-de-contenedores-de-moin-recibio-segundo-embarque-de-gruas-porticas-y-de-patio.

The Government of the Republic of Costa Rica. 2015. *Costa Rica y China fomentan crear Zona Económica Especial*. Retrieved from https://presidencia.go.cr/comunicados/2015/01/166-costa-rica-y-china-fomentan-crear-zona-economica-especial/.

The Government of the Republic of Costa Rica. 2018. *Inician intervención en Ruta 32 que dará vida útil de 10 años al tramo*. Retrieved from http://gobierno.cr/tag/ruta-32/.

Trejos, Alberto. 2013. Country Role Models for Development Success: the case of Costa Rica. In Fosu, A.K. (Ed.), *Achieving Development Success: Strategies and Lessons from the Developing World*. Oxford University Press: United Kingdom.

Yong, Marlon and María Villalobos. 2009. *Análisis de los flujos comerciales y el comercio e inversiones entre los países del ASEAN, China y Costa Rica*. Costa Rica: IICE-UCR.

RETROSPECTIVE AND PROSPECTIVE OF DOMINICAN REPUBLIC AND CHINA RELATIONS

Eduardo Klinger Pevida

Introduction

The announcement came on May 1st 2018. The world found out that the Dominican Republic had formalized its diplomatic relations with the People's Republic of China, recognizing it as the legitimate representative of China as a whole. That meant the end of this Caribbean nation's official ties with the Republic of Taiwan that it had maintained since the communist triumph in China, when the hitherto government of the then Republic of China, headed by General Chiang Kai-shek, was transported by the United States and its allies to the Chinese island of Formosa, today Taiwan. For more than 20 years practically everyone had continued to recognize this as the government of China until, in the decade of the nineteen seventies, President Richard Nixon took actions that brought the Chinese communist government closer to the US position towards the Soviet Union.

The conditions imposed by Mao Zedong, and accepted by the United States, led to the expulsion of Chiang Kai-shek's government from the United Nations and the recognition of the government seated in Beijing –then Peking– as the true and only representative of the Chinese nation. It involved turning over the permanent seat on the Security Council to the government of the People's Republic of China, with the corresponding veto power.

For the government located on the island of Formosa, it marked the beginning of its diplomatic isolation and, while abandoning the pretense of continuing to be recognized as the only voice for the Chinese nation, it proclaimed itself as the Chinese Republic of Taiwan and declared the existence of "two" Chinas. A progressive and incessant process began in which the international community gradually broke ties with Taipei, the "capital city" of Taiwan, and formalized its official links with one of the most dynamic economies of the twenty-first century and the world's second largest in terms of GDP.

By 2017, only 20 countries maintained their diplomatic recognition of Taiwan. In June of that year Panama broke its ties and recognized the People's Republic of China and, in May 2018, the Dominican Republic decided to end its relationship with Taipei and recognize the government in Beijing. A few weeks later El Salvador also terminated its relationship with Taiwan and initiated relations with the PRC. These actions, of a Caribbean island and two Central American countries, left Taiwan with only 17 allied governments –including the Vatican– more than half of which are in Latin America and the Caribbean, namely: Belize, Guatemala, Haiti, Honduras, Nicaragua, Paraguay, Saint Kitts and Nevis, Saint Lucia and Saint Vincent and the Grenadines; another six are in Oceania: Marshall Islands, Solomon Islands, Kiribati, Nauru, Palau and Tuvalu; and in Africa only Swaziland, recently renamed Esuatini. In Europe the only "government" that remains faithful to Taiwan is the Vatican.

The detachment of the Dominican Republic from the group of nations that still hold together regarding Taiwan had special significance, since it was the most relevant country of that group. The argument that these relations were established almost "77 years ago" was an inconsistent reference to why diplomatic ties had been sustained. This would trace the situation back to 1941 when the "Republic of Taiwan" did not yet exist. In fact, the date refers to the moment when many countries established official relations with what is now the People's Republic, recognized by more than 170 nations as the true and only China. The decision recently made by the Dominican Republic finally led this country to a real, legitimate and consistent path. It was absurd to pretend to continue ignoring the presence of a key figure in the world's geopolitical scenario.

Consequently, the Dominican decision to recognize its connections to the People's Republic of China represents the closing of another Cold War chapter that had remained open, and resets the country within the reality of the current global scenario. In fact, the relations between the PRC and the Dominican Republic really began in 1997 when they both signed an agreement to formally establish a commercial representation in the other country.

In 2016 the Organization for Economic Cooperation and Development (OECD), the Economic Commission for Latin America and the Caribbean (ECLAC) and the CAF (Development Bank of Latin America) jointly prepared the study "Economic Outlook 2016" in which they recommended that the Dominican Republic –along with the other countries of this region– should "deepen and improve its partnership with China".

Prior Chinese Interest in the Dominican Economy

During the years when the exchanges between Chinese and Dominican companies and entrepreneurs began, expressions of interest were manifested which, for the most part, could not prosper due to the absence of appropriate mechanisms derived from the lack of diplomatic relations.

One example is the situation that presented itself in 2010 when Chinese investors expressed willingness to invest about 800 million dollars for the construction of a 600-megawatt coal-fired plant in Monte Cristi, in the north of the island. The deal could not be brought to fruition despite the interest expressed by the Dominican Corporation of State Electric Companies (CDEEE).

In 2012, the Dominican Republic's Center of Export and Investment (CEI-RD), announced that the Chinese company HAYCO –a well-known manufacturer of mass consumption products, including liquid supply systems, water purification devices, electric toothbrushes and household cleaning items– intended to open a plant in the DR. At the time it would have been the first of such factories to open outside of China. However, in the absence of official relations the project was postponed.

In 2013, the Institute of Innovation in Biotechnology and Industry (IIBI) in the Dominican Republic attracted the attention of a Chinese enterprise because of a novel technology it had developed to process cassava starch and flour, and given the possibility, as well, to dehydrate widely available bananas to make flour. On occasion, Chinese companies with investments in the Caribbean sugar industry also came forth with proposals to invest in the local sugar industry, since sugar is a product of great interest to China given its importance for the food and pharmaceutical industries.

Through the efforts of the respective trade and investment promotion offices that the two countries had mutually opened, long before bilateral relations were formalized –China opened its Commercial Office in Santo Domingo in 1997 and the Dominican Republic opened one in Shanghai in 2011– expressions of interest and even proposals for collaboration had been manifested by the Chinese. Multiple delegations of Chinese businessmen had visited the DR. Several commercial fairs had been held under the patronage of the national business sector and representation agreements had been signed, among other initiatives.

Even before diplomatic relations were formalized, the Chinese had expressed their interest in various projects with investments totaling more than 800 million dollars and with relevant socioeconomic impacts, namely:

- The PowerChina entity proposed a multipurpose project for the Yuna River that would prevent recurrent flooding in the area, and provide potable water and water for irrigation, as well as a hydroelectric plant. The total investment would reach $350 million dollars and could employ up to 2 thousand workers.
- An electricity generation plant based on biomass and natural gas with an investment of $300 million dollars.
- A central waste incinerator for more than $100 million.

- Also reported was the willingness to build 10,000 low-cost houses with an investment of $200 million dollars. It has been pointed out that the project could be expanded up to the construction of 30 thousand housing units (Commercial Office of the People´s Republic of China in the Dominican Republic).

Before the establishment of diplomatic ties, the Chinese authorities had already stated their interest in building 30 thousand houses with a serial methodology, addressing the Dominican Republic's needs in that sector. The Chinese had also mentioned the availability of scholarships for Dominicans in several fields. According to the Commercial Office of China in Santo Domingo 80 Dominicans had benefitted from training programs in China in 2016, and it was intended that in 2017 they would host three times more as part of their commitment to the development of the DR's human resources. According to this same office, China was both interested in and willing to support the Dominican Republic's development and poverty reduction efforts. Through the Academy of International Business Officers and/or the Training Center of the Ministry of Commerce, training courses are offered in economics, business, administration, commerce, telecommunications, transportation, construction and technology, among others.

Years ago Chinese entrepreneurs had expressed interest in eventually becoming involved in infrastructure projects in the Dominican Republic. Among these is the development of a freight and passenger railway system with national coverage, extending along 908 kilometers with an estimated cost of $5,670 million dollars. This train system would interconnect the main ports and airports and even the Santo Domingo metro. In addition to connecting with the binational market in Dajabon, it would connect the cities of Barahona, San Juan de la Maguana, Santiago, Punta Cana and Samaná.

Likewise, Chinese businesspeople have expressed interest in building a 30 km "express train" route Santiago-Puerto Plata, a distance that would be covered in just 25 minutes. The project also includes a four-lane tunnel and 14 km of road, all with a cost of one billion dollars.

Even without formal relations, the country was frequently visited by groups of Chinese businessmen exploring the potentialities of the Dominican economy for investing capital and technology in sectors that could increase exports such as pork, chicken and beef, as well as in bauxite production. They were also interested in possible investments in agro-industries, mining and tourism.

On several occasions the Chinese commercial representation in the DR complained about the difficulties Chinese companies faced when trying to move forward with their investment interests, stemming from incidental obstacles, posed by officials for imprecise reasons, or those of a bureaucratic nature due to the absence of formal relations. In 2015, the Head of China's Office of Commerce, Promotion and Investment in Santo Domingo publicly appealed to the President of the Dominican Republic to eliminate the obstacles blocking procedures to install a shoe factory to initiate production targeting the Latin American market, acquisition of a hotel under the administration of the state entity Corphotel and even investments of a social nature.

Dominican Interest in Negotiating with China

For a long time the Dominican government and entrepreneurs have been aware of the PRC's economic potential and they realize that attracting Chinese investments in the DR's productive sectors would probably facilitate increasing the supply of exportable goods directed mainly towards the Chinese market, and thereby contribute to decreasing the DR's enormous and growing trade deficit. At the First Ministerial Meeting of the Community of Latin American and Caribbean States (CELAC) and China, held in Beijing in 2015, Dominican representatives expressed interest in deepening relations with China and hopes of attracting Chinese investments in key sectors of national interest such as manufacturing, agro-industries, tourist services and others in general.

The Chinese government must surely have visualized the Dominican Republic's potential for extending the Belt and Road initiative in Latin America and the Caribbean. The DR's strategic location in Mesoamerica, its vicinity to the Panama Canal and the port and airport facilities available might enable it to become a trade hub for the Caribbean. The DR might, in fact, possibly become a large logistics center for the collection and distribution of cargo that could make trade more efficient for the smaller surrounding islands. The tiny scale of Caribbean island economies makes international trade extraordinarily burdensome. Keep in mind that the Caribbean has the highest concentration of small states in the world.

In 2014, a ministerial delegation participated in the footwear multinational Wolverine's Suppliers Summit, held in the Chinese city of Macao, and shed light on the ease and advantages offered by the Dominican Republic for international investments in the footwear sector, in particular. Free zone industrial parks annually export several hundred million dollars in footwear to the United States and European markets, taking advantage of the preferential trade agreements in force with those destinations. It is a sector of great interest for the Dominican economy

The "1st China-DR Cooperation Symposium", a bilateral seminar held in October 2015, was particularly relevant. It addressed the issues of investment, tourism and cooperation between important entrepreneurial groups in these two nations, through business rounds, seeking to stimulate and expand the economic and trade relations already underway. For the DR's Minister of Economy, the meeting was laden with intentions "to establish a broad communication channel that would allow strengthening of scientific, technical and cultural cooperation relations, as well as economic, commercial and investment exchange." During his speech the minister affirmed that the country was considering, "when the time was right, to promote a strategic alliance between the People's Republic of China and the Dominican Republic, that would allow to diversify trade and open a new horizon for Chinese investment" in the DR (Presentation by the Minister of Economy 2015).

Since 2015 the Dominican government has called for the opening of new horizons for Chinese investment in the country, which would be an alternative way of compensating, to some extent, for the trade deficit it faces. Oil prospecting and exploration is of maximum interest for the national economy. Seven sedimentary basins have been identified on land. Five of these are open for eventual concessions, while in the case of the other two there are possibilities for negotiating strategic associations with companies willing to provide investment and technology. It has also been indicated that "all the marine territory is available for concession". Among investment projects that would be very well received, given the country's urgent needs, are those aimed at electricity generation, especially from clean sources. Energy, nowadays, constitutes two of the weakest links in the national economic structure: dependence on fuel imports and limited electricity generation capacity.

For the Dominican Republic it is of maximum strategic interest to continue diversifying its generation matrix. If in 2000, 88% of the generation depended on liquid petroleum derivatives, by 2017 liquid fuel consumption, for this purpose, derived from petroleum had dropped significantly to 33.55%: 29.5% from number 6 and 4.1% from number 2. By then 34.68% was produced with natural gas; the hydroelectric plants contributed 14.24%; the weight of coal was 13.86%; 2.47% was produced with wind energy; 0.90% came from biomass and 0.31% was solar energy. (Source: Dominican Association of the Electrical Industry (ADIE). For the Dominican economy it is vital to continue decreasing the dependence on oil imports and expanding the diversification of electricity generation. China has achieved indisputable global leadership in energy and previously Chinese companies had expressed interest in investing in that sector in the DR.

The Dominican Republic presented an extensive inventory of investment opportunities to its Chinese counterpart, highlighting mining with options in gold, silver and copper as well as oil exploration and exploitation and priority for the electricity sector.

Trade between the Dominican Republic and China

With the beginning of official relations, both parties have significant interest in promoting business activities in the commercial sector –where there is already a strong relationship– and investments in infrastructure, ports, and roads, as well as in education, culture, and finance among several others. From the point of view of trade in goods, the Chinese have shown interest in local products and traditional national goods such as tobacco, cocoa, pineapples and coffee among others, which may be in high demand. For example, the Chinese are great smokers and the Dominican homegrown cigar enjoys great prestige and international acclaim. Two emblematic Dominican stones, larimar and amber, are widely appreciated in China.

Undoubtedly, long before establishing diplomatic relations, the aspect where the relationship had already reached a high level and intensity was in bilateral trade. In 2002, the commercial flow between the two nations amounted to 210 million dollars, of which the Dominican Republic imported 207.7 million and exported only 2.3 million. If we observe that in 2017 the exchange reached US$2,603 million dollars, of which US$145 million were exports from the DR and US$2,458 million reflected imports from China, we can see that in 15 years trade grew 12.4 times. Dominican exports to China increased 63 times and their imports from China, which still remain far above their exports, grew only 12 times. That same year, the last of commercial and formal ties with Taiwan, Dominican imports from that market reached US$119.8 million –only 4.9% of what was imported from the People's Republic of China– and exports destined for the "rebellious" island were only $ 34.3 million, 23.7% of the total exported to the mainland.

Since 2009 the People's Republic of China is the second source of imports for the DR and since 2011, the Asian giant has become the third destination for DR exports only surpassed by the United States and Haiti. However, the DR has accumulated a trade deficit of US$6,445 million between 2013 and 2013, period in which the total of exports of the DR reached US$862 million, 13.4% of the volume of trade with China.The main products that the

DR imports from China are cell phones, motorcycles, sports shoes, machines for reception and voice conversation, and data transmission, fans, air conditioners, tires, vehicle parts and accessories and plastic articles for manufacturing.

The Dominican Republic mainly exports mining products such as copper and aluminum minerals and their concentrates, copper waste and scrap, ferronickel, zinc minerals and their concentrates, as well as medical and dental instruments and equipment and disposable materials –needles, catheters and cannulas– and raw paper or cardboard kraft or corrugated paper or cardboard for recycling, which combined constitute up to 74% of its exports to China. It also exports tobacco, coffee, cocoa, rum and other similar products. The contraction of exports sent to the Chinese market, which fell from US$355.6 million dollars in 2012 to US$145.0 million in 2017, was due for the most part to reductions in shipments of bauxite and scrap metals.

Among almost 170 industries established in the DR's free zones, the textile industry is a sector that offers great export possibilities. Similarly, the country has great export potential in tropical fruits and vegetables. The Dominican Republic exports Sanchez type cacao which has a high demand in the global cocoa and chocolate industries.

The PRC and the DR have made progress in talks on relaxing restrictions and expediting trade as well as fulfilling phytosanitary requirements to create better conditions for Dominican agricultural sector exports, which offers great possibilities.

In 2017 the DR's main exports to China consisted of telephones and telephone sets for US$47.88 million (33.0% of total exports); copper minerals and concentrates, US$22.43 million (15.5%), medical instruments and devices US$13.88 million (9.6%); ferrous alloys US$11.11 million (7.7%). Other exports totaled US$49.7 million (33.2% of total exports). That same year, Dominican imports from China consisted of cell phones, motorcycles, sport shoes, data transmission machines, air conditioners, fans, tires, vehicle parts and plastic articles, among others (National Bureau of Statistics).

Since 2015 the World Bank had recognized that the Dominican Republic has "untapped opportunities to increase its exports to China ..." and suggested that they begin to explore an eventual increase in exports other than those obtained in the extractive industries, noting opportunities in the pharmaceutical industry, plastics and medical equipment, in addition to iron and steel, ranking these as sectors well positioned to export not only to China but also to Brazil, Ecuador and Venezuela among other possible destinations. According to the authors of the study cited here, the Dominican Republic has "a comparative advantage" in these areas.

Free -Trade Zones

The Dominican free-trade zones structure is leader of the sector throughout the entire Caribbean area, havint exported some $5,695 million USD in goods in 2017 and having directly created 165,724 formal jobs. In 2017, 665 companies operated in the different industrial parks participated with US$2,365 million dollars. These companies accounted for an investment of US$4,474 million mainly from the US, Canada, European Union, Brazil, Taiwan and South Korea (ADOZONA and CNZFE).

Between the years 2010 and 2017, and according to ADOZONA, the Dominican Free-Trade Zones exported $40,869 million USD, with the United States as the main destination. In 2017, medical products were the leading export, representing $1,485 million USD, 26% of the total; textile and garments followed with $1,068 million USD or 19%; electrical and electronic products $883 USD, for 16%; $794 million USD worth of tobacco and derivatives were exported equal to 14%, and $391 million USD of footwear and its components equal to 7% of the total exports from the free zones (CNZFE).

It should be noted that the establishment of the so-called Special Economic Zones (SEZs) has played a fundamental role in China's own development strategy, and they have begun to replicate this model in some of the countries where they invest. In the

Dominican Republic's case, presumably taking advantage of the undisputed virtues of the national laws binding for the free zone system, the port structure that already exists and the potential for development this sector offers, as well as the proximity and ease of access to the North American market, we can assume that Chinese entrepreneurs, both public and private, will see this as a relevant niche for their interests.

In April 2018, just days before the announcement of the establishment of diplomatic relations, a "first" Chinese company opened for business in the DR under the free zones system. This is the Kingston Aluminio company, with an initial investment of 11 million dollars and which during its first year will generate 420 direct jobs and a thousand indirect ones. This is a manufacturing industry with cutting-edge technology to produce aluminum profiles for markets in the United States, Europe and Asia (Source: CEI-RD). However, in some other reports it appears that there is another Chinese company in the free-trade zone sector, Good Box Dominican, E. I. R. L., and three others with both Dominican and Chinese capital: Adomchin S. A., Copen United DR, S. R. L. and SML, Dominican, S. A.

Outside the limits of the free-trade zone only two other Chinese companies are confirmed to be established in the country. This is the case of the most important Chinese investment registered in the Dominican Republic, the Cerro Maimón mine (COMIRDOM), a producer of gold, silver and copper, 53% of which is owned by the Chinese company Shenzhen Zhongjin Lingnan Nonfemet Co., Ltd ("Zhongjin Lingnan"). Also Huawei Technologies Dominican, S. R. L. was established in the island some years ago.

For both parties it would be of great potential to identify joint actions in projects to add value to Dominican agricultural products, which have significant weight in national exports but mainly as consumables or as primary products.

Tourism

Tourism is perceived as a sector of widespread incidence, since China declared the Dominican Republic as a "destination". This is an important legal requirement to promote the visit of Chinese citizens to the DR, which will stimulate investments in the sector, possibly lead to a direct flight and facilitate visas or other entry documents.

The interrelation between the DR and China in the tourism industry is particularly interesting for both parties. The DR is the main tourist destination in the Caribbean region with more than 6 million tourists arriving every year and the country aspires to reach the 10 million annual visitors mark as soon as possible. China is the main source of outbound travelers worldwide with more than 130 millions of its citizens traveling around the world in 2017. In only a few years' time, it is expected that about 500 million Chinese will be traveling abroad as tourists. Given Chinese idiosyncrasy, the most attractive aspect of a tourist destination is what it has to offer in cultural and historical aspects as well as the possibility for adventure and new experiences. The Dominican Republic has much to offer in the way of attractions; it is the place "where everything started". Santo Domingo is the "First City" of the Americas; it has many interesting sites to visit and numerous indigenous manifestations capable of attracting the attention of Chinese visitors. According to the World Tourism Organization (UNWTO) Chinese tourists have the highest incidence of expenditure in the places they visit. Furthermore given the distance and duration of the trip from their continent to the Caribbean, the length of their stay will probably be considerable.

Consequently, given that China includes the DR as a destination to promote for its outbound travelers, arranging a more direct air connection and facilitating financial transactions for them is highly urgent for both countries.

Taking into account that the Dominican government hopes to receive up to 10 million tourists annually, this sector offers ample possibilities for investment by Chinese companies.

Financial Relations

Also since 2015, through the Banco de Reservas (BR), the Dominican government has reached a series of financial agreements with public and private banks in China. The aim is for the BR to become a channel between companies from both nations, thus facilitating payments and other reciprocal banking transactions in which Chinese entrepreneurs could use their national currency. This objective, without a doubt, will require great ingenuity to overcome practical obstacles that will inevitably arise.

However, the new scenario created with the establishment of diplomatic relations and a deepening of bilateral ties will be beneficial for both countries. For China it will mean furthering its goal of increasingly internationalizing the Yuan, and for Dominican entrepreneurs it will enhance conditions for more competitive prices. These agreements made it possible to begin creating a financial platform for accessing means of payment used in China, thereby facilitating the development of the DR as a destination for Chinese tourists.

The agreements reached between the Dominican BR and the Chinese export and development banks –state entities oriented towards promoting trade, investment and financial cooperation– made it possible for them to focus their attention on clusters of public and private companies interested in exploring possibilities in the manufacturing, energy and infrastructure sectors. Doors were opened so that Chinese banks can finance local projects in the DR and support Chinese companies that settle on Dominican soil.

Shortly after bilateral relations were formalized, both Governments participated in conversations aimed at providing practical support for agreements that had thus far been identified and concretized. A Bilateral Joint Commission was created to provide follow up to the proposals that were being introduced, with emphasis on trade, foreign direct investment, and cooperation in and development of the tourism sector. As stated above, tourism is of particular relevance for the Dominican Republic given its status as the most important destination in the Caribbean region. The DR currently receives-more than 6 million tourists yearly and is working to reach its goal of 10 million visitors, upon initiating the relationship with China, the world's leading outbound market.

Right from the start Dominican counterparts made clear their interest in attracting Chinese capital for the execution of infrastructure projects, especially for port development for commercial cargo and berthing for tourist cruises, as well as economic development zones and new industrial parks, renewable energy, electricity distribution and transmission systems, roadside and emergency assistance, sanitation of rivers, land transportation projects and urban development in general and education and technical training programs. On their part, the China Trade and Investment Promotion Office in Santo Domingo announced that the Chinese government had $25 billion dollars available for investments in infrastructure and tourism, as well as for other areas (Fu 2018).

The Chinese authorities consider economic and commercial presence in the Dominican Republic to be attractive because of this county's status as the most important economy in Central America and the Caribbean, its continued pace of economic growth, socio-political stability, and having certain competitive advantages, as well as having free trade agreements with the United States, Europe, Central America and the CARICOM nations. Once official ties were established, China began work on drawing up more than ten agreements, being drafted by three bilateral technical committees, which both parties would sign on the occasion of a state visit by the Dominican President to Beijing shortly thereafter.

The Dominican Republic views very positively that it is being considered as part of the "New Silk Road", an idea which also seems to be attractive to China.

Conclusions

Obviously, for many years, in spite of the fact that the Dominican Republic had maintained relations with Taiwan, Chinese authorities and businessmen had expressed interest in investing in and establishing a presence in the Dominican economy.

The first Chinese ambassador to Santo Domingo has insisted on China's interest in increasing their imports from the island and has identified some traditional Dominican exports as being of interest in addition to other products from the national economy and from the free zone sector. He also offered a donation of 10 million dollars for the national electrical sector and stated his government's willingness to collaborate in such a key and problematic sector for the Dominican economy.

Three months after diplomatic relations were established no agreements had yet been signed. It had been announced that during President Danilo Medina's visit to Beijing near the end of 2018, approximately 10 agreements were to be considered.

There is no doubt that having established formal relations will be relevant for investment in infrastructure development and other activities and that the new situation will further enhance trade.

References

Fu, Xinrong. 2018. Interview. Commercial Representative of the People's Republic of China in the Dominican Republic, June 29th.

Presentation by the Minister of Economy, Planning and Development entitled "China-DR cooperation relations in politics, in the international community, commercially, in tourism and in culture", 1st Cooperation Symposium China - DR, October 27, 2015.

Report of the World Bank [http://www.elcaribe.com.do/2015/03/18/cita-potencial-exportador-para-china brasil#sthash.b3CpMcuS.dpuf).

THE IMPACT OF CHINESE OUTBOUND FOREIGN DIRECT INVESTMENT IN JAMAICA (2000-2017)

TWO CASE STUDIES

Jevon Minto

At the end of 2017, Jamaica was the leading recipient of outward foreign direct investment inflows (OFDI) in the English-speaking Caribbean, with the greatest amount directed at greenfield projects (World Investment Report 2018). According to data from the Bank of Jamaica, the country received US$ 928 million in total OFDI inflows in 2016, the highest amount since 2008, and the second highest amount since 2002. Chinese OFDI played a significant role in reverting the country's FDI stock to pre-crisis levels. With a 2016 acquisition of US$ 360 million, the stock of Chinese investments in Jamaica reached US$ 839 million dollars, the highest ever recorded, tripling the investment stock for 2015 when the volume of Chinese OFDI peaked at US$ 225 million. These investments have increased in both quality and quantity since the beginning of the current decade and century, facilitated and encouraged by both governments, and th eir state agencies. Since the first flows were recorded in 2007, Chinese OFDI has become a critical feature of Sino-Jamaica relations, reflecting the wider growth, development, and integration of the Asian giant in the global economy that led to an expansion of its overseas investments facilitated by a strategic commercial policy agenda. While these investments have become more and more critical, they are not the only form of Chinese investment in the island. Infrastructure investments also play an increasingly important role in the bilateral relationship. As Beijing embarks on exporting its industrial capacity and its companies look to expand market access, its OFDI is emerging as a new priority in Jamaica, creating new realities for the 46-year old relationship.

This study examines the economic relation between China and Jamaica, analyzing the stock and flows of Chinese OFDI to the Caribbean island between 2000-2017 through the lens of two case studies. This is one of the first studies that looks at the bilateral investment relationship. In analyzing the relationship, the key questions discussed are: in what sectors are Chinese FDI flows directed? What are the motivations behind these flows to Jamaica? Is the output targeted at the domestic or external market? What type of Chinese firms are investing in the country? How does its stock of FDI compare to trade and cooperation flows? Is there a reciprocal FDI flows to China from Jamaican companies? This paper will discuss the wider China-Jamaica relationship, then present two case studies that afford a window into the impact of Chinese OFDI on the Jamaican economy, and then conclude with policy suggestions and a look at opportunities for the future.

China Jamaica Relations (Trade, Aid, Financing, and Infrastructure Projects)

Since the start of the current century, bilateral economic cooperation between Jamaica and China has developed at an unprecedented level. Following the launch of the 1999 Chinese "going out" policy, Jamaica became China's biggest trading partner in the English-speaking Caribbean (Richardson 2013). According to data from the Statistical Institute of Jamaica, STATIN, in 2000, China-Jamaica bilateral trade volume[1] was US$ 58 million. By 2004, it increased six-fold, totaling US$ 396 million (see Figure 1). At that time, Jamaica was a net exporter, recording a trade deficit of US$ 54 million. That trend would be short-lived when the

1 Trade data referred to through this report do not include re-exports except where otherwise specified.

balance of trade shifted considerably in China's favor beginning in 2007. Since then, Jamaican exports have dropped significantly while imports from China have grown substantially and rapidly, with some notable fluctuations. Consequently, the trade deficit has grown substantially.

Figure 1. Jamaica-China Trade Volume (US$ million)

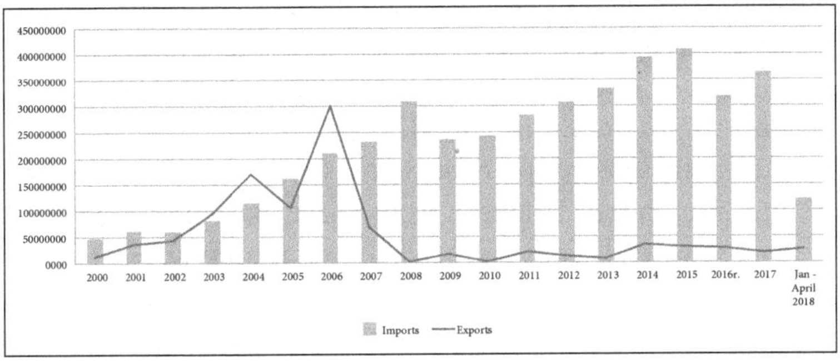

Source: author's elaboration based on data requested and obtained from the Statistical Institute of Jamaica, STATIN.

At the end of 2015, China held a trade surplus with Jamaica that had reached a record high of an estimated US$ 385 million, up from US$ 355 million the previous year. The goods composition of these imports is heavily concentrated around manufacturing, machinery, and transport equipment. Jamaica mainly exports aluminum, waste, and scrap to China. Overall, total bilateral trade in 2017 reached US$ 382 million, recovering from the fluctuation recorded in 2016 when the volume dipped to US$ 345 million.

Since 2004, China has moved from being Jamaica's seventh import destination to fourth in 2009 (Lei 2016) and second since 2017, behind the United States of America. Over the same period, China moved from being Jamaica's third largest export destination to not being featured among the country's top ten export destination (STATIN 2018). There are two primary factors responsible for this development. First, the 2008 financial crisis, which led to a reduction in global demand for Jamaican exports and services, crippled bauxite plants (Kouame and Reyes 2010). In January 2006, bilateral trade amounted to an estimated US$ 500 million, increasing from US$ 270 the previous year. Notably, Jamaican exports outpaced Chinese imports during this period. Since then, the export volume has failed to keep pace with increasing imports. Secondly, the robust engagement of Chinese authorities has promoted closer China-Latin America and Caribbean trade (Chinese State Council 2008). This engagement has been boosted by lines of credit as well as loans and grants that effectively promote Chinese exports to Jamaica. In 2009 for example, as part of a US$ 118 million aid package extended to Jamaica from the Chinese Government, 84% or US$ 100 million was designated to a line of credit for short-term trade financing (JIS 2009).

Before these developments, Bernal (2012) noted that imports from China to the Caribbean would have likely increased based on three factors: 1) both the merchant community and consumers in Jamaica and the wider Caribbean were becoming more familiar with products from China, 2) the competitive price and quality of Chinese exports and 3) a decline in exports from the Caribbean Community (CARICOM) to Jamaica. In terms of the impact that Chinese imports are having on Caribbean economies, Díaz (2016:175) concludes that the growing trade ties between China and the region pose a growing threat to and could weaken intra-CARICOM trade. Díaz also finds that Chinese imports have displaced some imports from the United States, Latin America, and the European Union.

Development and Infrastructure Projects

Jamaica is a small country with big needs. The island nation has a population of 2.8 million people and is classified as an upper middle-income country. However, it struggles with low growth (0.5% in 2017), high public debt (114% of GDP[2] and the second highest in all Latin America and the Caribbean (OECD 2017)), climate vulnerability, and external shocks. Financing those needs weighs heavily on the public purse since the country is unable to

2 2017 estimates according to World Bank data.

access low-interest rate concessional financing (Edmond 2018). Chinese financing eases some of that pressure as it assumes the risks in financing projects in the region and uses innovative financial schemes to lower debt obligation (Gallagher 2016).

While China remains Jamaica's second trade partner, it is the main provider of development assistance to the country, contributing more than twice the amount of financing to Jamaica between 2008 and 2016 compared to development finance from countries on the Development Assistance Committee (DAC) of the Organization for Economic Co-operation and Development, OECD.[3] This trend reflects heightened bilateral engagement from both sides and a reduction in aid flows from traditional development partners to Jamaica due to its reclassification from lower-middle to middle-income country (UNDP Evaluation Office 2011). From 2008-2016, China provided an estimated US$ 1 billion[4] in development finance to the Jamaican economy (see Figure 2). Most of that amount related to loans rather than grants, according to the Planning Institute of Jamaica (PIOJ) and most of that financing was

Figure 2. Chinese – DAC Development Assistance Flows to Jamaica (2008-2016)

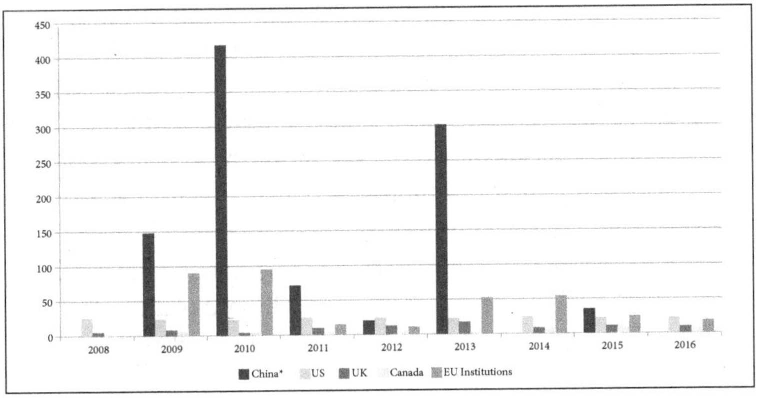

Source: author's elaboration based on Peng Liu and Minto Jevon (2018).

3 Chinese and DAC aid are measured differently. While most flows from DAC to developing countries are non-reimbursable, Chinese financing to developing countries like Jamaica are in the form of low-interest rate loans.

4 This data only includes government-to-government financing and excludes public private partnership projects such as a Chinese built US$ 730 million highway.

for infrastructure projects (Economic and Social Survey Jamaica 2015). Chinese financing to Jamaica has also easily surpassed financing from multilateral partners including the Inter-American Development Bank and the World Bank (Jackson 2016).

Two Case Studies

Despite a 1994 Bilateral Investment Treaty and the 1996 Double Taxation Avoidance Agreement, Chinese investments in Jamaica remained low in the first decade of the current century until 2007. In 2004, China was the eighth most important FDI source for the developing world and other advanced middle-income economies (Buckley, Clegg, Cross, Liu, Voss, and Zheng 2007). In 2005, the stock of Chinese investment in the Caribbean amounted to an estimated US$ 81.2 million (Bernal 2016).

The picture gradually changed as Chinese companies began to invest in Jamaica in 2007. Since then, Chinese investments in Jamaica have increased steadily with 2010 flows equaling the combined 2008 and 2009 stocks. In 2011, Jamaica recorded approximately US$ 40 million in Chinese investments, representing a 9-fold increase on the year before and making up 8.3% of total Chinese OFDI in the Caribbean that year. The next five years, 2012-2016, saw an even more robust profile of Chinese investments with 2012 stocks almost doubling those of the previous year. The 2013 numbers doubled 2011 figures, pushing Jamaica's share of Chinese Caribbean investment to a high of 13%. Since then, Chinese investments in Jamaica have risen progressively both qualitatively and quantitatively. At the end of 2016, the stock of Chinese investments in Jamaica reached US$ 839 million dollars (see Figure 3).

Chinese OFDI in Jamaica is motivated by the same market and resource seeking incentives seen in the rest of the region (López and Ramos 2014). Large state-owned enterprises have a strong presence in the sectors targeted by these investments. In Jamaica, the entire stock of current and prospective Chinese OFDI is focused on four sectors: agriculture, manufacturing, mining, and

Figure 3. Chinese Investments in Jamaica and the Caribbean 2007-2016

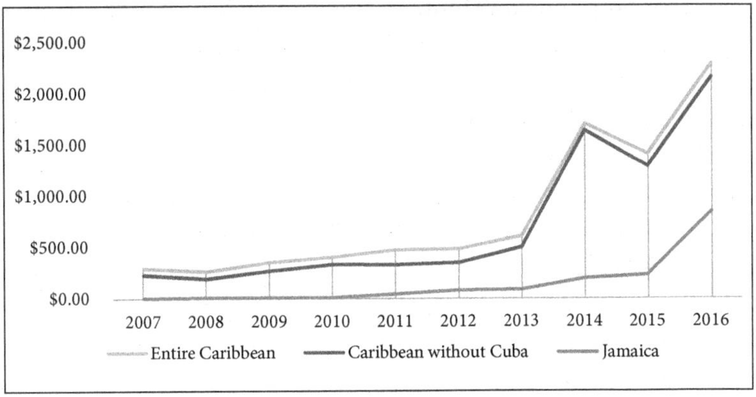

Source: author's elaboration based on data from the "Statistical Bulletin of China's Outward Foreign Direct Investment 2016", pp. 50-54.

Table 1. Chinese Foreign Direct Investments in Jamaica

Company	Sector	Investment		Location	Direct Employment Generated (August 2018)
		Value	Date		
China National Complete Plant Import-Export Corporation	Agriculture (cane farming)	US$ 260 million[5]	2011	Multiple	850[6]
	Manufacturing (sugar)	US$ 9 million[7]	2011	Multiple	
Jiuquan Iron and Steel Company (JISCO)	Mining (acquisition)	US$ 300 million[8]	2016	Nain, St. Elizabeth	900[9]
	(Plant reopening)	US$ 60 million[10]	2016	Nain, St. Elizabeth	

Source: author´s elaboration.

5 See Chinese Fed Up - Investors Want Out Of Monymusk Sugar Deal: http://jamaica-gleaner.com/article/lead-stories/20170830/chinese-fed-investors-want-out-monymusk-sugar-deal

6 See Sugar Workers Learning Chinese Out West: http://jamaica-gleaner.com/article/news/20170911/sugar-workers-learning-chinese-out-west

7 Ibid.

8 See JISCO makes first shipment of alumina today http://www.jamaicaobserver.com/news/jisco-makes-first-shipment-of-alumina-today_121115

9 Ibid.

10 See the 2018 Briefing Paper on Foreign Direct Investment in the region published by the Economic Commission for Latin America and the Caribbean (ECLAC).

tourism, all of which are the most important sectors for the Jamaican economy and contribute the most foreign exchange earnings.

The next section will analyze the following two investments in Jamaica, made by the China National Complete Plant Import-Export Corporation and Jiuguan Iron and Steel (JISCO), by looking at their value, social impact, and future. From a macroeconomic standpoint, these investments have already had a positive effect on the Jamaican economy. For example, JISCO acquired Jamaica's largest bauxite mining refinery form the Russian conglomerate, UC Rusal, in 2016. JISCO then invested a further US$60 million to reopen the plant, which was closed in 2009 as the global financial crisis deepened. The investment added some 800 new jobs to the economy and represents one of the largest investments undertaken

China's Complant International: Acquisitions in the Sugar Sector

In 2007, the Jamaican Government initiated measures to sell the five companies that made up the Sugar Company of Jamaica due to mounting financial losses, years of rising debt, and the resulting consequences of an EU decision to reform its sugar regime (Jamaica Information Service 2010).[11] Three years later, in 2010, the Chinese government-owned Complant International Sugar Company entered into an agreement for the lease and purchase of three sugar estates and two factories, namely the Frome Sugar Estate and factory, the Monymusk Sugar Estate and factory, and the Bernard Lodge Estate, which was handed over in 2011. Complant established the wholly-owned Jamaican company, Pan Caribbean Sugar Company Limited (PCSC) to manage the assets. Complant group also owns and operates other sugar businesses in various African countries as well as in China.

11 In 2009, the "sugar protocol," a long standing-agreement which provided Jamaica and other sugar producers from African, Caribbean and Pacific (ACP) states duty-free and quota-free access to the EU sugar market, came to an end. Until 2012, ACP countries were still allowed to export sugar duty-free to the EU, but prices and quantities were not fixed.

Under the sugar divestment agreement with Jamaica, Complant leased roughly 18,000 hectares (44,478 acres) of cane fields over 49 years. In exchange, Complant paid US$ 9 million for the three factories and control of surrounding sugar cane lands. PCSC also agreed to renovate and rehabilitate the sugar mills and fields by installing new equipment such as boilers, centrifugal baskets, and cane conveyor systems. Both sides agreed also that PCSC would invest a minimum of US$ 156 million within four years of acquiring the assets. Two years before the deadline, the Development Bank of Jamaica reported that PCSC had invested more than US$ 260 million in the factories (Hill 2013). To facilitate the transaction, the Jamaican government provided a 20-year tax holiday on five categories[12] of taxes to the company (Luton 2012). A cap was also imposed on the number of foreign nationals PCSC could bring into the country and enumerated which categories of employees could be brought in to Jamaica. Additional provisions were also made for Jamaicans to be trained in various disciplines by PCSC foreign experts, and the power of unions was significantly reduced (Hill 2013).

The decision by the Chinese to take over the estates and factories was a surprise to local experts given the high debt, low productivity, and operating costs associated with the industry. Nonetheless, the Chinese were convinced that their modernization plans would improve the industry and allow them to maximize their profit margins. Jamaica, in comparison to the African factories, was very attractive to Complant, given its 200 years of sugar history and continuous operation of the factories (Titus 2017). Despite these vast concerns, Chinese executives had a plan to restructure and cut operation costs by around 30% to enhance productivity and improve efficiency at the estates. These included the development of idle cane fields, improving the irrigation system, producing their own electricity, and providing a lower rate for harvesting, reaping, and transportation. They also sought to exit a cooperative agreement to sell sugar through Jamaica Cane

12 These categories are general consumption tax (GCT), corporate income, withholding tax, customs duty and stamp duty or transfer tax.

Product Sales Limited (JCPS), the agency that markets Jamaican sugar locally and internationally (Grant 2014). Data from the Jamaica Sugar Industry Authorities, SIA, shows that those modernization plans are yet to yield positive results. Sugar production has nose-dived, and output is at its lowest levels since 2007 (see Figure 4).

At the end of 2016, approximately 385 workers had been made redundant at the Monymusk estate (Jamaica Observer 2016), the same year that Complant suspended certain agricultural and factory operations at two Bernard Lodge and Monymusk Estate sugar estates as well as the sugar factory at Monymusk. The decision left the Jamaican Government scrabbling to save the livelihoods of hundreds of affected cane farmers. Both parties entered into a short-term management agreement for the Government to operate the factory. By 2017, PCSC was only operating the Frome Sugar Estate and Frome Sugar Factory and had announced plans to completely offload the Monymusk estate to a new operator. Company executives say their investment in Jamaica has far

Figure 4. General Trends in Foreign Direct Investment Flows to Jamaica US millions (2000-2017)

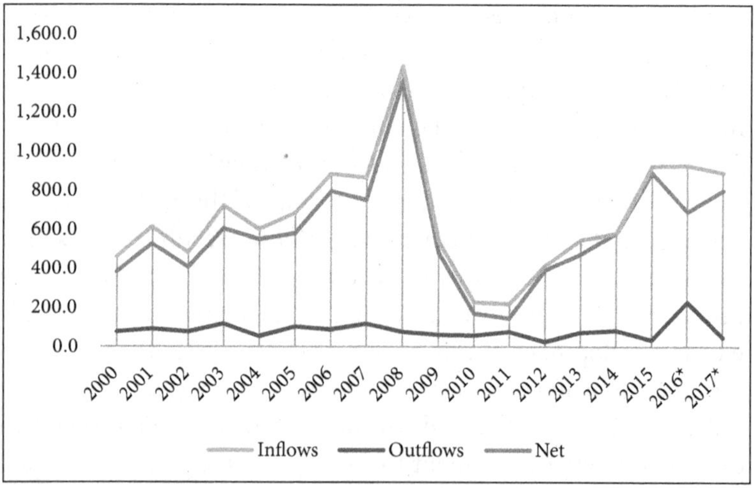

Source: author's elaboration based on data from the Bank of *Jamaica External Statistics.*[13]

13 See http://boj.org.jm/uploads/excel/Table_37a.xls

exceeded their commitment since Monymusk has the capacity to process 600,000 tons of sugar cane but annual production capacity was amounting to less than 200,000 tons, resulting in a cumulative loss of US$ 60 million ($J 7.3 billion). This decline in production was exacerbated by the decline in global sugar prices, adverse weather condition, illicit cane fires, and theft. Sugar production has reached historic low rates under Chinese management (see Figure 4). The Monymusk estate accounted for $J 5.5 billion of the total reported losses between 2010 and 2015. PCSC and the Government of Jamaica have initiated a search to find investors to take over operations of the Monymusk assets. Local media have reported that another Chinese company and PCSC are in the second phase of negotiations for the factory (Titus 2018).

The Chinese conglomerate's decision to invest in Jamaica's sugar industry mirrors the investment pattern of Chinese OFDI in regional agricultural products. This pattern is generally market-oriented (seeking new markets, profit, and cheap labour) and occurs alongside the exploration for resources (Myers and Guo 2018). China's National Bureau of Statistics reports that foreign investment in farming, forestry, and fishing grew fivefold between 2010 and 2016. According to China's Ministry of Agriculture, the country had over 1,300 agricultural, forestry, and fisheries enterprises with registered overseas investments valued at 180 billion yuan (US$ 26 billion) at the end of 2016 (Farmer's Daily, 2017a). Still, despite the billions recorded in losses, data from the Honk Kong-based Joyful Right Group, the holding company of PCSC, shows that Jamaica remains the principal market for the Group (see Figure 5 below). In Jamaica, the average selling price of products is still higher than that in the international market (Poyser 2016).

Figure 5. Joyful Right's Group Revenue from External Customers, HK million (2012-2017)

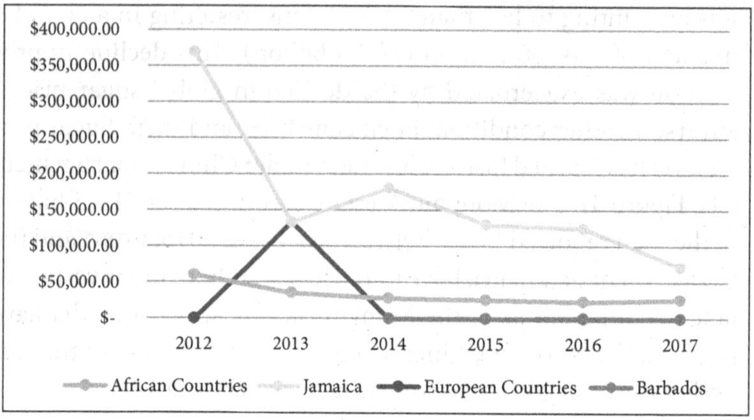

Source: author's elaboration based on data compiled from the annual reports[14] of Hua Lien International Company Limited, the parent company of PCSC.

Figure 6. Tons of Sugar Produced Annually by PCSC for Crop Years 2006-2016.

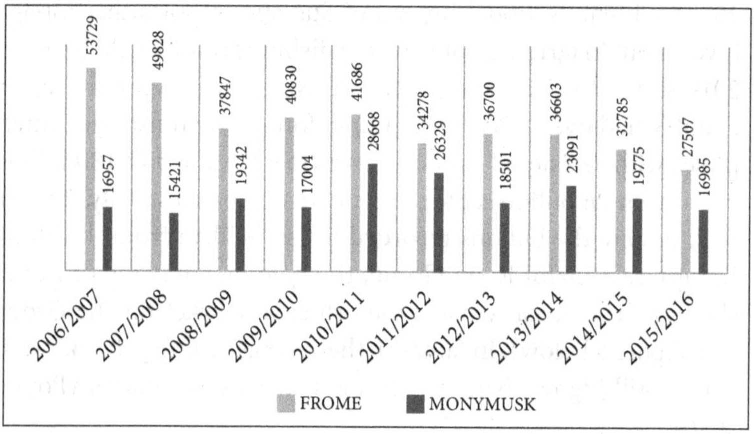

Source: author's elaboration based on data from the annual reports of Jamaica Sugar Industry Authority[15]

14 See list of annual reports at - http://www.irasia.com/listco/hk/hualien/annual/index.htm

15 See https://japarliament.gov.jm/attachments/article/1539/2015%20Ministry%20Paper%20122.pdf

1. JISCO Alumina Jamaica II Limited (Alumina Plant): Exporting Industrial Capacity

One of the most crucial investments by Chinese state-owned companies in Jamaica was the 2016 purchase of the Alpart Bauxite-Alumina Refinery, formerly owned by a Russian company, UC Rusal. Jiuquan Iron and Steel Company (JISCO), based in Gansu Province, Northwest China, invested US$ 300 million to acquire the plant which has a capacity to produce 1.65 million metric tons of alumina, making it the largest refinery in Jamaica.[16] JISCO is listed among China's top 7 firms (private and SOEs) with production capacities that exceed 1 million metric tons. In addition to the US$ 300 million for the acquisition, JISCO invested another US$ 60 million to open the plant. JISCO's rehabilitation and expansion plans could see an additional US$ 2 billion in investments flows for the development of the downstream capacity of the plant, the building of alumina refineries and aluminum smelters. Experts have estimated that the expansion plans could increase the annual production capacity of the plant to a maximum of three million tons of alumina, pushing the combined output of the refinery to 5 million tons (Gleaner 2018).

Aluminum production in China rose from 3.1 million tons in 2001 to 30.8 million metric tons in 2015, quadrupling China's share of global production (from 13% to 54% during the same period). The increase in production has largely been driven by rising domestic demand for unwrought aluminum (CRU Group 2018). Today, China remains the largest global producer of both primary and wrought aluminum and is a substantial producer of secondary aluminum. It intends to grow its production capacity to 52 million tons by 2020, which would represent a 25% increase in comparison to 2016 figures (The Aluminum Association 2008). This capacity growth exceeds growth in Chinese domestic consumption (Hendrix 2014), resulting in China's excess primary aluminum capacity of some 10 million tons as of 2017, with another 3.3 million tons expected in 2018. This excess capacity has forced

16 Data from Jamaica Bauxite Institute.

several regions in China to implement stringent environmental and regulatory guidelines that will result in seasonal cuts for aluminum smelting and alumina refining, primarily to protect the air quality across China (Daly and Burton 2018).

As these problems emerged at home and Premier Liu Keqiang intensified a war against smog, the Chinese government began exporting the extra capacity, adding international capacity cooperation (国际产能合作) to the "Go Global" policy suite in 2014 (Kenderdine and Ling 2017). Under the capacity cooperation framework, China seeks to offshore excess capacity as OFDI through a variety of infrastructure investments. Provincial governments are the main actors targeted under this policy. To date, China's National Development and Reform Commission, the body coordinating capacity cooperation, has signed agreements with multiple provincial-level governments, including Gansu and 12 other provinces (Tristan 2017). Beijing has billed its industrial capacity export cooperation as an alternative form of technology transfer and foreign direct investment. But for experts, the motivations behind this policy is two-fold: on one hand, it is an attempt by China to bring whole industrial clusters to its external markets in order to develop the industrial bases of its trading partners. On the other hand, it is perceived as a a move by China to offshore its excess industrial capacity. JISCO's acquisition of Alpart can be explained by these two motivations. A third explanation is the 2014 ban by the Indonesian Government[17] on the export of mineral ores as it moves to develop national downstream processing capacity. The decision reverberated in Beijing, leading large state-owned companies like JISCO to scour the globe for new sources of supply (Nolad 2013).

Currently, Jamaica mines bauxite into alumina but due to high energy costs, it is unable to develop the commodity further into aluminum or its related products. As JISCO settles in the country, it also plans to build a LNG plant to facilitate a second alumina

17 In January 2017, Indonesia's Ministry of Energy and Mineral Resources announced that it would allow the export of several minerals, including bauxite, to resume but under certain conditions.

refinery and aluminum smelters as part of a larger plan to develop an industrial park and a special economic zone. The special economic zone is expected to integrate six main functions: processing and manufacturing, modern logistics, international trade, research and development, professional services, and urban support. The company will likely spend an anticipated US$ 3 billion to construct and operationalize these new facilities. Earlier this year, both the Chinese Central Government and the Gansu Provincial Government approved a framework agreement, clearing the way for JISCO to go ahead with the investment. The acquisition, in addition to the expansion of the plant, is projected to bring an overall investment value of US$ 6 billion to the Jamaican economy and generate approximately 60,000 jobs, according to government estimates. Based on the agreement, 70% of the jobs will be taken by Jamaican employees (Linton 2018).

If JISCO can deliver on its planned expansion of the refinery, the Jamaican economy should improve its competitiveness and increase alumina production, which is an output leading to increased domestic exports and expanded foreign exchange earnings. Currently, bauxite and alumina demand in China significantly exceeds domestic production capacity, making China import-dependent (Hendrix 2014). Local employment should also increase both in primary and secondary terms. Experts have already questioned whether JISCO will be able to execute these ambitious plans due to Jamaica's high reliance on imported energy, weak electrical capacity, and numerous failed attempts, dating back to the 1950s at developing downstream capacity (Hendrix 2014).

Conclusion and Policy Recommendations

Upon the acquisition of the Alpart Refinery and the three sugar assets, JISCO and Complant became not only major players in the industries but the principal actors. Alumina, bauxite, and sugar are ranked consistently as Jamaica's most traded commodities and in addition to tourism, they are the largest net earners of foreign exchange for the country, contributing significantly to government revenues. Thus, more than in any other period in history, the stability of the Jamaican economy is tied to Chinese domestic industrial and agricultural policies. These linkages have also ushered in a new phase in the bilateral relationship: A new pattern has emerged in Chinese investments in Jamaica. Large SOEs are establishing and exerting a dominant sectoral presence in the economy. These firms, backed by Chinese Government state policies, are also showing a growing interest in cultivating complementary services in the form of new investments in order to capture the potential spillover effects created by their investments. But notwithstanding the spillover benefits, specifically in the bauxite and alumina industry, expectations must be gauged against the learning curve and the domestic reality that confronts large Chinese SOEs in the Jamaican market.

In terms of JISCO's acquisition of the Alpart refinery and its planned expansion, this investment presents long-term Chinese control over local operations. These investments are driven mainly by China's need to secure, access, and acquire key commodity assets and capture under-exploited markets. For China, Jamaica is strategically located to leverage those objectives and to provide its companies with greater and easier access to the North American market. For Jamaica, many of the expected spill-over effects of the investment, like downstream capacity development, the transfer of technology, etc., are speculative. As experts have pointed out, due to issues related to local infrastructure, high reliance on imported energy, weak electrical capacity, and numerous failed attempts at downstream capacity development, the expected benefits do not have much credibility and may well remain a pipe dream. *The Global Energy Architecture Performance Index (*See Global Energy Architecture Performance Index Report 2017 (2018) has consistently ranked Jamaica as a low energy performer because of these issues. Conversely, due to high local energy costs, previous multinational corporations, such as Rusal and Alcoa, have at times temporarily shut down their Jamaican alumina refining plants (Hendrix 2014). In fact, JISCO was able to acquire the Alpart refinery due to its previous closure by UC Rusal.

In the case of Complant, why would Chinese companies go through the trouble of acquiring these sugar assets, given that both the risks and the costs involved were known to be very high? The most plausible answer to this question is twofold: 1) initial optimism by the Chinese that the economic advantages would offset the high transaction costs and that its position in Jamaica would provide expanded market access and; 2) the aggressive nature of Chinese agricultural investments. With the support of Chinese government policies, Complant demonstrated that it was willing to undertake an investment in an industry that experts believe face a very uncertain future (Wint, A. G., Baghaloo, Wilfred., & Henriques, Marjorie, 2010). At the same time, their incursion into the sugar sector provides an insight into the long process of adaptation and learning that Chinese companies confront in the local market.

In Jamaica, the long-term viability of the sugar industry is worrying. A 2010 Government commissioned report offered "no consensus position on the long-term sustainability of a private Sugar Industry future," (Wint, A. G., Baghaloo, Wilfred., & Henriques, Marjorie, 2010). But the industry is also the fabric of the rural economy. The resources invested by Complant have modernized the Monymusk factory. Now, as a new Chinese company looks to acquire the assets, the policy making environment in Jamaica will have to create an enabling environment that bridge the gap between the learning curve faced by Chinese companies in understanding local industry operations. Equally important, the policy environment must direct the viability and future of the industry by promoting the diversification of production –away from sugar and into other secondary products. In bauxite and mining, government policies will have to factor in civil society interests in legislation that give Chinese firms the green light to develop downstream capacities. Extractive investments of this nature are typically dogged by controversy and oftentimes face backlash from political and civil society concerns relating to human rights, working conditions, and corporate social responsibility, could lead to the politicization of these investment (Hendrix 2014).

To mitigate the risks facing Chinese investments in Jamaica, to capture their spillover effects, the following policy recommendations are useful:

a) Jamaica should consider upgrading ties with China from a strategic to a comprehensive strategic partnership, which would reaffirm the significance of the bilateral relationship and expand it into new directions. A deeper relationship would incentivize Chinese companies to participate in the transfer of technology towards new industries and the capture of potential spillover effects. Other benefits expected to emerge from Chinese OFDI include the augmentation of domestic capital, the transfer of knowledge and skills, promotion of competition and innovation, employment and enhanced output, and export and revenue performance.

b) To monitor and evaluate these efforts, Jamaican authorities should also consider establishing a specialized unit at the Jamaica Promotions Corporation, JAMPRO. China has the excess capacity while Jamaica needs the capital to build self-development capacity. Closer bilateral ties could close those gaps but institutional safeguards must also be implemented to make investments socially and environmentally sustainable. As noted earlier in this study, China's industrial capacity cooperation policy was in part provoked by domestic environmental concerns. Now that Chinese is offloading the excess capacity to markets like Jamaica and reduces internal pollution at the same time, Jamaica must institute strong safeguards to ensure that similar concerns are not triggered locally by the production process of these SOE s.

References

Arana, Rumile. 2009. *The World Aluminium Market: An analysis of Market Structure and Price Developments.* Jamaica: Bank of Jamaica.

Bernal, Richard. 2016. *Chinese Foreign Direct Investment in the Caribbean: Potential and Prospects*. Washington, D.C.: Inter-American Development Bank.

Buckley, Peter, Jeremy Clegg, Adam R. Cross, Liu, Xin, Hinrich Voss, and Ping Zheng. 2007. *The Determinants of Chinese Outward Foreign Direct Investment*. Journal of International Business Studies, 38(4), 499-518.

Cann, Vicki. (2016). *China's Jiuquan Iron & Steel boosts Jamaican economy* | CCTV News. Available at: http://english.cctv.com/2016/08/11/ARTIKvfrWrgGTwzARYVgHL93160811.shtml

Cru Group. 2018. JISCO*'s dependence on the third-party alumina market*. Available at: https://www.crugroup.com/knowledge-and-insights/insights/jiscos-dependence-on-the-third-party-alumina-market/

Daly, Tom and Melanie Burton. 2018. *China's winter cuts heat up aluminum market*. Available at: https://www.reuters.com/article/us-china-pollution-aluminium/chinas-winter-cuts-heat-up-aluminum-market-idUSKBN1CM11C.

Díaz, Raymer. (2016). La nueva relación de América Latina y el Caribe con China: ¿integración o desintegración regional? El caso de la CARICOM. In, Enrique Dussel Peters. (coordinator), La nueva relación comercial de ALC con China: ¿integración o desintegración? (pp. 141-194). Cuidad de Mexico: Red Académica de América Latina y el Caribe sobre China.

Dussel Peters, Enrique (coord.). 2010. *La inversión extranjera directa de China en América Latina: 10 estudios de caso*. Red ALC-China, UDUAL, UNAM, Cechimex, México, pp. 13-59.

Dussel Peters, Enrique and Samuel Ortiz Velásquez. 2017. Monitor of China's OFDI in Latin America and the Caribbean. Mexico: Academic Network of Latin America and the Caribbean on China (LAC-China Network)

Economic and Social Survey Jamaica. 2015. Planning Institute of Jamaica. Available at: https://webstore.pioj.gov.jm/images/PreviewDocument/20243.pdf.

Gallagher, Kevin. 2016. The China Triangle: China and the Fate of the Americas. New York and London: Oxford University Press.

Hendrix, Cullen. 2014. *Chinese Investment in Bauxite and Alumina: How Credible Are Promises of Processing Development?* | Korbel School of International Studies & Peterson Institute for International Economic.

Hill, Aubyn. 2013. *Chinese investment improving sugar industry* | Development Bank of Jamaica. Available at: http://dbankjm.com/news/chinese-investment-improving-sugar-industry/

Jamaica Gleaner. 2017. *FULL STATEMENT: Chinese Embassy hits back at Bunting.* Available at: http://jamaica-gleaner.com/article/news/20170811/full-statement-chinese-embassy-hits-back-bunting.

Jamaica Gleaner. 2018. Growth & Jobs | Why the future of Alpart matters to you - Projected Increased Alumina production is a near-term game changer, says Small-Ferguson. Available at: http://jamaica-gleaner.com/article/news/20180306/growth-jobs-why-future-alpart-matters-you-projected-increased-alumina

Jamaica Information Service. 2010. *Gov't Finalising US$9 Million Sale of Last 3 Sugar Factories* - Jamaica Information Service. Available at: https://jis.gov.jm/govt-finalising-us9-million-sale-of-last-3-sugar-factories/].

Jamaica Observer. 2016. 385 lose jobs. Available at: http://www.jamaicaobserver.com/news/385-lose-jobs_49203

Jamaica Observer. 2018. *Bunting insists Chinese 'taking over' Jamaica.* Available at: http://www.jamaicaobserver.com/latestnews/Bunting_insists_Chinese_taking_over_Jamaica?profile=1470.

Jamaica Observer. 2018a. *Ground to be broken for Jamaica-Gansu industrial park in December*. Available at: http://www.jamaicaobserver.com/latestnews/Ground_to_be_broken_for_Jamaica-Gansu_industrial_park_in_December_?profile=1373

Kenderdine, Tristan and Han Ling. 2017. *International Capacity Cooperation-Financing China's Export of Industrial Overcapacity*. Global Policy, 9(1), pp.41-52.

Kenderdine, Tristan. 2017. *The PRC's international capacity cooperation exports both industrial capacity and financial risk* | Asia Pathways. Available at: https://www.asiapathways-adbi.org/2017/07/the-prcs-international-capacity-cooperation-exports-both-industrial-capacity-and-financial-risk/.

Kouame, Auguste and Maria Ivanova Reyes. 2010. *The Caribbean Region Beyond the 2008-09 Global Financial Crisis* | International Monetary Fund.

Lian, Ruby and Melaine Burton. 2018. *China orders aluminum, steel cuts in war on smog*. Available at: https://www.reuters.com/article/us-china-pollution/china-orders-aluminum-steel-cuts-in-war-on-smog-idUSKBN1683G6

Lei, Lui. 2016. Jamaica-China Ties Reaping Harvest. Jamaica Gleaner. Available at: http://jamaica-gleaner.com/article/commentary/20160315/liu-lei-jamaica-china-ties-reaping-harvest

Linton, Latonya. 2018. Ground-Breaking for Jamaica-Gansu Industrial Park Year-End - Jamaica Information Service. Jamaica Information Service. Available at: https://jis.gov.jm/ground-breaking-for-jamaica-gansu-industrial-park-year-end/.

López, Andrés and Daniela Ramos. 2014. "*Argentina y China: nuevos encadenamientos mercantiles globales con empresas chinas. Los casos de Huawei, CNOOC y Sinopec*". In,

Luton, Daraine. 2012. *Waivers galore for Chinese firm*. Jamaica Gleaner. Available at: http://jamaica-gleaner.com/gleaner/20120530/lead/lead3.html

McIntosh, Douglas. 2018. Bilateral Trade Between Jamaica and China Expanding. Jamaica Information Service. Available at: https://jis.gov.jm/bilateral-trade-between-jamaica-and-china-expanding/

Myers, Margaret and Guo Jie. 2018. *China's Agricultural Investment in Latin America: A Critical Assessment* | The Inter-American Dialogue. Available at: http://www.thedialogue.org/wp-content/uploads/2015/06/Chinas-Agricultural-Investment-in-Latin-America.pdf

OECD. 2018. *Latin American Economic Outlook 2018: Rethinking Institutions for Development* | OECD Publishing. Available at: https://read.oecd-ilibrary.org/development/latin-american-economic-outlook-2018_leo-2018-en#page1.

Peng, Liu and Jevon Minto. 2018. *Chinese Foreign Aid to Latin America and the Caribbean – the case of Jamaica* (forthcoming). The Inter-American Dialogue

Poyser, Andre. 2016. *Aluminum consultant says Alpart restart will add downward pressure on prices.* Available at: http://jamaica-gleaner.com/article/lead-stories/20160824/aluminium-consultant-says-alpart-restart-will-add-downward-pressure.

Richardson, Julian. 2018. *'Jamaica now top Caribbean trading partner for China'* | Jamaica Observer. Available at: http://www.jamaicaobserver.com/business/Jamaica-now-top-Caribbean-trading-partner-for-China_14928589.

STATIN. (2018). Jamaica's Top 10 Import & Export Destinations 2014-2018. Statistical Institute of Jamaica. Unpublished data.

The Aluminum Association. 2018. *Aluminum excess capacity: time to act.* Available at: https://aluminium.ca/uploader/publications/roadmap_aluminiumexcesscapacity_timetoact-letterfinal.pdf

Titus, Mark. 2017. *Chinese hit hard by realities in local sugar industry.* Available at: http://jamaica-gleaner.com/article/lead-stories/20171121/chinese-hit-hard-realities-local-sugar-industry.

Titus, Mark. 2018. *Another Chinese firm eyeing Monymusk sugar factory.* Available at: http://jamaica-gleaner.com/article/lead-stories/20180109/another-chinese-firm-eyeing-monymusk-sugar-factory.

UNDP Evaluation Office. 2011. *Assessment of Development Results: Evaluation of UNDP Contribution.* United Nations Development Programme.

Wint, A. G., Baghaloo, Wilfred., & Henriques, Marjorie. (2010). Report of the Sugar Industry Enquiry Commission. Kingston: Ministry of Agriculture.

World Investment Report 2017. 2018. United Nations Conference on Trade and Development, UNCTAD. Available at: http://caribbean.cepal.org/content/world-investment-report-2017.

CHINA'S OVERSEAS FOREIGN DIRECT INVESTMENT IN MEXICO (2000-2018)

Enrique Dussel Peters

Mexico, together with China and a few other countries, has been one of the most successful international cases in attracting inflows of foreign direct investments (FDI) in the recent decades. In the context of China's growing global presence, its outflows of foreign direct investments (OFDI) have become increasingly relevant. The goal of this chapter is to analyze the characteristics of China's OFDI to Mexico since 2000 and discuss the bilateral learning process in this field.

This chapter is divided into three sections. The first section examines the political and economic context of the rapidly evolving bilateral relationship between Mexico and China, including politics, trade, financing, infrastructure, and other relevant topics since 2000. The second section highlights the volume of China's OFDI to Mexico and its main characteristics and structures in terms of annual transactions, employment, ownership structure, and sectors of the respective transactions. Finally, the third section discusses some of the main conclusions of the analysis and presents a series of proposals regarding China's OFDI in Mexico.

The Socioeconomic Context of China's OFDI in Mexico

Mexico was one of the first Latin American countries to extend diplomatic recognition of the People´s Republic of China. That relationship dates back to February 14th, 1972 (Anguiano Roch 2012; Ventura Valero and Meléndrez Armada 2016). Formally and diplomatically, the Mexico-China relationship has grown and matured substantially in the last decades.

There are significant meetings and commitments at the Latin American and Caribbean-China level, such as the Community of Latin American and Caribbean States (CELAC)-China Forum, active since 2015 (Cui and Pérez García 2016). The Cooperation Plan of 2015 (for the period 2015-2019) and 2018 (for the period 2019-2021) offers a wide range of concrete opportunities for cooperation, specifically in the fields of trade, infrastructure, and Chinese investments in LAC. The relationship has also improved in extension and depth, particularly since China's adhesion to the World Trade Organization (WTO) in 2001. Between 2013-2018, presidents of both countries met seven times, in addition to hundreds of meetings at all levels (Ventura Valero and Meléndrez Armada 2016). In this period, both countries also achieved dozens of sanitary and phytosanitary agreements on specific products (including berries, pork, and dairy products), as well as the denomination of origin of tequila. A set of bilateral instruments to enhance tourism has existed since 2013: three airlines now have direct Mexico-China flights. Finally, an Agreement for the Promotion and Reciprocal Protection of Investments was signed in 2008. The bilateral relationship today operates via four key institutions: the High Level Group (since 2004), the High Level Group in Business (since 2013), the High Level Group in Investments (since 2013) and most importantly, the Binational Commission (since 2004). In theory these institutions meet at least once a year, although their efficiency and results has been debated (Anguiano 2018; Dussel Peters and Levy-Dabbah 2018).

Since the Trump administration took office in January of 2017, the "new triangular relationship" (Dussel Peters, Hearn and Shaiken 2013) has been extremely tense. Under Trump, the United States has so far renegotiated the North American Free Trade Agreement (NAFTA) at the end of 2018 (also known as the United States-Mexico-Canada Agreement or USMCA), which has to be ratified by the legislatures of the three countries. After imposing unilateral tariff on sectors such as steel and aluminum and over 50% of Chinese imports, the Trump Administration began trade negotiations with China in January of 2019, with no concrete results until the first quarter of 2019. The new Mexican administration of Andrés Manuel López Obrador, who took office December of 2018, has been extremely cautious about avoiding confrontation with the Trump Administration on any matter, including the USMCA and immigration. The ratification process of the USMCA could prove extremely difficult for Mexico and may generate massive political and economic tensions throughout 2019-2020.[1]

China is Mexico´s second trading partner since 2003, displacing countries and regions such as Canada, the European Union, and Latin America. The topic has been analyzed in depth in recent years (Dussel Peters 2018; Dussel Peters and Ortiz Velásquez 2016; Ruiz Durán 2018). On the one hand, China's presence in Mexico´s trade has increased substantially, from levels below 1% of Mexico´s total trade before 2000 to 9.74% in 2018 (see Figure 1). On the other, this process has occurred primarily through massive Chinese imports, which increased from less than 1% up until 1996 to 17.64% in 2018. That process occurred in parallel to a massive displacement of US imports during the same period, particularly in electronics, auto parts and automobiles, the main imported items from China. Mexico´s massive trade deficit with China –in 2018 the import/export coefficient accounted for 11.2 or more than US$ 76 billion– is a result of Mexico´s difficulties in exporting to China and the manufactured goods, which account for practically all imports, flowing from China .

1 Each of the legislative powers will have to ratify USMCA, which includes an article that explicitly excludes the possibility of any of its members negotiating free-trade agreements with "non-market economies," meaning implicitly the People´s Republic of China. The NAFTA region, from this perspective, could become the first international "anti-China" region (Dussel Peters 2018/a).

Figure 1. Mexico Trade with the United States and China (1993-2018)
(percentage over respective total)

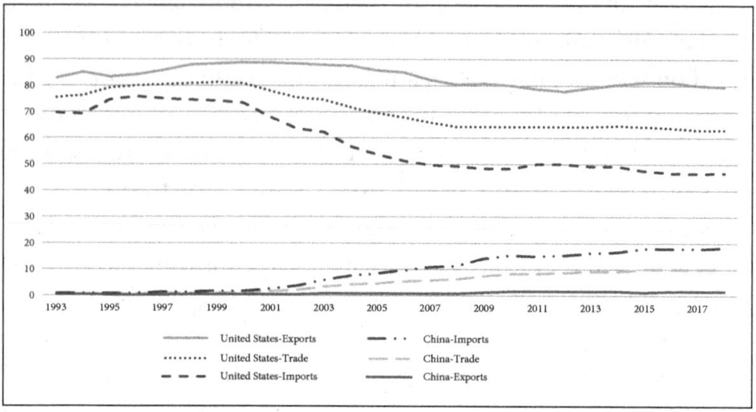

Source: author's elaboration based on Secretaría de Economía

Contrary to many other Latin American and Caribbean countries, Mexico has received practically no financing from China, with very few exceptions (IAD 2019; Zamora Torres 2016). Firms established in Mexico are limited in their access to domestic and international financial markets. Relatively high costs and other conditions have also been a limiting factor. China's experience with Mexico in the field of infrastructure projects has also been very limited and full of misunderstandings. In recent years, two major infrastructure projects, the high-speed train from Mexico City to Querétaro in 2014 and the hydroelectric plant Chicoasén II in 2016, failed (Dussel Peters 2018/b).

China's OFDI in Mexico (2000-2018)

China and Mexico have been some of the most outstanding international cases in attracting FDI in the last decades. Since 2000, Mexico registered in average $US 27 billion FDI annually during 2000-2017, 2.1% of global FDI); Mexico´s FDI was highest in 2002 with 4.1% of global FDI and accounted for around of a quarter of LAC´s FDI for 2000-2017. China's FDI, on the other hand, has constantly increased for the period 2000-2017, accounting for 6.5% and 8.1% for 2000-2010 and 2011-2017, respectively, and achieving its highest annual level with almost $US 140 billion in the period 2015-2017. While the relevance of Mexico's and LAC's FDI has remained relatively stable —at around 2.7% of their respective GDPs— it has fallen substantially for China. In the early 2000s China's FDI over GDP achieved levels above 3.5% and decreased substantially since then to levels closer to 1% in 2016 and 2017. Interestingly, FDI in both China and Mexico contracted in terms of its importance as a share of gross fixed capital formation (GFCF). In the case of Mexico, FDI accounted for levels above 14% in the first decade of the 21st century and less than 10% for several years during 2010-2017. The trend was particularly marked for China: in the early 2000s FDI/GFCF was above 10% and registers less than 3% for 2013-2017 (see Table 1).

Both countries have substantially increased their outflows of FDI (or OFDI). OFDI as a percentage of FDI increased from 21.34% in 2000-2010 to 33.72% in 2011-2017 for Mexico and from 31.99% to 95.21% for China, respectively. While the US is still the most important country in terms of global OFDI (with 21.76% percent during 2011-2017), in the years since 2015 China has become the second global source of OFDI, displacing Japan.[2]

Information provided by Mexican authorities (SE 2019/a) indicates that Mexico's FDI from China rose to $US 1,144 million for 1999-2018, with an average annual growth rate (AAGR) of 21.5% during 2010-2018, compared to an AAGR of 1.3% and 1.8% for FDI coming from the US and total FDI, respectively.[3] So far, Mexico's FDI from China accounts for 0.21% of Mexico's total FDI (and 0.38% if we include Hong Kong) during 1999-2018. Chart 2 suggests that since 2016, FDI from China (and Hong Kong) has picked

2 Only in 2017 was China's OFDI below Japanese OFDI, for reasons that have already been discussed (Dussel Peters 2018/c; MOFCOM 2018). If we include Hong Kong and Macao with China, Chinese OFDI is the second global source of OFDI and has been above Japan since 2009.

3 Mexico's FDI coming from China and Hong Kong accounted for 2,043.7 $US million and for an AAGR of 26.8 percent.

Table 1. Mexico´s and China's FDI (2000-2017)

	2000	2005	2010	2011	2012	2013	2014	2015	2016	2017	2018 /a		2000-2010	2011-2017	2000-2017
FDI inflows (billions)	1,359	949	1,372	1,568	1,575	1,425	1,339	1,921	1,868	1,430	--		12,247	11,125	23,372
China	41	72	115	124	121	124	129	136	134	136			801	903	1,704
LAC	80	77	167	198	190	180	171	169	140	151	--		982	1,199	2,181
Mexico	18	26	27	25	22	48	29	35	30	30			270	218	488
FDI inflows (percentage over total)	100.0	100.0	100.0	100.0	100.0	100.0	100.0	100.0	100.0	100.0	--		100.0	100.0	100.0
China	3.0	7.6	8.4	7.9	7.7	8.7	9.6	7.1	7.2	9.5	--		6.5	8.1	7.3
LAC	5.9	8.1	12.2	12.6	12.1	12.6	12.7	8.8	7.5	10.6	--		8.0	10.8	9.3
Mexico	1.3	2.7	2.0	1.6	1.4	3.4	2.1	1.8	1.6	2.1	--		2.2	2.0	2.1
FDI inflows (percentage over GDP)	4.05	2.00	2.08	2.13	2.10	1.86	1.70	2.58	2.48	1.79	--		2.31	2.09	2.22
China	3.35	3.14	1.89	1.65	1.41	1.29	1.22	1.21	1.19	1.13			2.81	1.30	2.22
LAC	3.64	2.85	3.24	3.38	3.19	2.93	2.79	3.23	2.79	2.59	--		2.93	2.99	2.95
Mexico	2.58	2.97	2.58	2.14	1.81	3.80	2.18	2.98	2.76	2.58	2.60		2.80	2.61	2.73
FDI inflows (percentage over gross fixed capital formation)	17.34	8.54	8.88	8.90	8.63	7.57	6.88	10.32	10.09	--	--		9.87	8.73	9.47
China	10.05	7.83	4.18	3.65	3.12	2.83	2.72	2.80	2.81	--	--		7.34	2.99	5.81
LAC	19.31	14.90	15.80	16.13	14.98	13.77	13.40	14.91	14.21	--	--		15.10	14.57	14.91
Mexico	12.00	14.32	11.97	9.59	7.92	17.90	10.38	13.23	12.05	12.28	14.90		13.38	11.85	12.84
OFDI flows (billions)	1,164	833	1,374	1,564	1,370	1,381	1,262	1,622	1,473	1,430	--		12,313	10,101	22,415
China	1	12	69	75	88	108	123	146	196	125	--		256	860	1,116
LAC	8	19	54	52	42	35	31	36	9	17	--		234	222	456
Mexico	--	6	14	13	23	15	5	11	2	5	--		58	74	131
OFDI / FDI (percentage)	85.65	87.82	100.13	99.75	86.97	96.88	94.28	84.42	78.89	100.01	--		100.54	90.80	95.91
China	2.25	16.93	59.97	60.21	72.52	87.03	95.81	107.42	146.70	91.42	--		31.99	95.21	65.49
LAC	10.18	24.45	32.58	26.36	22.06	19.26	18.19	21.05	6.68	11.45	--		23.82	18.53	20.91
Mexico	--	24.86	52.61	52.63	105.37	30.38	18.84	30.60	5.39	17.12	--		21.34	33.72	26.88

/a Information for 2018 was obtained by SE (2019) and …

Source: author´s elaboration based on UNCTAD (2019)

up significantly, but still constitutes very low absolute levels compared to other economies.[4]

Figure 2. Mexico: FDI From China (1999-2018) (as a percentage of total Mexican FDI)

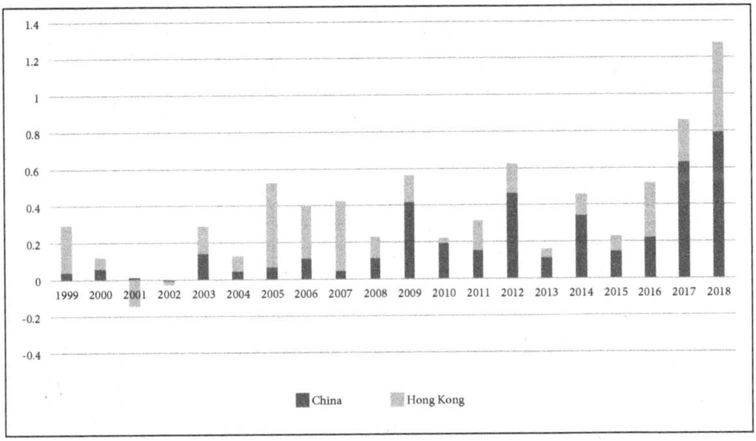

Source: author's elaboration based on SE (2019/a).

Table 2 refers to the sectorial characteristics of Mexico's FDI from China and Hong Kong: by far the most relevant sectors are transport and warehousing (37% of total Chinese FDI in Mexico for 1999-2018) and manufacturing (25.9%). In the transport and warehousing subsectors, water transport (17.4%) and storage services (19.6%) are the most substantial activities, while in manufacturing, activities related to the manufacturing of computer equipment (16.5%) and transport equipment (3.6%) are the most sizablet sectors. These two sectors account for 62.9% of Chinese FDI in Mexico during 1999-2018 and have increased their share since 2007.

Table 3 demonstrates the geographical concentration of China's (China and Hong Kong) FDI in Mexico during 1999-2018: two main cities (Mexico City and Veracruz) and six states of Mexico accounted for 50% and 81% of total FDI from China. China's

4 As a comparison, FDI coming from the US accounted for 48.16 percent during 1999-2018.

Table 2. Mexico: FDI from China and Hong Kong by Sectors (1999-2018)

		1999	2005	2010	2015	2016	2017	2018	1999-2018
		$US millions							
TOTAL		41.2	137.0	60.3	82.8	160.2	277.0	403.2	2,043.7
Sector	21 Mining	0.0	0.0	8.2	2.1	0.0	27.0	50.7	197.0
Subsector	211Oil extraction and gas	0.0	0.0	2.3	2.1	0.0	27.0	50.7	107.0
Branch	2111 Oil extraction and gas	0.0	0.0	2.3	2.1	0.0	27.0	50.7	107.0
Subsector	212 Mining of metallic minerals and non-metallic, except oil and gas	0.0	0.0	7.2	0.0	0.0	0.0	0.0	100.7
Sector	22 Generation, transmission and distribution of electrical energy	0.0	0.0	0.0	11.1	19.8	0.0	57.4	88.4
Sector	31-33 Manufacturing industries	7.6	14.4	33.5	27.5	44.9	35.0	171.2	528.3
Subsector	315 Manufacturing of garments	2.6	1.1	0.2	0.1	0.3	0.4	0.0	22.7
Subsector	325 Chemical industry	0.0	10.5	0.0	7.4	0.0	0.0	0.0	26.3
Branch	3254 Manufacturing of pharmaceutical products	0.0	10.5	0.0	0.3	0.0	0.0	0.0	15.6
Branch	3259 Manufacturing of other chemical products	0.0	0.0	0.0	0.0	16.5	0.0	0.0	18.1
Subsector	326 Plastics industry and rubber	0.4	1.2	0.0	0.1	16.6	17.1	-1.9	39.2
Subsector	334 Manufacturing of computer equipment and others	1.0	0.0	32.5	5.2	35.9	40.8	87.4	331.9
Branch	3341Manufacturing of computer equipment and peripherals	0.1	0.0	30.7	4.7	6.5	38.7	87.4	337.2
Subsector	336 Manufacturing of transport equipment	0.5	0.0	0.0	14.4	-8.9	-24.5	85.6	73.3
Branch	3363 Manufacturing of parts for motor vehicles	0.0	0.0	0.0	14.3	0.1	-24.5	85.6	75.5
Subsector	337 Manufacturing of furniture, mattresses and blinds	0.8	0.0	0.0	0.0	0.0	0.0	0.0	1.0
Sector	48 y 49 Transport and warehousing	12.6	118.3	1.2	14.4	60.3	67.3	93.6	757.1
Subsector	488 Services related to transport	12.6	22.5	-10.3	14.4	58.3	67.3	72.8	355.4
Branch	4883 Services related to water transport	12.6	24.1	-10.3	14.4	58.3	67.3	72.8	355.1
Subsector	493 Storage services	0.0	95.8	11.5	0.0	2.0	0.0	20.6	401.5
Sector	51 Information in mass media	0.0	0.0	7.3	0.0	0.1	98.2	1.7	107.4
Subsector	517 Telecommunications	0.0	0.0	0.0	0.0	0.1	100.0	0.0	100.1
Sector	52 Financial services and insurances	0.0	0.0	0.0	0.0	0.0	49.3	2.3	102.4
Subsector	522 Non-securitization credit and financial intermediation institutions	0.0	0.0	0.0	0.0	0.0	49.3	2.3	102.1
Branch	5221 Multiple bank	0.0	0.0	0.0	0.0	0.0	49.3	1.9	101.6

		percentage over total							
		100.0	100.0	100.0	100.0	100.0	100.0	100.0	100.0
Sector	21 Mining	0.0	0.0	13.5	2.5	0.0	9.7	12.6	9.6
Subsector	211Oil extraction and gas	0.0	0.0	3.9	2.5	0.0	9.7	12.6	5.2
Branch	2111 Oil extraction and gas	0.0	0.0	3.9	2.5	0.0	9.7	12.6	5.2
Subsector	212 Mining of metallic minerals and non-metallic, except oil and gas	0.0	0.0	11.9	0.0	0.0	0.0	0.0	4.9
Sector	22 Generation, transmission and distribution of electrical energy	0.0	0.0	0.0	13.4	12.4	0.0	14.2	4.3
Sector	31-33 Manufacturing industries	18.4	10.5	55.5	33.2	28.1	12.6	42.5	25.9
Subsector	315 Manufacturing of garments	6.3	0.8	0.4	0.1	0.2	0.1	0.0	1.1
Subsector	325 Chemical industry	0.0	7.6	0.0	9.0	0.0	0.0	0.0	1.3
Branch	3254 Manufacturing of pharmaceutical products	0.0	7.6	0.0	0.4	0.0	0.0	0.0	0.8
Branch	3259 Manufacturing of other chemical products	0.0	0.0	0.0	0.0	10.3	0.0	0.0	0.9
Subsector	326 Plastics industry and rubber	1.0	0.9	0.0	0.1	10.4	6.2	-0.5	1.9
Subsector	334 Manufacturing of computer equipment and others	2.3	0.0	53.9	6.3	22.4	14.7	21.7	16.2
Branch	3341Manufacturing of computer equipment and peripherals	0.2	0.0	50.9	5.6	4.0	14.0	21.7	16.5
Subsector	336 Manufacturing of transport equipment	1.2	0.0	0.0	17.5	-5.6	-8.9	21.2	3.6
Branch	3363 Manufacturing of parts for motor vehicles	0.0	0.0	0.0	17.3	0.0	-8.9	21.2	3.7
Subsector	337 Manufacturing of furniture, mattresses and blinds	1.9	0.0	0.0	0.0	0.0	0.0	0.0	0.1
Sector	48 y 49 Transport and warehousing	30.6	86.4	1.9	17.4	37.6	24.3	23.2	37.0
Subsector	488 Services related to transport	30.6	16.4	-17.1	17.4	36.4	24.3	18.1	17.4
Branch	4883 Services related to water transport	30.6	17.6	-17.1	17.4	36.4	24.3	18.1	17.4
Subsector	493 Storage services	0.0	70.0	19.0	0.0	1.2	0.0	5.1	19.6
Sector	51 Information in mass media	0.0	0.0	12.2	0.0	0.1	35.4	0.4	5.3
Subsector	517 Telecommunications	0.0	0.0	0.0	0.0	0.1	36.1	0.0	4.9
Sector	52 Financial services and insurances	0.0	0.0	0.0	0.0	0.0	17.8	0.6	5.0
Subsector	522 Non-securitization credit and financial intermediation institutions	0.0	0.0	0.0	0.0	0.0	17.8	0.6	5.0
Branch	5221 Multiple bank	0.0	0.0	0.0	0.0	0.0	17.8	0.5	5.0

Source: author´s elaboration based on SE (2019/a).

Table 3. Mexico: FDI from China and Hong Kong by State (1999-2018)

	1999	2005	2010	2015	2016	2017	1999-2018
	$US million						
TOTAL	41.2	137.0	60.3	82.8	160.2	277.0	1,640.5
Mexico City	1.1	5.3	2.3	10.7	36.0	80.1	240.5
Veracruz	0.0	0.0	-7.3	6.3	49.2	75.4	240.4
Aguascalientes	0.2	0.0	0.0	0.1	0.0	4.9	8.9
San Luis Potosí	0.0	0.0	0.8	14.3	0.0	-23.2	-8.0
Nuevo León	0.0	0.0	13.6	0.1	1.2	3.3	31.6
Michoacán	0.0	119.9	9.4	0.0	2.0	3.1	404.5
Rest	39.9	11.7	41.5	51.3	71.9	133.4	722.7
	percentage over total FDI from China and Hong Kong						
TOTAL	100.0	100.0	100.0	100.0	100.0	100.0	100.0
Mexico City	2.7	3.9	3.7	13.0	22.5	28.9	14.7
Veracruz	0.0	0.0	-12.1	7.6	30.7	27.2	14.7
Aguascalientes	0.5	0.0	0.0	0.1	0.0	1.8	0.5
San Luis Potosí	0.0	0.0	1.4	17.3	0.0	-8.4	-0.5
Nuevo León	0.0	0.0	22.6	0.1	0.7	1.2	1.9
Michoacán	0.0	87.5	15.6	0.0	1.2	1.1	24.7
Rest	96.8	8.5	68.9	61.9	44.9	48.2	44.1

Source: author´s elaboration based on SE (2019/a).

FDI to Mexico has been diversifying away from Mexico City and to states such as Veracruz and Aguascalientes (see Table 3).

The following section will deepen the characteristics of Chinese FDI in Mexico for 2000-2018 based on the dataset elaborated by Monitor of China's OFDI in LAC 2019 (Dussel Peters 2019). Given the methodological approach of Mexican official sources (SE 2019/b) and the transaction level statistics elaborated by Monitor of China's OFDI in LAC 2019, the differences are substantial. As Table 4 indicates, the official Mexican source (SE 2019/a), and the official Chinese source (MOFCOM 2018) represent 27.2% and 13.62% of FDI´s values for the period 2004-2017 of Monitor of China's OFDI in LAC (Dussel Peters 2019). In 2006 and 2015, for example, the difference is of the sign of China's FDI to Mexico. While Mexican and Chinese official statistics document $US 1.571 and 0.786 billion, respectively, the Monitor of China's OFDI in LAC registered $US 5.775 billion for 2004-2017 (see Table 4).

Table 4. Mexico: Chinese FDI by source (2000-2018)

	2000	2001	2002	2003	2004	2005	2006	2007	2008	2009	2010	2011	2012	2013	2014	2015	2016	2017	2018	2004-2017
	$US millions																			
Secretaría de Economía (SE 2019)																				
China	11	3	-2	26	12	17	24	16	33	76	53	39	102	55	101	53	69	203	250	852
Hong Kong	11	-42	-5	27	19	120	61	121	35	27	8	42	35	22	35	30	92	74	153	719
China and Hong Kong	22	-39	-7	53	31	137	85	136	68	103	60	81	138	77	135	83	160	277	403	1,571
MOFCOM					27	4	-4	17	6	1	27	42	100	50	141	-6	212	171	786	786
Monitor of China's OFDI in LAC (Dussel Peters 2019)	20	450	0	0	30	63	45	109	331	40	84	39	70	8	1,140	1,001	81	2,733	398	5,775
	Percentage (Monitor of China's OFDI (Dussel Peters 2019) = 100)																			
Secretaría de Economía (SE 2019)																				
China	55.69	0.60	--	--	39.68	26.54	52.42	14.53	10.09	189.37	62.53	98.29	146.36	685.83	8.83	5.30	84.34	7.45	62.92	14.75
Hong Kong	52.51	-9.34	--	--	62.25	190.87	135.83	110.67	10.44	68.52	9.18	107.39	50.42	272.11	3.04	2.97	112.76	2.69	38.48	12.46
China and Hong Kong	108.20	-8.74	--	--	101.94	217.41	188.25	125.20	20.53	257.89	71.71	205.68	196.78	957.94	11.88	8.27	197.09	10.14	101.40	27.20
MOFCOM	0.00	0.00	--	--	89.74	5.63	-8.20	15.74	1.70	2.05	31.78	105.81	143.46	621.63	12.33	-0.63	260.57	6.27	197.79	13.62

Source: author´s elaboration based on Monitor of China's OFDI in LAC (Dussel Peters 2019)

Considering these substantial discrepancies and the benefits of registering FDI by transaction (Dussel Peters 2019), the main results for China's FDI in Mexico highlight at least five important characteristics.

China's FDI in Mexico, although relatively small as a percentage of total FDI, has increased in importance and dynamism since 2000 (see Table 5). The period from 2000-2018 saw 81 transactions and $US 6.642 billion in investments, with more than 42,000 generated jobs as a result of these transactions. The years 2015 and 2017 were especially dynamic. In the Mexican case 82.63% of China's FDI during 2000-2018 (and 53.7% of total generated employment) came from new (or "greenfield") investments , suggesting that Chinese greenfield investment in Mexico is much more capital-intensive than mergers and acquisitions (M&A). The 16 M&A transactions generated during 2000-2018 an average of 1,233

Table 5. Mexico: Chinese FDI (2000-2018)

	Transactions (number)	Amount ($US millions)	Employment (number of employees)	Amount / Transactions ($US millions)	Amount / Employment ($US millions)	Employment / Transactions (employees)
			Total			
2000-2005	4	563.2	6,354	140.8	0.089	1,588.5
2006-2009	10	524.9	6,166	52.5	0.085	616.6
2010-2018	67	5,554.5	30,098	82.9	0.185	449.2
2000-2018	81	6,642.6	42,618	82.0	0.156	526.1
2015	9	1,001.3	4,915	111.3	0.204	546.1
2016	4	81.3	1,455	20.3	0.056	363.8
2017	23	2,745.6	1,759	119.4	1.561	76.5
2018	9	385.2	4,059	42.8	0.095	451.0
			Merger and Acquisitions			
2000-2005	1	450.0	5,500	450.0	0.082	5,500.0
2006-2009	4	385.1	4,150	96.3	0.093	1,037.5
2010-2018	11	318.1	10,083	28.9	0.032	916.6
2000-2018	16	1,153.2	19,733	72.1	0.058	1,233.3
2015	1	23.7	3,000	23.7	0.008	3,000.0
2016	1	0.2	0	0.2	0.000	0.0
2017	3	184.0	5,030	61.3	0.037	1,676.7
2018	0	0.0	0	0.0	0.000	0.0
			New Investments (greenfield)			
2000-2005	3	113.2	854	37.7	0.133	284.7
2006-2009	6	139.8	2,016	23.3	0.069	336.0
2010-2018	56	5,236.4	20,015	93.5	0.262	357.4
2000-2018	65	5,489.4	22,885	84.5	0.240	352.1
2015	8	977.6	1,915	122.2	0.510	239.4
2016	3	81.1	1,455	27.0	0.056	485.0
2017	18	2,487.0	11,269	138.2	0.221	626.1
2018	9	397.6	2,628	44.2	0.151	292.0

Source:author´s elaboration based on Dussel Peters (2019).

jobs, while the 65 greenfield transactions generated an average of only 352 jobs). The share of greenfield investments has increased substantially during 2015-2018.

Latin American and Caribbean Mexico represents an unusual case in the sense that most Chinese FDI does revolve around the acquisition of raw materials. During 2000-2018, manufacturing and transactions related to services and the domestic market

Table 6. Mexico: Chinese FDI by Sector (2000-2018)

	2000-2005	2006-2009	2010-2018	2000-2018	2015	2016	2017	2018
Raw materials								
Transactions	0	2	4	6	0	0	1	0
Amount ($US millions)	0	239	686	925	0	0	50	0
Employment	0	393	4,500	4,893	0	0	3,500	0
Amount / Transaction ($US millions)	0	119.5	171.5	154.2	0	0	50.0	0
Amount / Employment ($US millions)	0	0.608	0.152	0.189	0	0	0.014	0
Employment / Transaction	0	196.5	1125.0	815.5	0	0	3500.0	0
Manufacturing								
Transactions	3	8	43	54	5	3	17	5
Amount ($US millions)	113	286	4,174	4,574	950	81	2,627	323
Employment	854	5,773	23,608	30,235	4,088	1,455	13,088	2,370
Amount / Transaction ($US millions)	37.7	35.7	97.1	84.7	190.0	27.0	154.6	64.6
Amount / Employment ($US millions)	0.133	0.050	0.177	0.151	0.232	0.056	0.201	0.136
Employment / Transaction	284.7	721.6	549.0	559.9	817.6	485.0	769.9	474.0
Services and Domestic Market								
Transactions	1	0	20	21	4	1	5	4
Amount ($US millions)	450	0	894	1344.1	51	0	56	74
Employment	5,500	0	1,990	7,490	827	0	311	258
Amount / Transaction ($US millions)	450.0	0	44.7	64.0	12.8	0.2	11.2	18.6
Amount / Employment ($US millions)	0.082	0	0.449	0.179	0.062	0.000	0.180	0.289
Employment / Transaction	5,500	0	100	357	207	0	62	65
Purchase of Technology								
Transactions	0	0	0	0	0	0	0	0
Amount ($US millions)	0	0	0	0	0	0	0	0
Employment	0	0	0	0	0	0	0	0
Amount / Transaction ($US millions)	0	0	0	0	0	0	0	0
Amount / Employment ($US millions)	0	0	0	0	0	0	0	0
Employment / Transaction	0	0	0	0	0	0	0	0

Source: author's elaboration based on Dussel Peters (2019).

accounted for 54 and 21 transactions, respectively, while those related to raw Materials only accounted for 6% of transactions. The former constituted 68.85% and 20.23% of total Chinese FDI to Mexico during 2000-2018, respectively (see Table 6).

Mexico´s FDI coming from China is a relatively small share of Chinese public firms compared to LAC and the rest of the world. Chart 3 shows the increasing relevance of Chinese private firms for all the defined periods, with the exception of the period 2006-2009, in which private firms accounted for more than 70% of the transactions, the amount of FDI, as well as the generated employment for the period 2000-2018. In 2017-2018 the share of Chinese private firms in these variables has increased even further .

Chart 3. Mexico: Chinese Private FDI (2000-2018) (share over respective totals)

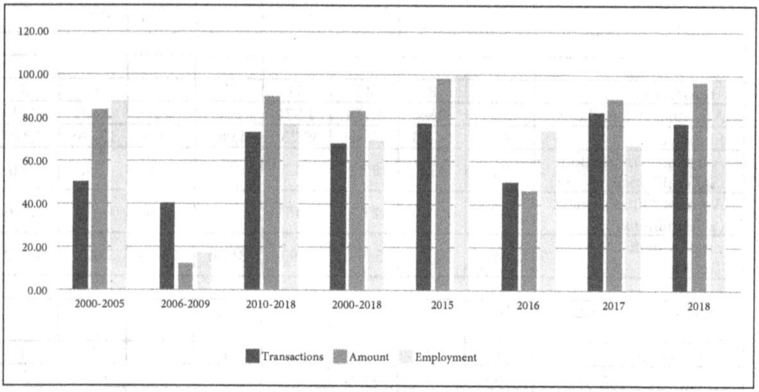

Sourced: author´s elaboration based on Dussel Peters (2019).

The same data set also highlights the main Chinese firms involved in Mexico. Considering the relatively small but dynamic Chinese presence in Mexico so far, firm-level results are very heterogeneous and trend toward single transactions, as in most of the cases in Table 7. Nevertheless, firms like Hutchinson Ports Holding, Minth, Huawei, and Lenovo have already established a tradition of investing in Mexico and have indicated their interest in continuing to do so in the future. The top ten firms noted in Table 7 have so far accumulated 74.55% of Chinese FDI in Mexico, as well

Table 7. Mexico: Chinese FDI by main firms (2000-2018)
(main 10 firms according to their FDI during 2000-2018)

	Transactions (number)	Amount ($US millions)	Employment (number of employees)	Amount / Transactions ($US millions)	Amount / Employment ($US millions)	Employment / Transactions (employees)
Total	81	6,643	42,618	82	0.156	526.1
JAC	1	1,000	4,400	1,000	0.227	4,400
Risen Energy	1	610	700	610	0.871	700
Sanhua Holding	2	615	621	308	0.990	311
Hutchinson Ports Holding	3	528	5,644	176	0.094	1,881
AMI PPM de México	1	500	100	500	5.000	100
Minth	3	403	2,010	134	0.200	670
Futong Group	1	400	455	400	0.879	455
Lenovo	3	242	1,926	81	0.126	642
Huawei	3	415	398	138	1.043	133
Jinchuan Group	2	239	650	120	0.368	325
Rest	61	1,691	25,714	28	0.066	422

Source: author´s elaboration based on Dussel Peters (2019).

as 39.66% of the jobs generated during 2000-2018. It is expected that with further Chinese FDI, this concentration will diversify substantially.

Firm-level analysis of Chinese investments in Mexico (Ando 2016; Dussel Peters 2014; Guerrero Vázquez 2018; Hua 2007; Micheli Thirion and Carrillo Viveros 2016; Schatan and Piloyan 2015;) shows that, with few exceptions, the time frame and respective costs for Chinese firms to learn in terms of local and domestic suppliers, clients, labor and environmental laws, etc. has been slow and difficult, but is improving quickly in Mexico, particularly for firms like Huawei, Hutchinson Ports Holding, Minth, FAW Trucks, JAC, and Sinatex, among others. Chinese firms are quickly improving in terms of their preparation to conduct business in LAC and Mexico and coordinating their experiences and knowledge to improve the results of their outbound FDI in LAC and other regions of the world.

Conclusions

Mexico and China have substantially intensified their bilateral relationship in the last two decades, becoming much more complex in terms of bilateral political institutions and in trade, financing, infrastructure projects, and Chinese FDI in Mexico. This relatively new relationship has not always been easy and has become increasingly complex.

China's FDI in Mexico is still relatively small, as highlighted by the statistical differences between official data from the two countries, but is expected to increase in the near future. Contrary to most of LAC, China's FDI in Mexico has concentrated in manufacturing and services related to Mexico´s domestic market. Private Chinese firms like Huawei, Hutchinson Ports Holding, Lenovo, and other firms in the auto parts and automobile manufacturing chain have, so far, dominated in terms of FDI amount and employment generation. Initial firm-level studies show that China's firms needed several years to understand the complexities of establishing themselves in Mexico, which has entailed understanding different rules, laws, and networks. That process has evolved quickly and more recently arrived Chinese firms have been able to shorten the time frame to integrate into local, national and NAFTA-networks. Given the potential impact of the USMCA on LAC markets and the limitations of countries like Argentina, Brazil, and Venezuela, Chinese FDI to Mexico will likely increase substantially in the short term.

In terms of proposals (Dussel Peters and Levvy-Dabbah 2018; Yang 2016) to enhance China's FDI to Mexico, both parties should improve the quality of the existing bilateral institutions to facilitate the learning process necessary for successful FDI. Mexican firms have also highlighted the importance of reciprocity, i.e. that Mexican firms should have the same opportunities to invest in China that Chinese firms have in Mexico. Finally, and most importantly, Chinese firms still need to improve their preparations for setting up new plants or M&A in Mexico and LAC by better understanding the organizational, social, environmental, and labor differences between countries and specifically in LAC and Mexico. Similarly

Mexican institutions at all levels, federal, state, and municipal, also need to improve their understanding of the "Chinese characteristics" of Chinese firms. One approach might be to set up specialized working groups to improve the establishment of Chinese firms in Mexico to lower the time and costs for their establishment.

References

Ando, Manuel. 2016. "La relación México-China: desempeño y propuestas, 2016-2018". In, Dussel Peters, Enrique (coord.). *La relación* México-China. *Desempeño y propuestas para 2016-2018.* México: UNAM/Cechimex and The Mexican Chamber of Commerce in China, pp. 77-79.

Anguiano Roch, Eugenio. 2012. "Sin sustento político, imposible construir relaciones económicas bilaterales sólidas". In, Dussel Peters, Enrique (edit.). *40 años de la relación entre México y China. Acuerdos, desencuentros y futuro.* México: UNAM/Cechimex, Cámara de Senadores and CICIR, pp. 37-48.

Anguiano Roch, Eugenio. 2018. "La relación México-China en el ámbito político". In, Dussel Peters, Enrique and Simón Levy-Dabbah (coord.). Hacia una agenda estratégica entre México y China. Mexico. AGENDASIA, COMEXI and CECHIMEX, pp. 47-58.

Cui, Shoujun and Manuel Pérez García (edits). 2016. *China and Latin America in Transition. Policy Dynamics, Economic Commitments, and Social Impacts.* New York: Palgrave MacMillan.

Dussel Peters, Enrique (coord.). 2014. La inversión extranjera directa de China en América Latina: 10 estudios de caso. México: Red ALC-China y UNAM/Cechimex.

Dussel Peters, Enrique (edit.). 2018/a. *The Renegotiation of* NAFTA. *And China*? Mexico: Red ALC-China and UNAM/Cechimex.

Dussel Peters, Enrique. 2018/b. "Chinese Infrastructure Projects in Mexico: General Context and Two Case Studies". In, Dussel Peters, Enrique, Ariel C. Armony and Shoujun Cui (coord.). *Building Development for a New Era. China's Infrastructure*

Projects in Latin America and the Caribbean. México: University of Pittsburgh and UNAM/Cechimex, pp. 58-76.

Dussel Peters, Enrique. 2019. Monitor of China's OFDI in Latin America and the Caribbean 2019. México: Red ALC-China.

Dussel Peters, Enrique, Adrian H. Hearn and Harley Shaiken (edits). 2013. *China and the New Triangular Relationships in the Americas. China and the Future of US-Mexico Relations.* Mexico: CLAS/University of Miami, CLAS/University of California Berkeley and UNAM/Cechimex.

Dussel Peters, Enrique and Samuel Ortiz Velásquez. 2016. "El Tratado de Libre Comercio de América del Norte, ¿contribuye China a su integración o desintegración?". In, Dussel Peters, Enrique (coord.). *La nueva relación comercial de América Latina y el Caribe con China, ¿integración o desintegración comercial?* México: Red ALC-China and UNAM/Cechimex, pp. 245-308.

Dussel Peters, Enrique and Simón Levy-Dabbah (edits.). 2018. *Hacia una agenda estratégica entre México y China.* México: Agendasia, Comexi and UNAM/Cechimex, pp. 47-57.

Guerrero Vázquez, René Andrei. 2018. *Las multinacionales chinas y sus estrategias de innovación en* México. MA Thesis presented at Colegio de la Frontera Norte, Tijuana.

Inter-American Dialogue. 2019. *China-Latin America Finance Database.* At: https://www.thedialogue.org/map_list/.

Hua, Li Jian. 2007. "El caso de Sinatex SA de CV en México". In, Dussel Peters, Enrique (coord.). *Oportunidades en la relación económica y comercial entre China y México.* México: CEPAL, pp. 239-244.

Jian, Shixue. 2016. "Revisiting China's Investment in Latin America". *China Quarterly of International Strategic Studies* 2(4), pp. 507-527.

Micheli Thirion, Jordy and Jorge Carrillo Viveros. 2016. "The Globalization Strategy of a Chinese Multinational: Huawei in Mexico". Frontera Norte28(56), pp. 35-58.

MOFCOM (Ministry of Commerce). 2018. 2017 Statistical Bulletin of China's Outward Foreign Direct Investment. Beijing: MOFCOM.

Ruiz Durán, Clemente. 2018. "Modernizing NAFTA: Transformation, Negotiation, and Unequal Results". In, Dussel Peters, Enrique (coord). *The Renegotiation of* NAFTA. *And China*? Mexico: Red ALC-China and UNAM/Cechimex, pp. 49-64.

Schatan, Claudia and Diana Piloyan. 2015. "China in Mexico: Some Environmental and Employment Dimensions". *Discussion Paper* (Boston University-Global Economic Governance Iniciative) 2015-7, pp. 1-44.

SE (Secretaría de Economía). 2019/a. Estadística official de los flujos de IED hacia México. At: https://www.gob.mx/se/acciones-y-programas/competitividad-y-normatividad-inversion-extranjera-directa?state=published.

SE. 2019/b. *Síntesis metodológica sobre la contabilización de flujos de inversion extranjera directa hacia* México. México: SE.

UNCTAD (United Nations Conference on Trade and Development). 2019. Data Center for Foreign Direct Investments. At: https://unctadstat.unctad.org/wds/ReportFolders/reportFolders.aspx.

Ventura Valero, Julián and Rodrigo Meléndrez Armada. 2016. "Relaciones económicas México-China: una agenda de oportunidades". *Revista Mexicana de Política Exterior* 108, pp. 27-49.

Yang, Zhimin. 2016. "México y China: condiciones y propuestas desde una perspectiva china". In, Dussel Peters, Enrique (coord.). *La relación* México-China. *Desempeño y propuestas para 2016-2018*. México: UNAM/Cechimex and The Mexican Chamber of Commerce in China, pp. 38-48.

Zamora Torres, Abraham. 2016. "Oportunidades de inversión en México: infraestructura y ZEE". En, Dussel Peters, Enrique (edit.). *La relación* México-China. *Desempeño y propuestas para 2016-2018*. México: MEXCHAM and UNAM/Cechimex, pp. 49-55.

ABOUT THE AUTHORS

Rafael Arias R., Ph.D., Associate Professor and Research Coordinator of the Economics School of National University and Associate Researcher of the Institute of Research of Economics Sciences of the University of Costa Rica. Member of the Red ALC-China.

Gustavo Bittencourt is a professor and researcher in the Department of Economics, Faculty of Social Sciences, University of the Republic, Uruguay. Author of numerous works on international economics and economic development, with an emphasis on FDI and development in Latin America, and Latin American relations with China. Alternate President of the South American Network of Applied Economics (Red Sur).

Linda Calabrese is a development economist and a Research Fellow at the Overseas Development Institute. Her research interests include trade and investment, industrial policy and economic transformation. A fluent Mandarin speaker, she is interested in China-Africa issues, in particular how Chinese and foreign investment promote economic transformation in Africa through the development of the manufacturing sector. At ODI she works extensively on industrial policy in East Africa. Prior to joining ODI, Linda worked as an economist for the Government of Uganda and as a country economist for the International Growth Centre in Rwanda.

Nehemías José Jaén Celada is a Panamanian consultant, political scientist, and international relations analyst. He graduated with a BA in political science specializing in international relations from National Taiwan University and obtained an MA in contemporary China Studies at Renmin University of China (RUC), where he also pursued a course of doctoral studies in international political economy with the School of International Studies. He also recently obtained an MBA with a specialization in finance from Hult International Business School. Member of the Latin American Studies Association (LASA) and Red ALC-China. He is the Vice Consul of the Republic of Panama in Shanghai.

Benjamin Creutzfeldt, Ph.D., is a scholar at the Woodrow Wilson Center in Washington DC, affiliated with the Kissinger Institute for China and the U.S. & the Latin America Program. Prior to this, he was Resident Postdoctoral Fellow for China-Latin America-U.S. Affairs at the SAIS Foreign Policy Institute, Johns Hopkins University. He is a sinologist by training, has extensive business experience managing start-ups in China, Panama and the U.S., and spent a decade in Colombia as a university lecturer in Chinese Studies. He is also a visiting professor at Universidad de La Sabana in Bogotá, Colombia.

Enrique Dussel Peters is a professor at the Graduate School of Economics, Universidad Nacional Autónoma de México (UNAM) since 1993. Research topics that interest him include economic development, political economy, industrial organization, and trade theory; NAFTA and CAFTA; and the evolution of industrial, trade, and regional patterns in Latin America and Mexico. He has conducted research on specific segments of commodity chains, such as pineapples, lemons, electronics, yarn, textiles, garments, auto parts and automobiles, and pharmaceuticals, among others. He served as coordinator of the Area of Political Economy at the Graduate School of Economics at UNAM from 2004 to 2008, and he is currently the coordinator of the Center for Chinese-Mexican Studies at UNAM. He also serves as the coordinator of the Academic Network of Latin American and Caribbean on China (Red ALC-China). Website: dusselpeters.com

Thilo Hanemann is a Director at Rhodium Group and leads the firm's work on global trade and investment, where he oversees the investment management, strategic planning, and policy analysis requirements of Rhodium clients within his fields of expertise. He is also a Senior Policy Fellow at the Mercator Institute for China Studies, Europe's biggest China think tank, located in Berlin. His research focuses on new trends in global trade and capital flows, related policy developments, and the political and commercial dynamics of specific transactions. One of his areas of expertise is the rise of emerging economies as global investors and the implications for host economies and the global economy. His most recent work focuses on the evolution of China's international investment position and the economic and policy implications of this new trend.

Adrian Hearn is an Associate Professor (University of Melbourne) and an anthropologist who researches urban multiculturalism and food systems. He is currently studying how trust affects localised food production in Beijing, Melbourne, Havana, Rio de Janeiro, and São Paulo. Funded by the Australian Research Council (ARC), the Commonwealth Department of Foreign Affairs and Trade (DFAT), and the São Paulo Research Foundation (FAPESP), his work brings together international teams to compare challenges, share success stories, and formulate solutions. His books include *Diaspora and Trust: Cuba, Mexico, and the Rise of China* and *Cuba: Religion Social Capital, and Development* (Duke Univ. Press 2016 and 2008), and (as editor) *The Changing Currents of Transpacific Integration* and *China Engages Latin America* (Lynne Rienner 2016 and 2011).

Celio Hiratuka is a professor at the Institute of Economics at the State University of Campinas (UNICAMP) and researcher at the Center of Industrial and Technology Economics and the Brazil China Studies Group at UNICAMP. He is also researcher of the South American Network of Applied Economics. Currently, he is the coordinator of graduate studies at the Institute of Economics. His research interests include the Brazilian industrial structure, international trade and foreign direct investment, and economic development and Brazil-China economic relations. Professor Hiratuka has several papers published in national and international peer-reviewed journal in his research areas.

Mikko Huotari is the Deputy Director of MERICS. His research focuses on China's foreign policy, China-Europe relations, and global (economic) governance. He has published on China's rise as a financial power, trade and investment relations with Europe, and geopolitical shifts related to China's emergence as a global security actor. Huotari studied in Freiburg, Nanjing and Shanghai. He holds a Ph.D. from Freiburg University and was a guest scholar at the University of California in San Diego in 2017/2018.

Eduardo Klinger Pevida is an economist and member of the Science Academy from Dominican Republic and coordinator of its Caribbean Studies Center. He is an ex-officer of the Economic Commission for Latin-American and the Caribbean (ECLAC) and was a professor and invited speaker at various universities throughout the region. He also served as deputy president of the Caribbean Economist from the Caribbean Association and member of the Executive Committee in the Latin-American Economists Association. Author of various books. Geopolitical adviser to the Defense Minister (2008 -2010) and special adviser in the Treasury Ministry from Dominican Republic (2013 -2017).

Jevon Minto is a recent graduate of the Benemérita Universidad Autónoma de Puebla with a Master's in Economic Development and International Cooperation. His research explores China's contribution to economic development in Latin America and the Caribbean through regional and subregional development banks (RDB s). Jevon is a Young Scholar with the Inter-American Dialogue-China/Latin America Program and a member of the China/Latin America and Caribbean Academic network. He is also a member of the Young Initiative on Foreign Affairs and International Relations. Jevon has written numerous articles on China-Latin America and Caribbean relations and is a former journalist for Nationwide Radio in Kingston, Jamaica where he closely monitored China's growing engagement with Jamaica and the Caribbean. He recently worked in the Inter-American Development Bank's Caribbean Department, where he helped develop communications strategies for Caribbean countries.

Carlos Eduardo Piña is a political scientist with experience in student conferences at national and international level, courses and training in diplomatic speeches, and the drafting of legislation. Recent research focuses on analyzing the international oil market, specifically in the area of oil geopolitics, and the Chinese-Venezuelan relationship. He is currently a research scholar at the Center for Chinese-Mexican Studies (CECHIMEX) at the School of Economics of the Universidad Nacional Autónoma de México (UNAM).

Xiaoyu Song is currently a Ph.D. candidate in Economics at the Universidad Nacional Autónoma de México (UNAM). She holds a master's degree in Economics from UNAM and earned her bachelor's degree in Hispanic Philology at Beijing Foreign Studies University (BFSU). She has received scholarships from the Consejo Nacional de Ciencia y Tecnología (CONACYT) of Mexico during her studies. Xiaoyu also studied at the Universidad Autónoma de Madrid with a scholarship during 2007-2008 and at the Institute of Latin-American Studies of Chinese Academy of Social Sciences (ILAS, CASS) as a visiting scholar in 2017 and has experience working in China's public sector in the international business. Her main research topics are the determinants of the Chinese Outward Foreign Direct Investment (OFDI) and Chinese OFDI in Latin America. She is a member of the Academic Network of Latin America and the Caribbean on China (Red ALC-China).

Leonardo E. Stanley is an associated researcher at the Center for the Study of State and Society (CEDES), an independent think tank in Argentina. He is a graduate in economics from the School of Economics, University of Mar del Plata, Argentina, and holds an MSc in economics from Queen Mary University, London, and an MsPhil/DEA (*Diplôme d'études approfondies*) from Université d'Evry Vald'Essone, France. Along with membership in many professional associations, he serves as an advisory board member at the Initiative for Financial Transparency (ITF) and as a member of the Institute of Latino American Centre, University of Rosario (UNR). His main fields of analysis involve economic development, international political economy, international financial architecture, and institutional design. He recently published his first book, *Emerging Market Economies and Financial Globalization: Argentina, Brazil, China, India and South Korea* (Anthem, 2018), which provides a comparative analysis of the capital account liberalization process.

Luis Vargas M., Ph.D. candidate, is a researcher at the Institute of Research of Economics Sciences of the University of Costa Rica and the International Centre of Economic Policy for Sustainable Development of the National University. Member of the Red ALC-China.

Universidad Nacional Autónoma de México
Facultad de Economía
Centro de Estudios China-México
Unión de Universidades de América Latina y el Caribe
Red Académica de América Latina y el Caribe sobre China

CHINA'S FOREIGN DIRECT INVESTMENT IN LATIN AMERICA AND THE CARIBBEAN
CONDITIONS AND CHALLENGES

Esta edición se terminó de imprimir en septiembre de 2019
en los talleres de Editores Buena Onda, S.A. de C.V.
Suiza 14, Col. Portales Oriente, Ciudad de México 03570
Su composición se realizó con las familias tipográficas:
Minion Pro 8:10; 9:15; 12:15; 11:15; 12:15; 18:20; 24:26; 32:34
El tiraje consta de 1,000 ejemplares
El cuidado de la edición estuvo a cargo de:
Megan McLean